THE MINERS' UNIONS OF
NORTHUMBERLAND
AND DURHAM

THE MINERS' UNIONS OF NORTHUMBERLAND AND DURHAM

BY

E. WELBOURNE, M.A.

FELLOW OF EMMANUEL COLLEGE,
CAMBRIDGE

Awarded the Thirlwall Prize, the Seeley Medal,
and the Gladstone Prize,

1921

CAMBRIDGE

AT THE UNIVERSITY PRESS

1923

CAMBRIDGE UNIVERSITY PRESS
Cambridge, New York, Melbourne, Madrid, Cape Town,
Singapore, São Paulo, Delhi, Tokyo, Mexico City

Cambridge University Press
The Edinburgh Building, Cambridge CB2 8RU, UK

Published in the United States of America by Cambridge University Press, New York

www.cambridge.org
Information on this title: www.cambridge.org/9781107641013

First published 1923
First paperback edition 2011

A catalogue record for this publication is available from the British Library

ISBN 978-1-107-64101-3 Paperback

CONTENTS

CHAPTER I

INTRODUCTION

PRIMITIVE coal-mining required no specially skilled body of workmen. Where the seams came to the surface on the sides of the hills coal could easily be won, and where by some chance shallow seams were discovered they were exposed by digging huge open trenches. It was in the early days of the thirteenth century, when the surface coal was almost all exhausted, that the pitman appeared. The name— in the north-country the collier is still a "pitman"—is at once a witness to the antiquity of the miner's calling, and a memory of his earliest method of work. He dug down until the seam was reached. Then the pit was widened in every direction, until the unsupported roof would stand no longer. The coal was carried to the surface in baskets, the pitman climbed up his short ladder, took it away, and dug a new pit. In 1256 deserted workings of this kind were so numerous near Newcastle that it was dangerous for a stranger to ride into the town.

The church was the pioneer in all mining enterprise. It needed lime for its building, and coal for the lime-kilns. Soon the pitmen, servants for the most part of the abbeys or of that powerful prince the Bishop of Durham, began to work deeper seams. They learned from the lead-miners a new word, shaft. They replaced the ladder by a windlass, a skep, and a rope.

In the fourteenth century sinking costs varied from
5s. 6d. to 40s., and leases which mention in turn roof
timber, surface damage, and a water-gate, shew that
regular workings were driven out from the shaft. But
there is little mention of the pitmen. During the
troubles of the Black Death, Bishop Hatfield issued
a warrant to John de Walgrave to seize workmen
and coal-bearers for his needs in Durham. And from
time to time officials are named. The pits were from
the first in the care of a viewer, who may at one time
have been a forest official. There were banksmen, and
once a banksman was promoted to a surveyor's place,
and given power to imprison his workmen. In one
place there was a clerk. The mines had plainly increased in size when in 1487 the monks of Finchale
spent £9. 15s. 6d. on a pump and its necessary horses.

It is probable that the first ship-load of coal was
sent from Newcastle to the Thames in the reign of
Henry III, but it was not until the later days of
Elizabeth that the coal trade grew to any great importance. In the sixteenth century chimneys became
common, and as the forests of the south country
disappeared fuel for the needs of London became in-
creasingly hard to find. Elizabeth's Privy Council
received a complaint that the coal-owners were
greedily raising the price of their commodity. One
man was reputed to have made £50,000 from a single
coal lease. A pamphlet has preserved the reply of
the Newcastle Corporation. Freights had risen, and
the coal-owners had been compelled by the high cost
of living to raise the wages of their workmen. For

those pore men who work ye Colles under ye grounde, having no other means to sustain ye necessities of themselves and families, then yr owne labours, are now compelled to paie 11d for the grasse of a Cowe, during the summer season, *wch* heretofore they were accustomed to hier for 3d or 4d, *wch* with the darth of other victualles, is ye cause, they cannot sustain yr lives with the allowance of yr former wages[1].

In 1602 the Newcastle Company of Hostmen was incorporated to regulate the coal trade. At that time the annual export to London was 190,000 tons. There were 200 hoys sailing between the Tyne and the Thames, and the coal dues brought the town of Newcastle a yearly income of £10,000. It was as a nursery of seamen and a source of revenue that the trade attracted the attention of the government. The Hostmen were among the culprits whom the Long Parliament attacked, those monopolists who "sheltered themselves under the guise of a corporation." But of the pitmen little is heard. An account book for 1530 shews that five hewers were paid, jointly, 21*d.* a day, while a man working with them removing stone received only 3*d.* They were no longer bondservants. Dr Kaye, the founder of Gonville and Caius College, Cambridge, noticed that some of the pits had "an unwholesome vapour" which would have destroyed the "hired labourers" had they not fled, warned of its presence by the blue flame at their lamps[2]. It is said that it was the enormous extension of the trade at this time which first made the employment of

---

[1] *Certain Matters relating to the Excessive price of Coals in the Time of Elizabeth.*

[2] *Joannis Caii Britanni de Ephemera Liber,* 1535.

women necessary, and to explain some curious sur-
vivals of folk-lore an antiquarian once suggested that
the Tynedale mosstroopers, driven from their home
in 1572, took to the pits.

James I made it known that he did not share
Elizabeth's dislike for "the foule smoke of the sea-
cole" and, in the boom which followed, there were
heard threats of rapid exhaustion of the supplies.
The coal leases were almost all in the hands of an
association which, through the society of Hostmen,
conducted for two hundred years a war with the
London consumer. Perhaps it was jealousy which,
in 1603, led the Newcastle Corporation to make complaint that the new society had "made congregation"
among other things for "the abridging of the wages
of the poore labourers"[1], for to some extent the
Hostmen protected the pitmen. In 1662 they put a
stop to the practice of paying wages in corn "at rates
farr above the markett price"[2]. Four years later they
closed all the pits, as a protest against the action of
the Lord Mayor of London, who had imposed a scale
of fixed prices. To relieve the "poore workpeople, like
to come to extreme want"[3] they at once imposed a
tax of a penny a chalder on all coal sold from stock.

Meantime, the tale of recorded accidents had begun,
with an entry in 1618 in the Register of St Mary's,
Newcastle, "Richard Backus, burnt in a pit." In
1658 two men were drowned by an inrush of water

---

[1] *The Company of the Hostmen of Newcastle* (Surtees Soc.),
1901, pp. 21 and 22.
[2] *Ibid.* Aug. 15th, 1662.   [3] *Ibid.* May 8th, 1666.

from an old working. The capital cost of mining had greatly increased, and there is steady complaint that mining was an uncertain business. In 1618 boring was introduced, in 1650 wooden ways, on which wagons ran from the pit-heads to the staithes. Roger North was told of an adit which cost £6000, and there were many stories of strangers who lost their whole fortune in unlucky ventures. Perhaps they were attracted by hopes of such profits as J. Hedworth lamented, in a letter to Sir Harry Vane. A minor during the troubles of the Commonwealth, he had been robbed by Hazelrigg of coal mines bringing in "£15 a day clear profit, and yet they sold the coals at 11s. the chalder, which now is at 13s."[1] A few pitmen were enlisted by the Scots to help in the siege of Newcastle. Some served among Newcastle's White-coats. But the war was a season of misery for all the people of the Tyne valley, for it brought the coal trade almost to a complete stop.

In 1708 the first treatise on mining was published, *The Compleat Collier*. Written by some anonymous Wearside miner, it was designed to encourage gentlemen to work coals by saving them from the exactions of their head servants. There were many reasons for the investment of money in mining; it increased at once the revenue and the national income, it added to the supply of fuel, it encouraged the growth of "that nursery of Saylors" the fleet of colliers, and it gave employment to many thousands of the poor

[1] *The Oppressed Man's Outcry*, 1651. (Tracts relating to the Civil War.)

"who must otherwise be beggars and starve." There
is an account of the sinking of a pit, and of the duties
and wages of every kind of workman and official.
The first men mentioned are the sinkers. Their pay
must have seemed high to the stranger, for the author
at once begins an explanation of the skill their work
demanded. In addition to the danger to the sinker
himself—he might be maimed, and rendered for ever
incapable of working, he might be blinded by a
splinter of stone, he might even be killed—a poor
workman would blunt and break tools, or "£1000
might be spent, and then by an ignorant man be
blasted by a strong blast"[1]. The sinker was no common labourer, but a man who understood the "nature
of stone, and stythe, and surfeit"[2].

A method of sinking through water-bearing strata
had already been devised. By lining the shaft with
wooden staves, behind which were stuffed uncured
sheep-skins, any ordinary difficulty could be sur-
mounted, but feeders, the powerful underground
springs tapped from time to time in mining opera-
tions, were a mystery to the *Compleat Collier*.
Contrary to the nature of water, they rose per-
pendicularly. He was driven to conclude that they
were fed from the sea, which lay like a fountain head
high above the land. Water was the miner's great
foe. To thirty fathoms, a hand pump would remove
it; beyond that, a horse pump was necessary. There

---

[1] J. C., *The Compleat Collier, or the Whole Art of Sinking,
Getting, and Working Coal Mine*. (Newcastle, 1708.)
[2] *Ibid.*

was too much reason to fear fire about a pit for the rumours of a fire pump to be welcome. A stronger pump was badly needed, and its inventor would meet with "such encouragement as would keep his coach and six," but fire was no trustworthy servant. As soon as the shaft was sunk a horse engine was required, with four relays of horses. To stint expense here was false economy, for if through lack of horses the pit stopped "the workmen, or at least some of them, will expect as much from their day's work, though it want a quarter of its quantity."

The chief official was the viewer, who was paid 15s. to 20s. a week, but as he was a skilled surveyor and could take three or four pits under his charge it was not an excessive wage. The overman, who placed the men at work, and who was actually in charge of the pit, drew only 8s. a week. There is no mention of the earnings of the corver, the man who repaired the large wicker baskets in which the coal was drawn to the surface, but his work was very important. Without his care, by the damage they received in the shaft, the corves would lose an inch a day in height, and fall rapidly in content. Of the two banksmen one was paid 16d. a day, his assistant 2d. less. They kept an account of the coals raised, setting aside the token, or small stick, by which each hewer below marked his corves. Badly filled corves were allowed to stand unemptied, until the hewers came out of the pit. Then the guilty man was reprimanded, and on occasion fined 6d. for his fraud or neglect. There were two classes of workmen underground, the hewers and the barrowmen. The hewers who with pick and shovel, maul and wedge, won the coal, were paid 12*d*. or 14*d*. a day. But it was usual to "agree with the hewers by the score of corves, by chance 10*d*. or 12*d*. a score, according to the tenderness or hardness of the coal, and what the mine will afford." For when the hewers were paid day wages each man might get but 13 or 15 corves a shift, but when they were paid by output "Good Hand" meant "Good Hire." It was in the payment of the barrowmen that the chief expense of coal-mining lay. It was their duty to fill the corves, haul them to the shaft, and hook them on the cable. For this they received 22*d*. a day, and as the workings advanced their demands increased. When it was an uphill journey to the shaft the barrowmen insisted on an additional payment of 2*d*. a day, and there was plain advantage in working upwards along a seam.

The dangers of the pit might justify the high wage but it was the profit of the owner which paid them. "For I have observed," said the *Compleat Collier*, "that where profit doth not arise, the wages are paid, though we venture our lives never so much, but grudgingly, if at all." As much skill was necessary to keep down the working costs as to overcome natural obstacles. The half yard seam was too low to work. The hewers and barrowmen would sometimes confederate together underground "and sometimes be so roguish, as to set big coals hollow at the Corfe bottom, and cover them over with small," and, where supervision was lacking, defraud the owner of great sums in wages. He on his side could make a great saving by working in winter, when many of the small pits were idle. "For then the labourers, rather than be idle, are prevailed upon, as is customary, to lower their wages."

Custom has long been the miners' guide, though now the men rely more on their own strength in dispute than on "the generosity of the owner." But from the tone of the comments on wages and working practice it is plain that the pitmen were in small fear of oppression or underpayment. By what means the barrowmen procured their periodic increase in wage is not explained, but there is no hint that the demands might be resisted. All the viewers' care was needed to keep down the working costs, but it is never suggested that the wages, admittedly so high as to need explanation, might be reduced.

It is easy to continue the story of the technical improvements in mining. There are a great many "Views," or surveys, of collieries, the older ones part picture, part plan, the later ones as exact as the compass could make them. Often a written description accompanies the plan, with calculations, and estimates, and well-stated arguments for some suggested course of action. The various costs, the profits to be expected, the difficulties to be overcome, are reviewed in turn. In 1712 the invention of Newcomen's Fire-engine provided the long desired pumping power. A seam much below 60 fathoms would have defeated the *Compleat Collier*. In 1786 coal was reached at Wallsend at a depth of 600 feet. As the depth increased, and with it the cost of sinking, it became necessary to work a much larger area from one shaft.

To reduce the cost of transport horses were taken
down the mines, and wooden tramways laid in the
more extensive workings, similar to those which had
long been common on the surface. Boys could drive
the horses, and push small sledges on the ways, and
about 1750, when the employment of boys became
common, the barrowmen lost their pride of place
as the best paid class in the pits. The boy putters
who supplanted them shared neither their name nor
their prosperity.

But it was not until 1780, when the steam engine
was already supplanting it, that the old Newcomen
pumping engine was adapted for drawing coal. To
get the coal out of the deep pits was a serious difficulty. In some places a bucket filled with water was
used as a counter poise to the corf, in others the
pump water, discharged from a height, drove the
wheel of a windlass. But horse gins long remained
the chief winding gear, and though in 1780 a square
iron tub replaced the corf in some collieries it was
an improvement which few viewers adopted. The
men rode up and down the shaft with a leg through
the loop of the rope. Even in 1840 children ascended
and descended clinging to one another "like a string
of onions"[1].

It was the increased capital cost of the deep shafts
which made it important to get as much coal as
possible from each seam. The old miners used to
drive parallel galleries and join them with cross cuts,

[1] J. R. Leifchild, *Children's Employment Commission* (1842),
p. 545.

leaving large square pillars to support the roof. Sometimes as much as half the coal remained permanently
underground. Later viewers saw that if they left
larger pillars most of the wasted coal could be removed by a second working. But it was not until
the nineteenth century was well advanced that it
became the rule to attempt to remove the whole of
the coal. The traditional method of working in the
north-country, "Bord and Pillar," was an improvement on the miner's earliest method. The hewers
worked singly, or in pairs, at the head of a gallery,
or the side of a pillar. This method of working had had
an influence mental, as well as technical. Each man
had a direct interest in his own forward progress, he
was neither checked nor encouraged by the speed of
visible companions. He worked for the coal-owner,
never as one of a gang engaged by a small contractor.
The "Butty" system has never had a hold in the
northern coal field. Officials were appointed who
visited each man at his work, but the hewer visited
from time to time developed a far greater skill and
self-reliance than did a man who worked constantly
under the eye of a foreman. Until very recent years
the north-country pitman had an unrivalled fame,
and even now he is apt to look upon the miners of
other districts as navvies rather than miners proper.

Meantime the isolation of the hewer became the
foundation of an exceptionally high standard of pit
discipline. It made necessary an unwatched obedience
to orders. It was the first cause of a minute division
of labour which is still unknown in other districts.

And four times a year lots were drawn to determine the place in which each hewer should work. This practice, known as "cavilling," has often been blamed as the foundation of the gambling habits of the pitmen, but it must often have assisted to maintain industrial peace. A good place, a bad place, came by fortune, not by the allotment of the officials.

In the old small pits there was a simple method of avoiding disastrous explosions. At the sign of gas the men left the pit. But in the deeper mines, large in area as they were, with immense tracts of exhausted workings or "goaf" upon which the roof was always settling, gas was always present. About 1730 the first attempts at ventilation were made. A furnace was built at the bottom of one shaft, its heat created an upward current of air, and as the pressure decreased in the workings, cold fresh air rushed down the second shaft. If the mine had but one shaft it was split into two by a wooden partition, known as the brattice. Not the least terror of an old mine was the descent through the smoke and hot foul air of the upcast shaft. In the eighteenth century two viewers at the Whitehaven collieries, Carlisle Spedding and his son John, slowly improved the system of ventilation. By doors and partitions they led the cold air into the furthest parts of the mines. But the pits "fired" with a frequency which is the best witness to the courage and perseverance of the men who worked them. The achievements of the Whitehaven viewers rendered the pits workable rather than safe.

But still there is far less to be told of the pitmen

than of the pits. The names common among them shew that they were recruited from the small farmers whom the agricultural revolution displaced. About 1780 the employment of women in the north-country pits ceased. Almost the last mention of a woman underground is in an account of a shaft accident. In 1772,

a woman employed in putting at South Biddick (was) riding up one of the pits (when) the other hook, in passing, caught her cloathes. The weight of the rope forced her out of the loop, and she fell to the bottom of the shaft[1].

At what date it became customary to hire the pit-men by a written agreement for a whole year's service is not known. A copy of a "bond" for the year 1703, made between the High Sheriff of Durham and the hewers of Benwell, is from its form obviously not the first of its kind. There is mention in turn of a price for each score of corves hewn, of an additional price for forward progress, and of exceptional payment "at the judgment of the viewer" for work of unusual difficulty. Such payment, known as "consideration," was a very treasured privilege in the north, where it survived until the invention of the statutory minimum wage. In the pictures of houses, by which the old plans represent a village, there are seen the familiar long rows of low cottages, with one window and one chimney to each door. Each cottage can have contained at most two rooms, probably in the majority of cases only one. It must have been very early in the eighteenth century that a free house

[1] *Newcastle Journal*, Feb. 8th, 1772.

became part of the hewer's wage, but the pitman's coal was hardly free in the days when 6*d*. a fother meant half a day's wage. But such agreed payments have a knack of standing still, despite alterations in wages and the value of money. Until late in the nineteenth century sixpence a fortnight remained the customary "off-take" from the miner's wage for his load of coal. Until 1740 the average daily pay of the hewer was about 1*s*. 2*d*. It rose in that year to rather less than 1*s*. 8*d*., and remained at that figure until 1790.

Mining engineers find in the long narrow stone drifts sufficient witness of the skill of the early pitmen. We can guess how laborious must have been their life when bodily strength and perseverance were their only weapons against natural obstacles. Gunpowder for blasting rock came into use in 1740, but it was not for many years that the miner dared to use powder for getting coal. After the face of the seam had been undercut with the pick the hanging mass was brought down by driving in wedges.

> Here, agyen, had awd langsyners
> Mony a weary, warkin' byen,
> Now unknawn te coaly-Tyners,
> A' bein' mell-and-wedge wark then.
>
> Aw've bray'd for hours at woody coal,
> Wi' airms myest droppin frae the shouthèr[1],

says the old pitman of his labours, and the work of the putters was as hard until the invention of plates, the iron rails which in 1808 took the place of the wooden "trams."

[1] T. Wilson, *The Pitman's Pay*.

Hobbes could well have learned his opinion of the life of savage man, "nasty, brutish, and short," from a study of the pitman. In the long rows of the colliery villages he lived almost unknown to the outside world. In the eighteenth century a visitor to the north found the pitmen

a rude, bold, savage set of beings, apparently cut off from their fellow men in their interest and feelings. They all have the same vocation, and stand out as a sturdy band apart from the motley mixture of common humanity[1].

Newspaper advertisements almost always describe them as of middle height, some 5 feet 7 inches, and slender build, with round shoulders. And inevitably there follow two phrases "wearing a striped waistcoat" and "walks like a pitman." Very few of them seem ever to have left the pits. Such boys from the collieries near the coast who ran away to sea quickly returned, for they found a sailor's life harder and more dangerous than the one they had left, and its discomforts more pronounced. And, in the drunken sprees which accompanied a trip to the town, pitmen occasionally fell into the clutches of the recruiting sergeant. In 1756 the artillery was so much in need of miners that it advertised in the Newcastle newspapers for them, offering 10s. a week as pay, with the prospect of 2s. a day as corporals, and half a crown as sergeants.

From the first the boys seem to have worked 14 to 18 hours a day, though in the recollections of

[1] R. N. Boyd, *Coal Pits and Pitmen*, 1895.

the old men work and absence from home seem to
be synonymous terms. As long as the hewers had
to break down the coal with maul and wedge they
worked in pairs, staying below rather more than
12 hours. Except in the very deep pits they kept no
regular hours, but came away when they were satisfied
with their day's work. When blasting came into use
the two men still remained "marrows," working
together and sharing their wages. But they worked
alone, the second man coming to the face to relieve
his fellow during the late hours of the morning, though
it was many years before the man in the "fore-shift"
left immediately he was relieved. Sometimes he stayed
for as much as two hours, for the hewers measured
their work rather by their forward progress than by
time. Still, blasting reduced the hewers' hours from
12 to roughly 8 though the rest of the pit's crew
remained below the whole day. But before the industrial changes brought a steady demand for coal
the pits worked very irregularly. There was a holiday
of about a month at Christmas, chiefly because at
that season the colliers were kept by adverse winds
in the Tyne. To mark the closing of the pit the last
hewn corf of coals was drawn up the shaft covered
with lighted candles, and the hewers gave Christmas
gifts to the lads who took away their coals. Two or
three times a year the lads proclaimed a "gaudy
day" and kept holiday, as for instance on the morning
on which they first heard the cuckoo.

Slack times might bring low pay, but the hewer
was secure against starvation. By his "bond" he

was "Upheld," that is, paid an agreed sum each fortnight, work or no work. But little excitement came to brighten life in the pit villages. There were weddings, celebrated with much eating and drinking and the firing of guns. There were christenings. And there was the fortnightly orgy at the Pay. Beyond this there was little but the rejoicings at the success of a new sinking and the processions which accompanied the first load of coals from the pit-head to the staithe. In 1802 the opening of Percy Main, won without the loss of a single life, was celebrated in a manner which long remained in local memory. The procession to the ship was headed by the master sinker, bearing a trophy. After him walked the sinkers, four and four, the smiths, and the enginemen. Then, accompanied by a band, and surrounded with colours, came the wagon of coals, on which sat a well-dressed lady to represent "the genius of the mine." There followed viewers, four and four, pitmen with cockades in their hats, wagonmen, enginemen, and staithe men. To a salute of artillery, and a triple round of cheers, the company drank to the success of Percy Main, and as the coal slid down the spout into the ship the band played the traditional song of the coal trade, "The Keel Row." The gentry, to the number of 150, sat down to dinner, and the pitmen went off "to be feasted with beef and plum pudding, strong beer and punch, and such of them as were sober, to finish off the night with music and dancing"[1].

[1] *Newcastle Courant*, Sept. 11th, 1802.

The pitmen were thought a violent, drunken, blasphemous race. They kept their fighting dogs and their cocks, they gambled, and delighted in performing feats of strength and endurance for wagers. In the midst of a blizzard "a one-eyed pitman, known by the name of Blenkar Will, undertook for the trifling sum of half a crown to go a mile along the public road, from Chester-le-Street to Sunderland, stark naked, which he performed in seven minutes"[1]. But Wesley, who on his first visit to the north was surprised at "so much drunkenness, cursing and swearing, even from the mouths of children, as never do I remember to have heard before," found their state was far less due to natural wickedness, than to neglect. The next time he came he

had a great desire to visit a little village called Plessey, about ten measured miles north of Newcastle. It is inhabited by colliers only, such as have been always in the first rank for savage ignorance, and wickedness of every kind. Their grand assembly used to be the Lord's Day, on which men, women, and children met together to play at chuck-ball, and spun-farthing[2].

Yet, in 1757, these people had become a pattern to all the societies in England. They had "no jars of any kind among them, but with heart and soul provoke one another to love and good works"[3].

It was during the eighteenth century that the pitman attained the height of his outward splendour. Though the full rig is rarely seen outside the small Northumberland villages the traditional working

---

[1] *Newcastle Courant*, Feb. 5th, 1814.
[2] *Wesley's Journal*, vol. III, p. 71.   [3] *Ibid.* vol. IV, p. 220.

clothes are not yet abandoned—a pair of short flannel trousers, white or blue checked; a blue checked shirt, with a red tie; a jacket to match the trousers; stout, square-toed shoes, and long knitted stockings of grey wool. But Methodist piety replaced the splendour of the holiday clothes by the respectability of Sunday blacks. The old-fashioned pitman wore his hair long, on week-days tied in a queue, on Sundays spread over his shoulders. At either temple was a curl, carefully rolled in paper over a small piece of lead, so that it would dangle in fantastic shape down his cheeks. Over a white shirt of fine linen was drawn a pair of blue velvet breeches. Next came long stockings, of pink, purple, or blue, clocked up to the knee; next, buckled shoes. The pitman's coat was of shiny blue, with an even brighter lining. His hat had several bands of yellow ribbon, into which were stuck flowers. But his greatest glory was his waistcoat of brocade, his "posy jacket," cut short to shew an inch or two of shirt above the waist-band.

> When aw put on my blue coat that shines se,
> My jacket wi posies sae fine, se,
> My sark sic sma' threed, man,
> My pigtail se greet, man,
> Odd smash, what a buck was Bob Cranky.
>
> Blue Stockings, white clocks, and reed garters,
> Yellow breeks, and my shoen wi' lang quarters,
> Aw myed wor bairns cry,
> Eh! Sartees! Ni! Ni!
> Sic very fine things had Bob Cranky[1].

[1] "Bob Cranky's Size Sunday," *The Newcastle Songster*.

CHAPTER II

EARLY STRUGGLES

UNTIL the reform in the franchise gave the workman political importance he had small opportunity of asserting his industrial claims. He was
hampered at every turn by the Combination Acts,
by the law of Master and Servant, and by an anti-
quated and partial interpretation of the common law.
The miner had other obstacles in his way, chief of
which was the Yearly Bond, the written agreement
which laid down the terms of his service. Except
during his few days of freedom at the annual hirings
the pitman who refused to work was risking arrest
and imprisonment for breach of contract. Fourteen
days in jail was the regular punishment for indiscipline, and almost every number of the old Newcastle
newspapers—three at least have been published since
the days of the Georges—heads its front page with
an offer of reward for the apprehension of some
absconding pitman. When it is remembered that as
late as 1882 the government inspector of mines suggested that all mining cases should be tried by a
stipendiary magistrate, the contempt of the pitmen
for the justice they received in more revolutionary
times can be well imagined[1]. Coroner and sheriff,

[1] *Report of H.M. Inspector of Mines, Newcastle District*, 1882.
And also, J. R. Leifchild, *Children's Employment Commission*
(1842), p. 520.

magistrate and grand jury, even the petty jury of
lick-spittle tradesmen, were all on the side of the
owners, and they seldom troubled to conceal a bias
which was at once a badge of respectability and a
witness to sound political principle.

But neither the fear of imprisonment nor the
certainty of speedy starvation could keep the pitmen
from strikes and combinations. It is a tradition that
the first widespread outbreak occurred in 1740, and
that it won an advance in wages most commonly
estimated at 30 per cent.[1] The number of advertisements for the arrest of incendiaries who were
burning the pit-head machinery suggests that in
1747 discontent was still rife. Eighteen years later
riot and destruction swept along the whole Tyne
valley. Trade was booming and employment was
plentiful. The coal-owners were afraid that competition for pitmen would drive up wages, or that their
men would be enticed from the deep and more
dangerous pits. They met and discussed an agreement by which managers were to bind no new men
who came to them unprovided with a certificate of
dismissal from their last colliery. In the middle of
August, long before the binding day, the pitmen
struck. Six hundred ships, and a hundred thousand
men, miners, sailors, keel-men, staithe men, even the
London coal-whippers, were laid idle[2]. In those
days "the course of a pitman's steek was traced in a
long line of wreckage, as the men proceeded from

[1] J. Bell Simpson, *Capital and Labour in Coal-Mining*.
[2] *Annual Register*, 1765.

Colliery to Colliery, and destroyed the winding gear
at the surface." The pitmen upheld their reputation
for ungovernable violence, setting fire to the pit-
heaps and caring little that here and there the mines
themselves were destroyed. The masters published a
denial that they had made any agreement. The men
replied that an agreement was known to exist, and
that the rise of prices had made their poverty too
great for them to submit to a more rigorous bond.
In October they returned to work, in part at least
victorious. If their wage remained unaltered—it is
seldom that a pitman's strike has been unaccompanied
by a wage-demand—they retained their freedom of
movement. In 1767 there was a little noticed sequel
of the strike. An amended Malicious Injuries to
Property Act made definite mention of "setting fire
to mines." The north-country coal-owners were not
without influence in the unreformed parliament.

If the recollections of the old pitmen are to be
trusted, at the binding day of 1800 there was a short,
indecisive strike. In the local newspapers there is no
record of disturbance, but the newspapers themselves
admit that at the request of the owners they had for
some little time ceased to mention mining matters.
It is significant that in 1800 the coal-owners were
provided with a new legal weapon against their men.
An act "for the security of collieries and mines, and
the better regulation of colliers and miners" made
mention of "the great fraud of stacking coal...by
which colliers obtain money beyond what they earn."
And it punished with imprisonment, or fine of 40s.,

breaches of the yearly agreement. It was an act which was often to be of use in later troubles.

The first strike of which we have any complete account occurred in 1810. The owners proposed to change the binding time from October to April:

for, as October was the period of the greatest trade, when a stock of coals was accumulated in the different markets, a strike or stoppage at that period was extremely inconvenient and objectionable[1].

Perhaps the alteration of the binding time points to a memory of frequent strikes, perhaps the owners wished to make some change in the bond which they knew would be resisted. It is impossible to separate the unrest of the times from the abnormal wage conditions.

The custom of giving two or three guineas per hewer as binding and bounty money had crept into the trade, but in consequence of the extraordinary demand for coals ...during the year (1804)...a general scramble for hewers and putters took place....The fears of procuring the necessary supply of men were industriously magnified to such a degree that from 12 to 14 guineas a man was given on the Tyne, and 18 guineas on the Wear, and progressive exorbitant bounties were paid to putters, drivers, and irregular workmen. Drink was lavished in the utmost profusion, and every sort of extravagance perpetrated. Nor did the evil end here, for a positive increase in rates and wages was established, to the extent of from 30 % to 40 %[2].

As a natural result there was an inrush of strangers to the trade. Over production brought down prices,

[1] Matthias Dunn, *An Historical View of the Coal Trade*, 1844, p. 30.
[2] *Ibid*. pp. 27 and 28.

at a time when high wages were giving the men extravagant tastes. The bounties were gradually discontinued, and wages fell to the old level.

Whatever may have been their reasons, and natural conservatism was in those days reason sufficient, the pitmen firmly refused to accept the change in the binding day. They struck, and the struggle lasted seven weeks. In the end the owners appealed to the law and won. At one time there were so many pitmen in jail that 300 had to be confined in the episcopal stables at Bishop Auckland[1]. Doubtless the men had signed the bond first in ignorance of its conditions, and then too late had begun their resistance. Among the prisoners must have been most of the leaders, for mediators, among them a Captain Davis of the Carmarthen militia, in vain attempted to persuade them to a compromise. The desired change was made. As an old pitman said in later days, the men lost the strike by an accident. Such memories of a compromise as persisted suggest that the renewal of the bounties was promised. That the men were not satisfied is clear, for next year the trouble threatened again. The Rev. M. Newfield, a well-known magistrate who had striven hard for peace the year before, called a meeting of the owners at Chester-le-Street[2]. His proposals of a conference with the men were at first unwelcome. The owners disliked the suggestion of a bargain with men who had no legal right to

[1] R. Fynes, *The Miners of Northumberland and Durham* (1873), pp. 13, 14.
[2] *Ibid.* p. 15.

combine, and whose actions, in days when the French Revolution was a vivid memory, seemed to promise widespread social disorder. But in the end they were persuaded to receive a deputation of two men from each colliery, and a bond, acceptable to both parties, was drawn up. If 1810 had brought defeat, 1811 was in the moral sense a memorable victory.

1825 was a year of activity, much of which centred round Hetton. There a man named Macintosh attempted to found a co-operative store, but the opposition of the owners and the distrust and ignorance of the men drove him in disappointment to America[1]. The unrest of the times is reflected in the sentences which the alarmed magistrates inflicted on defaulting pitmen; the traditional fourteen days imprisonment became for a time two months. Meantime Thomas Hepburn had founded the first miners' union "for the procuring of higher wages" says a contemporary writer[2]. There were many local strikes, outcome of the men's attempts to restrict their output. Restriction and union were for a long time to be synonymous in the minds of most of the pitmen, and indeed of many of the owners. But restriction at that time had no far-sighted political intent. It kept the young men from the exhaustion and premature enfeeblement which was the price they paid for their pride in their strength. It saved the old and the weak from dangerous comparisons. It was only here and

[1] R. Fynes, *The Miners of Northumberland and Durham*, pp. 16–17.
[2] Matthias Dunn, *An Historical View of the Coal Trade*, p. 33.

there that a man thought of restriction as a remedy against unemployment; its direct advantages were sufficient arguments in its favour. The men's contention in later years, that union was from the first a defence against the growing harshness of capitalistic industry, has unexpected confirmation in the words of almost the only impartial contemporary witness.

When the spirit of mercantile speculation was once turned to the collieries...when competition on the market, and the consequent diminution of profit induced the owners to aim at making better terms with their men...the latter sought to strengthen themselves with the dangerous bond of combination. From that time a series of conflicts, too painful to be dwelt on, as being in every way disastrous in their consequence, ensued[1].

For over two hundred years capital had played a part in coal mining almost unparalleled in a country where industry was in general still poorly developed. For ten generations the pitmen had been wage-dependent labourers, of a kind rare until the invention of the factory system. Yet, until the late eighteenth century, there had been small signs of wage manipulation. The strong hereditary influence in the coal trade, the completeness of the monopoly which the Newcastle Hostmen enjoyed in the London market, the absence of internal competition assured by the "Limitation of the Vend," a system of restriction of output which persisted until 1846, had made it the rule rather to accept labour costs as inevitable than to seek to diminish them except by engineering skill. At new collieries workmen's estimates fixed the

[1] J. Holland, *Fossil Fuel* (1835), pp. 298, 299, 300.

rate of wages, and few mining matters were free from the rule of local custom. It was the influx of new capital, the sudden extension of the Wearside collieries, and the success of a less hide-bound generation of viewers in working hitherto inaccessible seams, which persuaded the coal-owners to learn in the school of the Manchester manufacturers to treat labour as a commodity in a market subject to unalterable laws of supply and demand. Combination, strike, and restriction were the only weapons ready to the hand of the pitmen, weapons used with a vigour and success which kept the men, even in their later misery, from the worst evils of wage competition. Poor as they might think themselves, much as they might regret "the flesh-pots of their fathers"[1], the unanimous witness which almost every stranger gave of the miner's comparative well-being was a hard obstacle for the miners' leaders to overcome. Cobbett might be ill-informed, but it was not from "the coal merchant Vane Tempest" whose "right to sell and carry away the soil of the land given him in trust" he so loudly decried, that he learned that the pitmen lived on meal and bread, as people ought to do[2].

Union, and the general excitement which accompanied the campaign for political reform, gave the men a feeling of strength which encouraged them to two years of strife and led to their eventual defeat. In March, 1831, mass meetings were held to prepare

[1] Broad Sheet, Coal-Trade Offices, Newcastle: "Life, Character, Death of that Monster, Limitation of Coal Vend."
[2] W. Cobbett, *Tour of Scotland and the Four Northern Counties* (1833).

the men for the approaching binding day. Over twenty
thousand pitmen are said to have attended a great
meeting on Newcastle Town Moor, at which the men's
demands were finally stated. They asked for no increase in wages, merely for improved conditions of
service. They wished for some protection against the
viewers' right to lay the pits idle for a few days at
a time. They said that a day of fourteen to eighteen
hours deprived the boys of all hope of education.
Delegates were elected, weekly meetings arranged,
and a subscription of sixpence a man collected. In
turn suggestions were approved for a petition to
parliament, a claim to poor relief in idleness, and an
appeal to the magistrates. The men departed from
the meeting in good order, with the resolution to
continue at work unbound if the masters would allow
them to do so, but to be firm in their refusal to sign
the existing bond. In addition they pledged themselves to buy no more candles, meat, or drink from
the overmen.

The people of Newcastle had expected that mis-
chief would follow this assembly of savage pitmen.
Their Mayor appeared on the Moor to offer himself
as a messenger to the owners. His offer was of some
use to the men. It enabled their case to be stated
in the guise of an appeal for his worship's assistance
in mediation, as a leading member of the general
public. Six years before the infant union, under the
name of the Colliers of the United Association
of Northumberland and Durham, had issued two
pamphlets, as a plain statement of the grievances

which they wished to be considered, the fines, the
long hours of the boys, the frequent idleness of the
pits, and the increase in temperature due to the
neglect of ventilation which had followed the introduction of the Davy Lamp. Their action had been
passed over in silence, their desire for a meeting with
the owners ignored. But of the appeal which the
men issued at the beginning of the strike, an appeal
"replete with delusive and unfounded statements,"[1]
the newspapers thought fit to take notice. The editor
of the *Durham Chronicle*—using capitals to shew
where respect was added to obligation—thought it
his duty to concoct a reply, addressed to "the public,
the Coal-Owners, and the infatuated pitmen, dupes
as they are of a set of artful and designing rogues."

But this picture of the good fortune of the pitmen,
with their free coal, their free house, and an assured
income of 14s. a week, subject to fines and deductions
which seldom exceeded 1s. 8d. a fortnight, was neither
entirely true nor a good answer to a demand which
laid most stress on the need for a shorter day for
the boys. Fourteen shillings a week the owner was
compelled to pay, under the terms of the bond, but
if the pit were idle for not more than three days at
a time the men were entitled to no compensation.
This provision, devised to meet the case of an occasional accident, had suggested to astute managers a
method of economy in slack times. A pit could be
closed three days a week and the men left to depend
on the wages of their working time, a sum much

---

[1] *Durham Chronicle*, April 16th, 1831.

nearer 7s. than the 14s. named in the bond. And, if the testimony of survivors of the great strike is to be trusted, and every accidental circumstance supports the story which these men told in their old age, the "artful and designing rogues" who directed the strike were men of exceptionally high character and ability, Primitive Methodists whom recent conversion by a young man from Hull had given a new zeal for education and moral improvement. Three men met each week at the Cock Tavern, Newcastle: Thomas Hepburn, the president, a Hetton pitman whose father was killed in the mine; Samuel Wardle, of Backworth, the secretary; and Charles Parkin, of Hetton, who took the money[1].

By the time the owners thought fit to issue a reply to the union statement all the long-standing grievances of the men had been dragged into the battle, and general demands could be ignored in a general denial of hardship. For the lowness of wages the owners blamed the men. "Were they to bind such a number of men as they could find in full work not more than three-quarters of the pitmen would be employed"[2]. But they impaired the value of their statements by an assertion that during the preceding year the average wage of the pitmen had been 18s. 4½d. for a week of five days. Only two years before Mr Buddle, the best-known viewer in the north, had told a Committee of the House of Commons that miners' wages were 28s. a fortnight.

---

[1] *Newcastle (Weekly) Chronicle*, Dec. 25th, 1882.
[2] *Durham Chronicle*, April 23rd, 1831 (Owners' Advt.).

In an appeal addressed to the Mayor of Newcastle the men repeated their demands. A passage quoted from the bond proved that they were entitled to no compensation for odd days of idleness. It was said that a working day of even twelve hours meant for some boys an absence from home of seventeen. A new-felt hardship was the power of the owners to evict men from their houses; an old one, the weight of the fines, on which the men had no check, and which at times reduced their earnings to 20s. a fortnight.

The men were willing to go to work unbound, but they refused to sign the old agreement. Rather, they said, they would wait for an answer to the petition which their delegates intended to carry to parliament[1]. It is not surprising that here and there they broke into open violence. There were riots at West Jesmond, Chirton, and Netherton. A man on guard over the Fatfield pit was shot at, and dangerously wounded. A mob sacked the viewer's house at Cowpen, and wrecked the winding gear at Bedlington. As the poverty of the pitmen increased small parties wandered begging through the country-side, giving rise perhaps to more alarm than was warranted. Rumours were readily believed that they entered shops and inns and took by force what the less timid tradesmen dared to deny them. The people of Durham went in fear of an organised attack on their market[2]. The owners offered to increase the standing wage to 30s. a fortnight, but the delegates kept the men to

---

[1] *Durham Chronicle*, April 30th, 1831.
[2] *Ibid*. May 7th, 1831.

their original demands, in which no mention of wages
had been made[1]. Isolated men who returned to work
were threatened by huge crowds, but in June several
of the pits, notably those belonging to the Marquess
of Londonderry[2], had quietly started, under private
bargains which gave local satisfaction. This discord
in their ranks warned the owners that they could
hold out no longer. The refusal of their offer of an
increased wage had probably opened their eyes to
the true meaning of the discontent. Hepburn's chief
demand, that the boys' hours should not exceed
twelve, was granted[3]. A second reform, of almost
equal importance, was the abolition of truck and the
tommy-shop, a reform made rather at the expense
of the officials than the owners. Henceforth wages
were to be paid in ready money. Perhaps this is the
"very considerable advance of wages"[4] which they
accomplished, for no other trace of it can be found.
But the men were not satisfied with a victory which
must have rejoiced the leaders themselves. Here and
there the strike died hard. At Hetton, the centre of
all union activity, the pitmen came out again, demanding that no stranger should be employed, and
that a party of imported lead-miners, brought in
during the struggle, should be sent home[5].

[1] *Durham Chronicle*, May 14th, 1831.
[2] *Ibid.* May 21st, 1831. And also, R. Fynes, *The Miners of
Northumberland and Durham*, pp. 20–22.
[3] R. Fynes, *The Miners of Northumberland and Durham*,
p. 22.
[4] Matthias Dunn, *An Historical View of the Coal Trade*, p. 33.
[5] *The Durham Chronicle*, May 28th, June 4th and June 11th,
1831.

It was a mistake in tactics that the gains of the strike were accepted by the pitmen as an earnest of new victories to come. There is little doubt that their attitude warned the owners to prepare to make stouter resistance in the struggle which was plainly impending. During the autumn the cause of union was kept alive by local action. At Lambton, whose owner, Lord Londonderry, was the foremost opponent of the men, as perhaps he was their most enlightened employer, one or two of the banksmen were dismissed. The rest of the men struck, and seven of their leaders were arrested. "For refusing to work, and inciting others to do the same"[1] they were sent to jail, two for two months, the rest for a shorter time. The delegate whom the colliery had elected at the last strike was one of the two who received the heavier sentence. Hepburn for a time seems to have become a schoolmaster, and to have busied himself as much with political agitation as with the affairs of the union. "Only get the bill," he is reported to have said at a Reform meeting, "and every working man will have rum in his coffee every morning." The speech, little as it has in common with his other sayings, is doubtless a misremembered version of that view of political reform which many of the working men shared with Cobbett and the Chartists, that the vote would be the key to a new material prosperity, the fruits of a social and industrial revolution.

In a review of the events of the year the *Durham Chronicle* wrathfully remarked "it is a fact that the

---

[1] *Durham Chronicle*, Sept. 24th, 1831.

pitmen suppose they are omnipotent"[1] and deplored
the folly which led "the real tyrants, the well-paid
colliers,...to quarrel with their prosperity," at a
time when three-quarters of the country was starving[2].
Everywhere the owners began to complain that there
was an organised programme of restriction among the
men. To keep up the output they imported lead-
miners, whose intrusion the pitmen strongly resented[3].
It was with justice, for years of starvation in a
dying industry had made these strangers jump at
any chance of employment, however low the wage.
At Waldridge a mob of more than a thousand men
collected, and began to wreck the pit-head while the
lead-miners were below. Their lives were saved only
by the rumoured arrival of the military, which drove
the pitmen away and allowed the officials to re-start
the pumps[4]. At Cramlington, after due warning, four
men were beaten almost to death for the crime of
leaving the union[5]. In the conduct of the delegates
"bad and wicked men, skulking incendiaries who
planned in secret what they dared only order others
to do"[6] there was too often grave irregularity. The
pitmen of those days were ignorant men with a
reputation for savage violence. It is not strange that
here and there advocates of violence should have been
their chosen leaders. Seven men were arrested for the

---

[1] *Durham Chronicle*, Dec. 31st, 1831.
[2] *Ibid.*
[3] R. Fynes, *The Miners of Northumberland and Durham*,
pp. 25–26.
[4] *Durham Chronicle*, March 10th, 1832.
[5] *Ibid.* Feb. 18th, 1832.　　　　　[6] *Ibid.*

Waldridge outrage—a free pardon, and a reward of 500 guineas, had been offered as the price for information[1]. But it was doubtful if they were more guilty than many others, though at the assizes they were sent to prison for periods of from six to fifteen months. As Hepburn said, when he counselled the pitmen to keep order, "the owners were determined to punish someone, and it was enough that a man was a member of the union"[2]. At Coxlodge a persistent strike was countered by eviction[3], but though the newspapers continued their strictures on the dangerous pretensions, the foolish beliefs, and the outrageous violence of the pitmen, the judge at the Durham spring assizes could congratulate the county on its freedom from outrage such as was prevalent in the south[4]. For in 1832, among the starving rural population, rick burnings were common, and the comparative prosperity of the pitmen is reflected in their peaceful conduct.

A meeting on Boldon Fell was the only reply the pitmen made to an exhortation to seek protection "rather in the confidence and approbation of society than in the delusive promise of union"[5]. Hepburn, again elected leader, exhorted the men to order, sobriety, and the performance of their religious duties, and advised them to strive for the education

[1] *Durham Chronicle*, Jan. 21st, 1832.
[2] R. Fynes, *The Miners of Northumberland and Durham*, p. 26.
[3] *Durham Chronicle*, Jan. 21st, 1832.
[4] *Ibid*. March 3rd, 1832.
[5] *Ibid*. March 10th, 1832.

of their lads[1]. Over £10,000 had already been spent
by the union, yet there was still £1000 in hand for
the struggles to come. In March, 1832,

feeling a confidence in their union, and lacking the
prudence to be content with the advantages they had
gained the previous year, the pitmen commenced a more
general and formidable strike[2],

says Matthias Dunn, but in reality the strike was as
much the work of the owners as the men. Angered
by the men's persistent restriction of the output, and
perhaps even more by their general attitude of provo-
cative independence, the owners refused to rebind
the union men. The Brandlings—the head of the
family was in Anglican orders, and the name was
almost the oldest in the Newcastle coal trade—led
the way, at Kenton, Gosforth, and South Shields[3],
and to justify their action the associated owners
issued a statement of wages generally paid. In six
hours, they said, and without great exertion, two-
thirds of the hewers could earn 4s., a wage which the
weaker men could equal by a further two hours' work[4].
Boys were paid 10d. to 15d. a day, putters 4s. for
eleven hours' work, and shifters, men engaged on
repair work about the mine, 3s. for a day of eight
hours. The lead-miners, imported in the face of the
pitmen's opposition, were satisfied with their pay and
treatment, and almost at once they had become

---

[1] R. Fynes, *The Miners of Northumberland and Durham*,
p. 23.
[2] Matthias Dunn, *An Historical View of the Coal Trade*, p. 34.
[3] *Newcastle (Weekly) Chronicle*, Dec. 25th, 1882.
[4] *Durham Chronicle*, March 16th, 1832.

efficient workmen, a proof that pit-work required no long experience[1].

An anonymous pitman, calling himself Carbonarius, took on himself the duty of reply. Only the very best men, after eight hours' work in a favourable place, could earn the wage the owners said was so common, and one-fifth of the hewers were physically unable ever to earn so much, even if they toiled without pause for twelve hours. Three shillings, said this champion of union, whose letter has a ring of truth, was the average wage, and since the cranes which the boys attended worked 12 hours it was impossible that the boys themselves should work 11. Carbonarius hinted that the reason why gentlemen of repute had signed so untruthful a statement was that they were over-persuaded by their agents, through whose eyes owners always saw[2]. It is certain that Buddle, the acknowledged leader of the viewers, a man to whom the miners owed a new safety, for he had vastly improved ventilation, had a gift for manipulating figures, and by reason of long exercise of power, a strong dislike of any encroachment on his autocracy.

In April the last of the bonds expired and the strike became general, though at no time was the stoppage of work complete. Not all the pitmen were in the union. It was strong in a few places, such as Hetton[3] and South Shields. It was popular among the younger

---

[1] *Durham Chronicle*, March 16th, 1832.
[2] *Ibid*. March 30th, 1832.
[3] *Newcastle (Weekly) Chronicle*, Dec. 23rd, 1882.

men, who retained perhaps a more vivid memory of the slavery of their boyhood. While at some collieries the dismissal of the union men had small influence on the output, at others the owners took no share in the attempt to check the growth of combination among the men but bound all alike. Hepburn's policy was to tax the men employed for the maintenance of those idle through adherence to the union. Work was only stopped at pits where the majority of the men were in the union, and where the owner elected to share in the struggle. But this year the associated owners faced the strikers boldly. There was none of the hesitation of 1831. The pits were filled with "black-leg" labour, and after due warning the strikers were evicted from their homes. Special constables, soldiers, and the new London police were assembled in the villages to suppress every sign of disorder[1]. More and more men were enticed from the lead-mines, despite the efforts of the pitmen to scare them away by a recital of the dangers of the life[2]. Strangers were brought from Lancashire and Wales, though to prevent this second invasion the union sent delegates into the south. In some places they were well received. The Yorkshire miners had a union of their own. The Sheffield trade societies were always ready to help in a war against the masters. But at Alfreton the people, no doubt with the story of northern violence to black-leg labour

[1] R. Fynes, *The Miners of Northumberland and Durham*, p. 28.
[2] *Durham Chronicle*, May 25th, 1832.

in their ears, stripped and beat the delegates and dragged them through the village horse-pond[1]. Soon two or three thousand new men were working in the pits, and as the output rose the owners became more and more sure of victory.

The men had vague desires for an increase in wages but the owners from the first made recognition of the union the only issue of the strike. The adoption of the system of restriction of output had been a fatal mistake. An association which fostered such a breach of faith, said the owners, could not expect recognition. Had the leaders been content with demands for improved conditions, or for higher wages, they would not have been so bitterly opposed, but interference with the output and infringement of managerial control could not be borne. More and more strangers were imported, new districts such as Derbyshire sent their quota, and to account for their need of men the owners made no scruple of spreading stories of the decimation of the pitmen by cholera, or their decision to attempt to work a coal-field for themselves.

Under a persuasion that it was their duty to restore order many of the magistrates were active in opposition to the strike. In 1831 the newspapers had remarked on the unseemly conduct of Lord Londonderry, himself a coal-owner, in signing an official appeal for the preservation of the peace. In 1832 there was only praise for his actions when at the head of a troop of dragoons he rode to the pitmen's meetings to remind the men of their duty to refrain

---

[1] *Durham Chronicle*, June 6th, 1832.

from any breach of the peace. "Where is this great man of yours, your leader, Hepburn," said he, to stragglers on the outskirts of the crowd, but he went away peaceably, persuaded that no outbreak of violence was likely to follow the assemblies on the Fells. Later tradition says that the man who stepped forward to lead his horse through the crowd had a pistol ready to his hand in case the Marquess made any signal to the troops, and that in his later life Lord Londonderry was wont to say he had never seen a man with more influence over his fellows than the pitman's president[1]. But it was not long before the general peace of the strike was disturbed by outbreaks of local violence. At Hetton a man who left the union and signed the bond was attacked, and in the affray with the police a man was shot. At Fawdon and Tyne Main there was more shooting and it was thought necessary to guard the jails with military[2] while the violence gave excuse for the constables to break into every assembly of pitmen, and arrest the leaders[3]. In May the delegates offered to resign, a move which offered the newspapers fresh opportunities for abuse. "They have led their dupes to the brink of perdition, and now they will leave them to their fate"[4], said one editor, who in his next issue regretted the folly of the men who refused so good a chance of peace. In June, when the men at

[1] *Newcastle (Weekly) Chronicle*, Feb. 27th, 1875.
[2] *Durham Chronicle*, April 6th and April 27th, 1832.
[3] R. Fynes, *The Miners of Northumberland and Durham*, p. 28.
[4] *Durham Chronicle*, May 25th, 1832.

work were paying 6s. in the pound from their wages[1],
Hepburn said there were funds enough to support
the strike for ten more weeks. But the acclamations
which followed his speech were but the outcome of
momentary enthusiasm, for the struggle was "virtu-
ally at an end." The more violent spirits among the
men were safely lodged in jail. The men at work were
discouraged by the long continuance of the heavy
subscription, and alarmed at the prospect of further
violence, further evictions, and an increase in the
number of strangers. Every week the newspapers
began to chronicle fresh desertions. Every week the
statements of the owners took on a new tone of
assurance, as they published stories of the efficiency
of the new men and their satisfaction with their lot.
More and more stress was laid on the contrast between
the happy life of the pitman, with his short hours,
his high wage, his house, and his secure employment,
and the misery of the artisans of other parts of the
country. He had food other than oatmeal and bacon.
He could drink tea and coffee to his breakfast, the
whiteness of his bread was proverbial, and on his
return from work, after little more than four hours
actual labour, there was a dinner of fat mutton,
bread, potatoes, pudding and beer awaiting him[2].

The owners had taken to heart the advice of Lord
Londonderry, to treat colliery by colliery with their
men and so break up the combination. They repeated
their assertions of the folly of persistence in impossible

---

[1] *Durham Chronicle*, July 27th (and Fynes).
[2] *Ibid*. July 27th, 1832.

wage demands now that the northern coal field had
lost its monopoly of the London market. They sent
agents among the men to foment discord, and to
destroy their trust in their leaders. The strike dragged
on until August, when the men at Hetton consented
to be rebound and to sign the declaration against
adherence to any union which might question their
compact with their masters, but its collapse was made
certain in June by a crime which was to be remembered for over half a century[1]. Nicholas Forster[2], an
old man who as a magistrate had been active in the
maintenance of order, was stopped as he was riding
across Jarrow Slake, a flood area near the mouth of the
Tyne, dragged from his horse, and beaten to death[3].
A pitman, who was caught still bending over the
dying man, and who had been heard a few minutes
before to ask him for a drink, was arrested, tried,
and executed. Whether the pitmen approved of the
crime, or whether they were not satisfied that the
arrested man was the murderer—the evidence was
hardly conclusive and he persisted in his denial of
his guilt—is not certain. But as the doomed man
was led to execution a voice in the crowd cried him
farewell, and local tradition said the voice was that
of the real murderer who shortly afterwards left the
country. The body was hanged on a gibbet at the
edge of the Slake until, to the general relief, it was
secretly removed. Many years later the crime was

---

[1] *Durham Chronicle*, June 15th, 1832, 1832.
[2] Matthias Dunn, *An Historical View of the Coal Trade*, p. 34.
[3] *Durham Chronicle*, Aug. 10th and 24th, 1832.

still a subject of fierce discussion. The name of the
real murderer was freely quoted, and family tradi-
tions were exhausted in an attempt to account for
the disappearance of the gibbeted body. In the
end, to reconcile conflicting stories, it was agreed
that a first attempt to dispose of it by sinking it
in the Tyne failed, that it was washed ashore, and
eventually buried not far from the old church.

It was generally agreed that both sides had paid
too dear for their principles, that the strike had been
a disaster not only for the men, but for the owners.

The exertions of the coal-owners brought in an accumula-
tion of labour, which laid the foundation of that over-
plus...which has since produced so fatal results...in
the superabundant supply both of labour and coal[1],

said Matthias Dunn, who in 1844 wrote the first
history of the coal-mines. The union dwindled away.
The monopoly of the London market was lost for
ever. There was a last meeting in August, at Shadons
Hill, though next February it was rumoured that
Hepburn had made new efforts to gather the men
together[2]. But Hepburn himself had been starved
into submission. He was offered work by the manager
of the Felling on condition that he would advocate
no more the principles which once he had seen
triumph. He kept his promise and disappeared into
obscurity[3]. During the Chartist troubles there were
rumours that he had again been seen at public

[1] Matthias Dunn, *An Historical View of the Coal Trade*, p. 34.
[2] *Durham Chronicle*, Feb. 8th, 1833.
[3] R. Fynes, *The Miners of Northumberland and Durham*,
p. 36.

meetings, rumours which the newspapers thought worthy of denial. In their hall, among the statues of their great men, the miners of Durham have placed a bust of this almost unknown man who was their first leader. But all that enquiry could discover was that he was born at Pelton, and that he once worked at Urpeth, and that at the Felling he was in turn a deputy, a lamp-inspector, and a master wasteman, until in 1839, robbed of his strength by an accident, he left the pit to die in poverty[1]. All that remains of him is the memory of his exhortations to order and sobriety, and his appeals for better education; that, and the tradition of union, which after his work could never entirely disappear.

[1] *Newcastle (Weekly) Chronicle*, Feb. 27th, 1875.

CHAPTER III

OUTSIDE INFLUENCE

IT was not entirely by his own act that the pitman emerged from the isolation of his village life; he was dragged into a wider world by the enormous extension of mining activity. The general use of iron machinery and of steam power, the adoption of gas lighting, and the rapid growth of the town population, combined to multiply the demand for coal and everywhere new methods and new machinery came into use. In 1780 the steam-engine began to take the place of the Newcomen despite the fact that until small coal became saleable low fuel consumption was an actual demerit in the eyes of the viewers. When the invention of the crank made it possible to use the new engine for winding coal the last obstacle in the way of working the deep seams disappeared. By the end of the eighteenth century the 600 feet of the Wallsend shaft was exceeded by half a dozen scattered sinkings. In 1832 seams which lay 1500 feet below the sea were being worked at Wearmouth[1].

That the coal-measures extended over a wide area in Durham and Northumberland was well known. Mining had been confined to the Tyne valley chiefly because of the small depth of the seams, and the ease of access to the sea. And south of the Tyne the coal was soft, and bore transport badly. But this soft

[1] R. Galloway, *Annals of Coal-Mining and the Coal Trade.*

Durham coal was well-suited for coking, though its gassy nature made mining more dangerous and added to the need for ventilation. But by 1820 the Tyneside collieries were declining in importance and the pitmen began a double migration, north to the district round Blythe, south to the Wear, the Tees, and the upland districts of central Durham. In 1832 Lord Londonderry founded his own coal port at Seaham with its attendant mining villages. The Town Moor at Newcastle ceased to be the natural centre for pitmen's meetings; the sacred places of the miners' union are Shadons Hill and Boldon Fell.

In the newly developed areas the pitmen were less an accepted part of the social order and an increasing number of them were new to the life in the colliery rows. Lead-miners who had left their exhausted workings to bind themselves at the coal-pits, colliers from Scotland, Wales, and the Midland counties, Irish peasants, and south-country labourers, knew little of the hereditary claim to steady employment and of the traditional high standard of life. They were expected to conform more closely to the other inhabitants, the farm hands whom they displaced and the coke-men and furnace-men who came to live in the iron towns which grew up near the pit-heads. They had no reason to claim the privilege of the old pitmen, "undisturbed quarters, respectful distance, and freedom from arrest"[1]. They had no pride in their calling. It was a means to a living, not a station in society.

[1] J. Everett, *The Allens of Shiny Row*, p. 25.

In every account of labour troubles it is plain that the centres of unrest were the new pits. The men had lately come, they were as ready to go. There was a high proportion of the young and adventurous. The good workmen, steady and fairly content, were loathe to leave their employment, the timid ones afraid. In a new pit village were congregated the enterprising, the dissatisfied, often, even, the idle and dissolute who found work the more easily where their character was unknown[1]. Most of the problems of the pit had yet to be settled. Where there was no memory of fair treatment on past occasions isolated misunderstanding was soon magnified into deliberate injustice. Where no established body of precedent existed there was natural fear among both men and officials that submission in any point would be quoted against them in later dispute. And naturally the men who rose to influence in a new colliery, destitute of social life, were men marked out for distinction by activity rather than by character, men who won support rather by words than by wisdom. And as naturally, words which won support in a new colliery were those of violence and decision.

As the shafts went deeper, the capital costs grew, until as much as £80,000 was spent on a single sinking. This increase in the initial expense made necessary a greater attention to the cost of working. Mining became less of a mystery, to be jealously guarded from the stranger's curiosity. By the skill of the leading viewers it was elevated to the dignity of a

[1] J. R. Leifchild, *Children's Employment Commission*, p. 530.

profession, and though experience was still a safer
guide than theory scientific thought began to take the
place of rule of thumb, and precaution, of a reckless
disregard for danger. Though desire to add to the
safety of the mine was in the main the stimulus to
improvement, from the efforts to avoid the disaster
of an explosion steady benefit accrued to the pitmen.
Despite the appalling frequency of accident it became
possible to work the soft, gassy coal in Durham, and
in the first decade of the nineteenth century improvements in ventilation encouraged the miner to begin the
use of powder for getting coal. Blasting reduced the
pitman's labour and almost halved the length of his
day. The pair of hewers who worked together divided
the day between them, and during the nineteenth
century two shifts of coal-getters to one of other men
and boys became the normal proportion in the north.
It was a good argument for the influence of short
hours on production that man for man the north-
country pitmen stood highest in the output tables.

The difference between Durham and Northumberland grew. The hard coal of the one, worked chiefly
for export, had a fluctuating demand, and a constantly moving market-price, but each year more
and more of the soft coal of Durham went straight
to the coke-ovens, and the prosperity of the Durham
pitmen came to depend on the state of the iron trade.
Moreover, as the soft coal was got with less labour
and less care, round coal being no great advantage
for coking, it was long thought that hewing in
Durham required little skill. Certainly strangers found

room in the Durham pits readily and the rate of wages was apt to be less than that current north of the Tyne, where the Northumberland men cherished a slight contempt for their southern neighbours. It was a division which, becoming apparent in trade dispute, was to become a permanent feature of union history.

Meantime other mechanical improvements came in turn to make their changes in the pitman's traditional habits of life. In the year of Waterloo the locomotive engine appeared on the wagon ways and this invention of a colliery mechanic was destined to make the fortune of many an inland coal-owner. Better screens added at once to the quantity of saleable coal, and to the number of men employed at the pit-heads. And in 1818 the launch of steam-tugs on the Tyne made an end of the annual holiday, for the mines could work steadily on while the tugs towed the colliers out in the teeth of the north-easters.

One unfortunate result of the increase in the depth and extent of the workings was the rapid growth of the number of fatalities. In 1710, an explosion at Bensham, the first place where the Low Main seam was worked, killed several men, and few years after that passed without some disaster. In the deep shafts a slip meant death. Not many men had the luck of the pitman who, after a fall of eighty feet, caught a rope end and was safely drawn up from the depths below. And as in the big mines the need for speed in the transport of the tubs grew, hurry brought a new crop of accidents. Drivers, passing at a trot, were trapped between the tub and the roof in low places. Men and boys were run over on the inclines. It was not by chance that the appalling loss of life first attracted public attention at Sunderland. The mines there were unusually deep and extensive, the pitmen lived almost among the townsfolk and the accidents of their trade were less a secret. Dr Clanny, a well-known local surgeon, began to enlist support for his attempts to construct a lamp which would burn safely in a gassy atmosphere. The steel mill, which the Speddings of Whitehaven had invented, a friction wheel which struck a rapid succession of sparks, was known to be useless. Sometimes, in sinking a shaft, the men worked for days in complete darkness. The viewers scouted the idea of a safety lamp, and pinned their faith on improved ventilation; it had done much, it was capable of more.

In 1813 Dr Clanny made a lamp which promised success. He had already formed a society to help him in his work, a society whose existence was advertised in the newspapers[1]. At a meeting it was resolved to ask the advice of some scientist of repute and Sir Humphry Davy was consulted. By hard work, and the exercise of great forbearance and tact, —" at the request of one proprietor the number of lives lost was erased from the resolution (*of formation*) for fear of giving offence "[2]—the Sunderland Society had

---

[1] *Newcastle Courant*, Oct. 9th, 1813.
[2] J. H. H. Holmes, *A Treatise on the Coal Mines of Durham and Northumberland*, p. 131.

succeeded in convincing the coal-owners of the honesty
of its intentions. Buddle, the well-known viewer, who
was listened to almost as an oracle, gave his encouragement to the research, and at the end of a year Davy
produced an efficient safety lamp. Its light was
barely sufficient, but the value of the lamp was
chiefly that by changes in behaviour it announced the
presence of gas. Sir Humphry Davy would accept
no reward for his invention, which to the surprise
of all was eagerly taken into use by the men[1]. The
Luddite riots had fostered the belief that the working
man, out of stupidity, resisted all innovation. But
the merits of the safety lamp were obvious though
its poor light increased the danger of falls of coal and
reduced the earnings of the men by as much as sixpence a day. It was reserved for a later generation
to turn its use into a danger.

The Sunderland Society dissolved, its object accomplished. But the gift of the lamp was perhaps
of less importance than the awakening of general
interest in the collieries. Local patriotism provoked
many an argument in the north on the relative merits
of the Davy and the Geordie, the lamp which Robert
Stevenson designed. It was something of a shock to
the old-fashioned viewers, to find that a scientist of
the schools could do in one year what they had so
often declared to be impossible. Contemptuous experience could no longer scorn enquiry. In 1835 the
House of Commons appointed a committee to report

[1] Matthias Dunn, *A Treatise on the Winning and Working
of Collieries*, p. 187.

on the causes of mine explosions. The county coroners, asked to send statistics of fatalities, almost ignored the demand. Many years later the pitmen, the government inspectors, and the general public joined in an appeal for the suspension of the Northumberland coroner whose old-fashioned view of his duty was a hindrance to proper investigation of neglect[1]. In earlier days, when the owners had influence enough to keep from publication all report of accident, and when they had the active assistance of the coroners, it was impossible to make any good estimate of the annual number of the killed. No inquest could be held until the bodies were recovered. In a general disaster an inquest on one body was thought sufficient and one death was recorded where perhaps fifty men had perished. And as yet it was thought the duty of no one to protect a man from his own folly. In this new public interest was born the demand for protective legislation and formal inspection. The Sunderland Society made the first breach in the wall of concealment which for a century had hidden, among much unavoidable ignorance, callous neglect and, at times, commercial greed.

Disinterested humanity was not the only cause of the new interest in the pitmen. All the political parties were engaged in destroying the transparent fabric of their opponents' dwellings. The manufacturers demanded the repeal of the corn laws: the Tory landlords devised the factory acts. And, with a foresight which told them that an extended franchise would

[1] Matthias Dunn, *Report of H.M. Inspector of Mines*, 1862.

not be confined long to the retail tradesmen, the radicals, the anti-corn law orators, and the advocates of political reform, appealed for the support of the pitman, voteless as he was to remain for half a century. From the politicians the pitmen learned many a lesson in the art of enlisting the support of popular enthusiasm. They learned the value of meetings and processions, of petitions and newspaper advertisements, of torches and bands and banners. They learned how to draft resolutions and to conduct with proper solemnity an orderly public meeting. Respect for parliamentary form is one of the most humorous features of trade-union history. Many a hastily called strike meeting began with a demand from the delegate that the men should move one of their number into the chair, and some unwilling hewer was pushed into unwelcome prominence, to shew by his stammering speech his bewilderment as to why the "agent" could not get on alone with the speech he had come from headquarters to deliver. And many a Radical was to be puzzled by the inconsistency of his political views and his industrial creed. Hepburn had not failed to remark on the difference of the magisterial attitude to a reform demonstration and a pitmen's meeting. In the strike of '32 the owners' newspaper champion tried in vain to reconcile this refusal of the right to combine with his late ardent assertion of the right of every man to a citizen's vote in a new democratic assembly[1]. And years later a pitmen's agent was to confound

[1] *Durham Chronicle*, June 15th, 1832.

a stiff-necked owner, who paid notoriously low wages,
and dismissed his men for reading union literature
and giving hospitality to union speakers, by a shew
of his inconsistency.

Joe is a free trader. What is a free trader? Why! ivvery
boddy knaws. The Manchester skule, what hires lecturers,
and that is to get us our bread cheap. Joe is a free trader,
and circulates tracts, and all that. These is his principles[1].

Convinced by the failure of their strike of the
"delusive promise of union," the pitmen turned their
attention to politics. Chartist agitation took the
place of trade action. The man who had been a union
delegate became a preacher of the gospel of the six
points. The pits which had been centres of industrial
unrest became "hotbeds of Chartist intrigue and infidel
teaching"[2]. Colliery smiths made pikes and caltrops,
and on his return from a tour of the north-country
collieries Julian Harney made report to the National
Convention that "the hand which swung the pick
could at need weild the sabre and the pike"[3]. But
though the Chartist teachings had a welcome among
the pitmen there was no readiness to sacrifice prosperity for political principle. The man who would
starve to raise his wages would not strike in the cause
of manhood suffrage. Here and there a colliery sent
its subscription to the National Rent. Here and there
the pitmen made a holiday of the first day of the
Sacred Month. But they went to work on the morrow,

[1] *Durham Chronicle*, Nov. 12th, 1863.
[2] Tremenheere, *Reports on the State of the Mining Population*.
[3] E. Dolleans, *L'Evolution du Chartism*; R. G. Gammage,
History of the Chartist Movement.

refusing to be misled further by the foolish promise of universal action.

It is probable that the Chartist movement did more than trade-union activity to attract the attention of the Government to the miseries of the working classes. The spirit of the reforms is shewn by the creation of a rural police, and the proposal to build churches in the neglected districts. Such social improvement as was attempted was intended less as a foundation for further progress than as a sop to keep quiet a people among whom revolution was feared. The middle classes joined a special constabulary which lived in groundless alarm of a general attack on lives and property. The tenant farmers sent their sons into a yeomanry which threatened to become a more dangerous instrument of oppression than any standing army. It was this yeomanry which charged the crowd at Peterloo, and against which the caltrops of the Chartists were designed. The hatred of the educated classes for all combinations, the strange idea which they had of their eventual purpose, the readiness to believe the most impossibly wild stories of the conduct and motives of men with whom they had lived as neighbours for many years began to pass away as the hysteria of the revolutions of 1832 declined. The newspapers began to print reports of workmen's meetings without adding their old outbursts against the folly and wickedness of union.

The coal-owners who fought the first union were many of them convinced that to encourage habits of thrift among their men would be a source of new danger, and that the amassing of savings would increase the readiness to strike and prolong the duration of the struggles[1]. But others had begun to hope that an increased material prosperity might bring a new steadiness, and higher wages make possible a better social life. It was a dim understanding of this which caused some of the men to suspect that housing improvement was often made out of a desire to restrict their freedom of movement. Meantime, though many people had been both alarmed and amazed to see the educated pitmen step forward as the leaders of the union movement, others had realised that it was not an unmixed evil. The more respectable were the strike leaders, the less was the danger of outrage. Experience brought the comforting assurance that where the educated men ruled violence was forbidden, and that if they dared to encounter the owners in argument, they were not less ready to face the men and persuade them to compromise. It was this which encouraged the more far-sighted owners to build schools and reading rooms where some of them hoped that "the truths of the laws of political economy" might be taught[2].

No influence had effects as important, or as little the object of hostile criticism, as the steady spread of Methodism. It was true that the management of their little chapels gave some of the pitmen a dangerous habit of self-sufficiency. It was true that the local

[1] J. R. Leifchild, *Children's Employment Commission*, p. 518.
[2] *Report on State of Popular Education* (Asst. Comm. A. F. Foster).

preacher stepped only too readily from the pulpit to the strike platform. It was this tendency which hastened more than one Methodist schism. As an old congregation increased in respectability, as the practice of frugality brought wealth to its individual members, secession gave the enthusiasts, and the poorer members, a chapel of their own. The Wesleyans had among them the tradesmen, the newer masters, even some of the local professional men. They had an educated ministry which steadily lost touch with the pitmen. The answers some of the Wesleyan preachers gave to Government enquiries shew them to be possessed of a social theory more rigid than that of the most upright evangelical who ever tainted his philanthropy with a misinterpretation of the catechism, or mixed Dr Watt's hymns with Harriet Martineau's economic platitudes[1]. The Wesleyans were never the leaders of strikes. It was the Ranters, as the Primitive Methodists were called even in official reports, who continued the real work of Methodism, the uplifting of the lowest ranks in society. They fought the evils of drunkenness, gambling, and improvidence. They took away from the pitman his gun, his dog, and his fighting cock. They gave him a frock coat for his posy jacket, hymns for his public-house ditties, prayer-meetings for his pay-night frolics. They drove into the minds of a naturally improvident race the idea that extravagance was in itself a sin, until the falling wage

[1] *Report on State of Popular Education* (Asst. Comm. A. F. Foster), and evidence (Rev. R. Brown and Colonel Stobart).

sufficed for an ever-advancing domestic comfort. The pit-wife who was to "take in the preacher" obtained her proud privilege by an acknowledged refinement.

It was the desire to read the Bible which was the first effective stimulus to education. The establishment of a Methodist class was at once followed by the opening of a Sunday school. In that Sunday school sat the converted hewers, side by side with their own children, new-found Christian humility overcoming shame at their ignorance, and impatience at their difficulty. Many a man was to "pass out of the Bible into the newspapers." Many a boy who had learned to read in the Scriptures was in his later life to reject the improving books of the colliery libraries, and prefer "exciting literature, Chartist and infidel tracts."

There was often no church in the colliery village. At first the Methodists met in the house of the class-leader. Then, as numbers grew, the congregation began to desire a new home. 1780 was the first year of chapel-building, and to many the building of the chapel was the first lesson in communal effort. In the management of the service was an opportunity for the natural leader, in the administration of the funds an education in business method. At the class meetings the men lost their fear of self-expression. In the pulpits the local preachers practised oratory. Later this gift of speech was to be used to recite the tale of the pitman's wrongs, and to stir the men to union and to strikes. The Bible furnished many an economic argument, many a warning to the rich, many a threat to the oppressor. The Sermon on the Mount is an education in social equality, the Old Testament a trumpet blast to the warrior. With Psalms the Roundheads and the Covenanters marched to battle. Under banners embroidered with texts the pitmen assembled, lodge by lodge, at their meetings. "He that oppresseth the poor, reproacheth his maker."

CHAPTER IV

THE SECOND UNION

FOR ten years Lord Londonderry's specific against combination continued to be successful. The policy of making a separate bargain with the men of each pit, reinforced by the demand for a promise of resignation from the union, was an insuperable obstacle to the demagogue's desires. The spare enthusiasm of discontent was expended on the Chartist cause, but, forgetting how often the Bible and the sword have been allies, the Methodists looked on Chartism with little favour. They feared the infidelity of its leaders; they opposed their demands for secular education. They disliked the attacks on property, and thought the Methodist hymn-book an ill neighbour for the pistol and the pike. The forty thousand pitmen who were to rally to the people's cause existed only in the imagination of the alarmists. Except at such places as Seghill and Thornley the Sacred Month passed unregarded.

At Hetton there was a strike in the spring of 1834, but evictions soon made an end of it[1]. At Bishop Auckland there was a meeting attended by about a hundred men, no sufficient number to give rise to alarm[2]. If the newspaper comments have any founda-

[1] *Durham Chronicle*, Feb. 21st, 1834.
[2] *Ibid.* March 14th, 1834.

tion the pitmen had been persuaded of the folly of subscribing their pennies that their delegates might live like gentlemen. Two years later, in April, a strike threatened in the whole of Northumberland[1]. The corf was being rapidly displaced by the tub and the cage, and the owners wished to discontinue the old method of paying the hewers by the measure of their output, and base their prices on weight[2]. As an innovation the change was unpopular, the more so as the men had cause to suspect that the new rates bore more harshly on them than the old.

In 1839 where the Chartists attempted any open action, "fine and imprisonment soon restored order[3]." But the prosperity of the next year—marked by the celebration of many new winnings—did more perhaps than the activity of the new rural police. But soon the new pits swamped the markets with coal. Stocks grew at the staithes, prices fell, wages were reduced, and the pits stood idle two or three days a week[4]. Fear of a fall in the standard of life has always been the strength of labour agitation. The cautious man who will take no risk to add to his wages will fight the hardest to maintain them. In the alarm at the growing poverty the cry of "Unite" was heard again. There was one leader who had no longer cause to fear the owners' resentment, Martin Jude, once a pitman, but at this time landlord of the Three Tuns, in the

[1] *Durham Chronicle*, April 1st, 1836.
[2] R. Galloway, *Annals of the Coal Trade*.
[3] *Children's Employment Commission* (Evid. Wm. Hunter, Viewer Walbottle).
[4] *Durham Chronicle*, July 23rd, 1841; June 24th, 1842.

Manor Chare, Newcastle. In his tap-room the delegates assembled. It argued ill for the peace of the
coal trade that among them were newcomers to the
pits, black-legs of 1832. Mark Dent, Hepburn's successor, had been enticed out of the lead-mines in that
year of disaster[1].

Among the old pitmen to be bound year after year
at the same colliery was a certificate of respectability,
and the bond itself a security against unemployment.
It was perhaps among the new men, less in love with
the customs of the pits, that the system of binding
came into disfavour, perhaps among them that the
brilliant idea was conceived of turning against the
owners their own weapon. If, under the bond, a
strike was possible only once a year, a legal battle
over some alleged breach of contract could always
be precipitated. The bonds, hitherto rigorously enforced in the courts, were many of them crude, badly
drawn agreements. The owners were to find them
poor weapons when the pitmen brought lawyers to
defeat the attempts to punish indiscipline by imprisonment. And in their turn the men began to
appeal to the law to protect them from encroach-
ments, and to bring actions for damages, in which
the sum demanded was a trifle as compared to the
trouble of the defence. For the owners were as much
trammelled by the yearly bond as the men. Wages
fixed in March were sometimes unwillingly paid in
September, if a fall in price had intervened, and

[1] *Tyne Mercury*, May 7th, 1842; *Newcastle Journal*, May 18th,
1842.

profits could only be maintained by mal-practice. The fines were increased. It was a condition of the bond that for a badly filled tub, or one in which there was too much stone, the hewer should be punished and receive no payment. By forfeiting tubs an unscrupulous official could always reduce his labour costs and the men had small check on the measurement of their work.

Hewers' wages were ruled by the clause in the bond defining the payment for each "score of corves" hewn. When, in 1832, weight took the place of measure in the London coal-market payment of wages by measure became an anomaly. Keeping the old payment and its old name "score price," many managers fixed a weight equivalent to the score of corves and removed the anomaly[1]. But there was a widespread suspicion among the pitmen that they had been defrauded by the change. Not only did they assert that the new weight was no fair equivalent for the old measure—in its fixing they had naturally not been consulted—but they distrusted the accuracy of the weighing machines the owners installed. In general these were beams, not the old-fashioned balance which every man could understand. Ignorance and conservative prejudice may have been in the main the cause of this distrust. It seemed an unworthy suspicion that coal-owners, noblemen and gentlemen as they were, could stoop to defraud their workmen by the beggarly device of the roguish tradesman, a false balance. In later years

[1] R. Galloway, *Annals of the Coal Trade.*

there was to be evidence sufficient that some men did not despise petty deceit where it was a way to fortune.

The second union was part of a general combination, "The Union of Miners of Great Britain and Ireland"[1]. But if the leaders were wise enough to see the weakness of isolation they were not far-sighted enough to repudiate the popular doctrine of restriction of labour. Indeed, a belief in the benefit of regulation of output had a foremost place in their economic creed. Partly to support their case that they were underpaid, partly to escape excessive labour and provide against unemployment, the men reduced the quantity which they thought fit to hew. To discover how much the fall in wage—in 1843 some 15 per cent.—was due to the action of the men is now impossible. It was a mistaken policy for the men to earn by election less than their customary wage. It placed at the command of the owners the argument that wages willingly reduced, could not be insufficient for the needs of life. If the union had from the first discouraged restriction the owners would have been without their most powerful weapons, appeal to the moral indignation of the public, scorn for false statistics, broken faith, and foolish theory.

A much wiser step was the institution of a law fund. £500 was collected, for the defence of pitmen who should incur arrest for breach of their bond[2].

[1] R. Fynes, *The Miners of Northumberland and Durham*, p. 37.
[2] *Ibid.*

By ill-luck the first important case was the outcome of a strike at Wingate over the introduction of a wire rope. Almost as soon as it was placed in the shaft the men refused to descend, saying they would not entrust their lives to anything but the old proven hempen cable, nor could the published opinions of well-known engineers shake their conservative prejudice. Their own chosen engineer, obviously an ignorant man picked because of his bias, supported them in their decision, and in truth the condition of the wire rope would have shocked a modern inspector. There was no question that many of the strands were broken, and that the outer covering shewed several signs of wear[1]. But in the eyes of all progressive men the wire rope was an improvement. It made possible an immediate increase in the speed of winding, and by the diminution of both thickness and weight promised a new ability for the working of deep mines. The strike was but another instance of the foolish opposition of workmen to all invention. The mine-owners offered to allow the timorous to descend by another, if less comfortable, way. In the dispute, complicated already by wage dissatisfaction, there was even a hint that the old cable would be put back if the men would forgo the claims for their arrears. In the end the strike came to an amicable conclusion; small concessions were made to the men, and the wire rope remained. The most important outcome of the quarrel was that Horner, the lawyer to whom the

[1] *The Durham Chronicle*, Aug. and Sept. 1843; and R. Galloway, *The Annals of the Coal Trade*.

pitmen had entrusted their case, gave up his position in disgust[1]. Of his four cases he had brought but one to a successful conclusion. Claims for damages against Sir William Chaytor, and the Thornley Colliery, had been defeated[2]. Only under the terms of the West Holywell bond had he upheld his contention that for unexpected days of idleness the pitmen were entitled to their pay.

At once a new man appeared, W. P. Roberts, a solicitor from Bath, who for the next twenty years was to be famous as "The Pitman's Attorney-General." How he came to the north is well described in the *Newcastle Journal*:

The agitation of Chartism brought to the surface of society a great deal of scum, which usually putrefies in obscurity below, and among the parties who assumed prominence in this turmoil was a man named Beasley[3].

When the Chartist cause collapsed Beasley became a professional agitator among the pitmen, and until the Methodists took exception to him he was editor of the *Miner's Advocate*, one of the two unstamped journals which were founded in 1843 to support the miners' union. When the pitmen grew dissatisfied with Horner, Beasley wrote to Roberts, whom he had known as a Chartist, and the west-country attorney seized the opportunity to leave a district where he too had come to unprofitable notoriety[4].

He was promised by the union a salary of £1000

[1] *The Durham Chronicle*, Aug. 21st, 1843.
[2] *Ibid.* July 28th, Aug. 3rd, 1843.
[3] *Newcastle Journal*, April 13th, 1844.
[4] *Ibid.*

a year. Beasley was articled to him at their expense, and together the two began to outrage all respectable feeling in the north. Roberts saw that once he had committed himself to the pitmen's cause, his professional ruin was certain. He could hope only for the success of the union, unless indeed he could obtain a bribe to silence, if by persistence he could drive the owners into so underhand a course. It is to be feared that the boldness of his fight and the excellence of his cause do not entirely clear this champion from the charge of being a rogue. That he was able there is no doubt: alone, he was more than a match for all the legal skill the owners could engage, though it had the favourable ear of a biased court. If he "lived like a lord on the pennies of the starving pitmen"[1], he gave them astonishing value for their money. He addressed their meetings, he drew up their resolutions, he edited their public appeals, he dictated their policy, he was their adviser in all matters. His letters to the newspapers were so frequent, so powerful, and so hard to answer, that in the end the editors were driven to refuse them insertion except as advertisements. He induced the men to appeal to parliament, he wrote their petitions and found a member willing to present them, he ignored every attack on his motives, he listened unmoved to the threats of the angry, he passed over accusations of dishonesty which the men themselves were not slow to make in times of disappointment. Perhaps he was not required to starve with his clients

[1] *Durham Chronicle*, Sept. 15th, 1843.

because he shared their principles. The owners and their lawyers were not unrecompensed for their belief in competitive economics and the rights of property. He could well jeer at their pretence of high motive and accuse them of a conscience which was not without its monetary reward. The worst that can be proved of the pitman's advocate was that he was unscrupulous, vulgar, and of unsurpassed thickness of skin. Every time he went into court he invited commitment for contempt, escaping at the last possible moment by a shameless withdrawal or more often by bullying the magistrates. If they roared and stamped, he roared and stamped even louder. If they threatened and beat upon the bench, he returned threat for threat and beat upon the table. If they availed themselves of their position to deliver lectures on political economy, he dragged into his case a violent exposition of the rights of man. Unused to contradiction the gentry on the bench threw away by undignified rage their judicial advantage, and blind to their folly the newspapers continued to publish, with minute particularity, speeches whose sentiments they were in general anxious to conceal. Better advertisement of their cause the miners could hardly have contrived.

Roberts' first great case was the outcome of a strike at Thornley. Exasperated by the unbearable weight of the fines and by the arbitrary manner of the viewer the men had struck, and sixty-eight of them were brought before the magistrates on a charge of breach of contract. To a bench, every one of whose members was directly interested in the coal trade, Heckles, the viewer, told his story of complaint, deputation, and strike[1]. His brutal frankness was witness sufficient that the injustice of which the men complained had been deliberately increased, and that the strike, if unsought, was not unexpected. " I don't doubt," said he, "that one man may have been fined 22s. in two days. I know that other men have been fined 8s., 7s., 6s., and 5s. a day." The men had asked for boxes to be put at the pit-head, in which the stone sent up by each man with his coal could be placed as a proof of the extent of his offence. It had been done and the fines had increased at once by a third. But it was quite evident that the viewer had kept well within the terms of the bond. The secret of the dissatisfaction was that for the first time an old contract, in itself impossible of fulfilment, had been strictly enforced. Year after year its provisions had been neglected, until the men had come to sign willingly a contract of the true nature of which they were ignorant. Now the only plea left to them was that a long-standing bond demanded a skill beyond human ability. It was on this that Mr Roberts based his case. He called the hewers, one by one, to testify on oath that, with the utmost care and skill of which man was capable, they could not avoid the fines for mixing too much stone with the coal. When the court grew weary of the repetition, and objected that no man would make a bargain which offered him such

[1] *Durham Chronicle*, Nov. 24th, 1843; and R. Fynes, *The Miners of Northumberland and Durham*, p. 39.

small advantage, he threatened to call every one of
the hewers, three or four hundred though there might
be, to confound this belief. As the men in the gallery
muttered their applause he grew eloquent:

Though in nine-tenths of the cases the pitmen swore that
the colliery weights were false, yet they were condemned.
Was it always to be imprisonment, imprisonment, imprisonment...as if the men were all criminals, the
owners all angels...was it to be reserved to this country
to have a law which gave the rich the power of inflicting
imprisonment, while it did not give the same power to
the poor?[1]

And when, despite his defence, the men were committed to prison for six weeks, there was a scene in
court which has not often been paralleled in our
orderly judicial history.

During the hearing witnesses had sworn in turn
that they had never earned the wages promised them
in the bond, that they had never been placed in the
house which was an essential condition of the hewer's
contract, and that when they had offered money as
payment for the debts they had incurred in fines it
had been refused. One man swore that Heckles had
offered to bribe him to bear witness to the justice
of the fairness of the contract. "If he could swear
he could work for a fortnight without having any
'laid-out' he should have easy work, he should have
his bread for doing nothing." Mr Roberts attacked
the honesty of the magistrates, one of whom in the
past had refused to issue a man a summons against

[1] *Durham Chronicle*, Nov. 24th, 1843; and R. Fynes, *The
Miners of Northumberland and Durham*, pp. 39–47.

his master because the sum at issue, 3s., was too small. But if the contract seemed impossible, the court biased, it should be remarked that in later days men were heard to boast that they had put stone among the coal to provoke a strike, and that the Thornley men of those days bore no very good character[1].

As the convicted men left the court Roberts rose to protest. As the magistrates stamped upon the bench, he beat upon the table, shouting above their orders:

Rather than submit to such a bond, the men they saw in the gallery would all go to prison. They would declare, so help them God, that they would not work until the men sent to prison were released.

ALL! ALL! roared the Thornley hewers, with such effect that the magistrates sought to quiet them by a bargain. If they would return to work the magistrates would petition the Home Secretary for the release of the offenders and later, on the grounds of a technical error, the men actually were released[2].

The pitmen's meetings began again. Forty thousand assembled at Shadons Hill, to be exhorted to order, and to listen to a recital of their wrongs. At the owners' annual meeting, held to discuss the terms of the bond for the coming year, an unexpected step was taken: the bond was abandoned and a monthly agreement put in its place. It was a natural consequence of the annoyance at the constant litigation, a

[1] *Durham Chronicle*, Nov. 24th, 1843.
[2] *Ibid.*; R. Fynes, *The Miners of Northumberland and Durham*, pp. 39–47.

tribute to the skill of Beasley and Roberts, but there was
general alarm among the pitmen, especially among
the older men who had been bound year by year since
they first kept a door. As a counter Roberts drew
up a specimen bond, the terms of which were widely
circulated and subjected to universal comment.

It made an attempt to enlist the support of every
class in the mines. The bond was to be made for six
months. The smart-money—a weekly payment during
incapacity which followed injury—was to be raised
from 5s. to 10s. Widows were to be given a pension,
and a grant towards their husband's burial. The new
fly doors, which required no small boy in attendance,
and diminished the employment of children, were to
be removed. The fines were to be limited, and no man
was to be punished for absence when attending
delegate meetings of the union. The hewers were to
be paid by weight, and given a plain statement of
their earnings. Moreover, they were not to be put
to any work which they were not accustomed to do.
It was a sore grievance, and one which was to persist
many more years, that in emergency the manager
could send the hewers to other employment. They
disliked tasks which they thought unworthy of their
strength and skill, and until the manager's power was
hedged in by a host of limitations they were apt to
lose money by the change. Roberts did not forget
himself; men were to be given a fortnight's notice
of intended prosecution. But it was the wage demand
which assured for the men's bond immediate refusal.
Not only were the men to be paid weekly, and their

wages made more stable, but the hewers were to be guaranteed steady employment, five days a week at 3s. a day, and 3s. a day was to be esteemed the measure of a fair day's work[1].

On a falling market it was too much. The demand meant an advance in wages of 30 per cent. The owners ignored the document, so plainly a challenge to battle, and in March, 1844, the third great strike began.

1832 had taught the owners more than one lesson in tactics. They had built up stocks of coal sufficient for the first weeks of disorganisation and the sale of these stocks at strike prices was ample compensation for a short period of idleness. But by the end of a month the pitmen were starving. Their prosperity was less deep-seated than in the past. In the last strike they had spent their savings and scattered their household treasures[2]. It was only the fortunate who had contrived to buy back the ornate mahogany furniture. It was only the provident who had regained the old high standard of domestic comfort[3]. In the new collieries there were few gardens and pig-crees and the men preferred to spend their leisure in pitch and toss rather than to busy themselves with more gainful occupation. The constant movement of the population had cut short the credit which in ordinary times the tradesmen were only too willing to offer. In fact, every resource was weakened, and the second

[1] Matthias Dunn, *A General View of the Coal-Trade since 1836.* (Appendix to *An Historical View.*) (1844). p. 226.

[2] Leifchild, *Children's Employment Commission*, p. 719.

[3] *Durham Chronicle*, April 5th, 1844.

union was a poor substitute for the old prosperity. It made no boast of a strike fund, such as in Hepburn's days had given the men an unwonted confidence. Indeed there had been small chance to create one, for the bulk of the subscriptions of its single year of life had been spent on Roberts and his legal activities. The very fact that the strike was more general was a source of weakness, for no union men were at work and no levies could be demanded for the support of the strikers.

There were the usual meetings on the hill-sides to strengthen the men's resolution but from the first the union sought a wider publicity for its demands. It held meetings in Sunderland and Newcastle where Dent and the other leaders quietly expounded the strikers' case to crowds which included even viewers and owners. Letters were sent to the newspapers, but the editors were less inclined to make room for them than ever now that the men had a journal of their own, the unstamped *Miner's Advocate*. A little to the men's astonishment, at the end of a month the owners were so far from wishing to treat that they commenced a vigorous opposition. Black-legs were imported from Wales, and Cornwall, and Ireland. South-country parishes encouraged their paupers to go north, where they were told that high wages could readily be earned. Weak-hearted men were enticed back to the pits by promise of favour. Soon, the owners were able to publish a weekly statement of the number of men at work, the number of new hands engaged, and the number of deserters from the union.

It was an advertisement of their triumph: each week
the figures grew. Next, in odd corners of every newspaper, as letters, as advertisements, and as news,
accounts began to appear of the high wages the
black-legs were earning. It was at once an appeal
to the cupidity of the men[1] and an imposition on the
credulity of the public. That men earned at times as
much as 7s. 6d. and 10s. a day was probable. In most
pits there are places where the coal is easy to get,
and such men as were at work were naturally sent
to those places, while their output was measured with
a generous hand. The strike had started in April. In
July Hetton was approaching its usual output[2] and
at most of the Durham collieries the owners were well
satisfied with their success. The black-legs worked
under the protection of the new rural police, and of
a force of special constables which consisted in the
main of colliery officials, who at the price of an oath
obtained magisterial protection, and the right to
carry arms.

There was little show of military force, and on the
whole less need for it than in the past, for the influence
of the Ranters, though on the side of union, was
against violence. Lord Londonderry was as active
as in the other troubles. He was grieved that the
ancestral pitmen of the house of Vane and Tempest
should strike, and yet admit to him, in conference,
that they had no grievance[3]. In a proclamation he

[1] *Durham Chronicle*, May 17th and 31st, June 7th, 1844.
[2] *Ibid.* July 26th, 1844.
[3] *Ibid.* June 21st, July 19th, 1844.

forbade the tradesmen of "My town of Seaham" to
assist such ungrateful and foolish men by extending
to them credit[1]. He threatened to bring over Irish
labourers, from his other estates, and in the end the
Irish came. His efforts to check the giving of credit
were generally imitated, and the tradesmen were
given long lectures on the folly of a mistaken kindness, which at once increased the miseries of the
men, and their own subsequent loss[2]. The readiness
of the shop-keepers to listen to the advice was the
cause of much of the enthusiasm for co-operation.
The men were slow to forget a step which they thought
a mean desertion, and they rejoiced at the chance
of delivering a blow to men who had shewn so little
sympathy with starvation. A few even foresaw the aid
which co-operative stores might be in later strikes.

But the owners' strongest weapon was the power
of eviction and it was by wholesale evictions that an
end was made of the strike. When the pitmen refused
their employers' pay they had no longer a right to a
house. If they would not be bound they could be
removed, to make room for willing men. It was
impossible to deny the legality of the owners' right,
difficult to question its justice, for room had to be
found somewhere for the black-legs. But it was the
power of eviction which caused most of the bitterness
of the strikes, which led to hate, and violence, and
outrage. Even had houses existed, other than in the

---

[1] R. Fynes, *The Miners of Northumberland and Durham*,
p. 82.
[2] *Durham Chronicle*, May 31st, July 5th and 12th, 1844.

colliery rows, they would have been closed to men who were without work or money. But pitmen on strike never entertained a thought of leaving their own village. They were the staff of the colliery, the newcomers were but temporary intruders who had interfered in a quarrel which in no way concerned them. Their coming was resented but it was resented the more when it had what seemed the unfair result of turning families from houses which by long occupation they had come to regard as their permanent home. When a force of bailiffs, recruited from the slums of the towns, burst open the doors and turned the furniture into the street it was hard for the men to keep their anger within bounds, and harder still for the "house-proud" women.

If the evictions had been carried out in good faith they would have produced ill-feeling enough. But families were turned from their homes with no thought of making room for strangers, publicans were threatened if they gave them hospitality, and the bivouacs which the men built in the fields and the streets were broken up on charges of trespass, of causing obstruction, or the excuse of public nuisance. But when the bailiffs—often well known as thieves and beggars—of design maltreated the furniture, abused the women, and jeered at the men, it was not strange that riot speedily followed. It was a refinement of later days to send a doctor with the candymen, as the evicting party were called. At first women and children, the sick, the aged, even the dying, were thrust ruthlessly into the streets.

As Mr Roberts said, the strike was "a trial between the long purses of the owners, and the hungry guts of the pitmen"[1], and hunger was not an ally to boast. By the end of June some 200 men were leaving the union every week. The Durham men were the first to submit[2]. The pits in which they worked were newer, bigger, and under less sympathetic management. They had been most affected by the wage reductions. They were the first to feel the full weight of the owners' displeasure. In the old Tyneside collieries master and man fought out the struggle alone. Only in the north of Northumberland was there much immigration. But to Durham Irishmen came in large numbers, and there eviction was general. There had been two great meetings south of the Tyne, at which 20,000 men listened earnestly to complaint of harsh treatment, dangers, discomforts, and fines, and to a strange new doctrine, that by their labour the pitmen deserved well of the community. When the scene of the meetings was changed to the Town Moor, at Newcastle, it meant that the strike was at an end. At the first of these meetings 25,000 men assembled, in a pouring rain, to give visible disproof of the rumour that desertion had defeated the union. A fortnight later but 5000 men were there[3]. They were the Northumberland men alone, for by the end of August every colliery in Durham was in full work at the old terms. It gave the death-blow to the union when in

[1] *Durham Chronicle*, May 10th, 1844.
[2] R. Fynes, *The Miners of Northumberland and Durham*, pp. 66–81, 102.
[3] *Durham Chronicle*, May 24th, June 21st, July 12th, 1844.

despair the Ranter preachers advised the men to submit and save what they could[1].

Here and there a feeble attempt was made to secure the re-engagement of the leaders. Here and there the strike ended in an outburst of violence. But eighteen weeks of idleness and starvation had made an end of the men's resolution. The delegates whom they had sent to London—jeeringly called the Twelve Apostles—had collected but a paltry sum. When the tradesman's credit was exhausted, the last dresser and eight-day clock sold, even the rings from the women's fingers pawned, "poverty and indigence, unable to cope any longer with wealth and affluence, gave up the combat"[2].

The second union gained nothing. It had made demands less definite and more far-reaching than had the first, confined by Hepburn's wisdom to practicality. Its complaints of oppression were in general disproved; the truth of its wage statements denied. Whether the daily wage was 3s. 8d., as the owners said, or 3s., as the men alleged, cannot be determined. Restriction had made the pay-notes worthless in argument. But the pitman had thrust himself further than ever before into public notice. For five months his deeds had filled the newspapers, and while the meetings in the towns had made the public familiar with his demands, on the whole, his good conduct had improved his reputation. It was after this strike that the coal-owners became possessed of

[1] *Durham Chronicle*, August 16th and 23rd, 1844.
[2] R. Fynes, *The Miners of Northumberland and Durham*, p. 93.

a new zeal for education and social improvement. Meantime the loyalty which the men had shewn to a beaten cause, and the endurance they had displayed in the long battle, were encouraging signs for leaders who should prepare before they began the fight. The boys who in this strike hung about the meetings, jeered at the police, hooted the black-legs, and shared in the starvation, were the men among whom a more enduring union was to be preached.

The strike had brought a second race of strangers to embarrass an already overcrowded trade; 4000 new men were at work in the pits. Some of them were navvies, who soon tired of their new life and returned to the railways, the roads, and the vagrant existence. Most of the others were unprofitable servants. A man bred and born to the pits was admitted to be better worth his wages, and as the old hands began to return and time to excuse their offence the owners forgot the debt they owed to the black-legs. The strangers who remained became shifters and screen-men, labourers rather than hewers, while the pitmen did their best to drive them from the villages. They were denied all social life: assaulted in the taverns, beaten in the quiet solitudes of the pits. Guns were fired through their windows and powder thrown down their chimneys. As Fynes, the first historian of union, remembered, "their poor, wretched lives at length became as bad as toads under a harrow"[1].

It was remarked in both the great cholera epidemics

[1] R. Fynes, *The Miners of Northumberland and Durham*, p. 110.

that the mortality was by far the highest among the newcomers. In the insanitary colliery village where families lived in one and two rooms, while at the back of the rows stretched a long heap of dung and household refuse, household pride was the only defence against frequent disease. The newcomers were without that scrupulous care for personal cleanliness which is the pride of the true north-country pitman and even more of his wife. Tremenheere, after a eulogy on the Scottish immigrants, who would deny themselves a meal to save the price of a book, could find no better conclusion than "after one generation they become nearly as clean as their English neighbours"[1]. Of the newcomers, it is doubtful whether more than half remained. Only one section was too strong for the native pitmen, the Irish. To add to the natural growth of their families every year more friends were brought over, allured by the tales of incredible prosperity. For years their low standard of life—their religion denied them the zeal for education, which was at once the danger and the merit of Methodism—was to make them the weapons of the owners, in every wage dispute.

[1] *Report—State of Population in the Mining District* (Tremenheere), 1856.

CHAPTER V

PHILANTHROPY AND STATE ACTION

ALMOST all the early mining legislation was dis-
ciplinary. In 1736 it was made felony, without
benefit of clergy, to set fire to a pit. In 1747 a new
Masters and Servants Act was so framed as to include
"miners and colliers, keelmen and pitmen." In 1736
an Act against Malicious Injuries to Property extended legal protection to the coal-mines. Both the
dates and the language of these amendments of the
law suggest north-country influence, but there was
little interference with the coal trade, despite the
perpetual strife between the Lord Mayor of London
and the Newcastle Hostmen. The London coal dues
were as heavy a burden on the consumer as the
merchants' profits, and a diplomatic peace as a rule
prevented untimely disclosures. But once, in 1696,
a petition was presented, praying for a bill in restraint
of "such extravagant rates for way-leave and staithe-
room as (are) no small prejudice to the trade, and
(tend to the raising of) the price of coale in the
kingdom"[1]. And once it was suggested that coal-
owners as well as men needed a reminder of their
duties. In 1756 so many people were killed near
Newcastle by falling into deserted workings that an
angry editor proposed "that the legislature should

[1] Mark Archer, *A Sketch of the History of the Coal Trade of
Northumberland and Durham*, 1897.

compell the owners...who can well afford the small
outlay to fill up such pits "[1].

Custom extended some protection to the victims
of mine disaster. Widows were left in quiet possession
of their houses, cripples found light employment,
hale survivors shewn a preference in small favours.
After a great calamity a public subscription was
raised, augmented a little by the charity of the
London merchants, though the well-kept silence which
surrounded all mining matters diminished both
the frequency and extent of such relief. In 1805 Dr
Chapman drew up a scheme for the establishment of a
permanent relief fund but until the matter was debated
by the Sunderland Society it attracted little notice.
In 1815 the owners met to consider a scheme which
had been proposed by an anonymous writer in the
newspapers, that a fund should be raised by placing
a tax on the sale of coal and adding to it a small
deduction made from the wages of the men[2]. But
the plan was never seriously tried; apparently the
owners were unable to overcome the suspicions of the
men, who saw in the Provident Fund a scheme to shift
to their shoulders the burden of the poor rate[3]. From
the pains one pamphlet took to refute what it thought
an erroneous belief there is reason to suppose that
many thought the occasional subscriptions an imposition on public benevolence, and shared the pit-

[1] *Newcastle Courant.*
[2] T. Whittell, *Pamphlet*, 1815; *Newcastle Courant*, May 13th,
June 15th, 1815.
[3] Matthias Dunn, *An Historical View of the Coal Trade*,
pp. 37–38.

men's belief that the support of the injured was a duty incumbent on the owners.

The Sunderland Society dissolved, content with the invention of the safety lamp, but the exertions of Dr Clanny had done a little to destroy the policy of isolation and concealment which the owners maintained out of "a mistaken view of self-interest." How difficult had been his task is shewn by an angry letter which he wrote to a friend:

I feel hurt at the conduct of the viewers, as they continue to sacrifice good principles at the mercenary shrine of self-interest, and willingly see hundreds of their fellow creatures hurled into eternity, rather than encourage any plans which might militate against their remuneration[1].

How fanatical was the opposition to interference is shewn by the refusal to adopt a system of registration of mine surveys, though Buddle, the foremost viewer in the north, gave it his support and pointed out how rapidly the danger of inundation from old workings was growing. But there was good reason for this stout belief in the efficacy of individual effort. The northern viewers had set a standard of careful working and rapid technical improvement which was a pattern to every other coal-field. Their pride was hurt by the suggestion that state interference could goad them to exertions greater than those which they had willingly undertaken.

At first the Davy lamp brought added safety, but when it became an excuse for neglect of ventilation

[1] J. H. H. Holmes, *A Treatise on the Coal Mines of Northumberland and Durham containing Accounts of Explosions* (1816), p. 132.

and men were habitually sent into places where a naked light would have brought instant disaster hints began to be made that the lamp was worse than useless. Through the interested insistence of two inventors of a rival device in 1835 the House of Commons appointed a committee to enquire into the frequency and cause of accidents in mines. It was but half-hearted in its enquiries, though its single decision that the Davy lamp was better than its rivals was sufficiently sound[1]. But accidents continued, for the poor light which lamps of every pattern gave prevented their wide adoption, while Davy's careful directions were forgotten, and no precautions taken in the use of a device from which miracles were expected. In 1839 a voluntary committee gathered in South Shields to conduct a new enquiry. Headed by Mather, one of the inventors of the life-boat, the members explored several pits, sometimes descending so soon after a disaster as to be present when the rescue party was still at work. The committee came to three conclusions; that many of the traditional methods of mining engineers had no foundation of reason; that improvement was both possible, and desirable, in the furnace system of ventilation, for ventilation was the only secret of security; and that legislation, and government inspection, would be of undoubted value.

From that time an increasing number of people were converted to a belief in state interference. The

[1] J. Mather, *The Coal Mines, together with a Report of the South Shields Committee*, 1868.

men were the loudest advocates of inspection. They did not share the owners' fear that it would add to working costs and by diminishing private responsibility increase the danger. They were inclined to welcome the restriction of the manager's authority. Nor did they take alarm at the thought that inspection might expose trade secrets to business rivals. The publicity which the owners opposed they had always desired, to shame bad masters out of malpractice. Before the Commons' Committee the one working miner called as a witness held stoutly to his claim for thorough inspection, though much argument was used to dissuade him. But the new school of engineers which succeeded Buddle was so far of the same mind as the men that its members were ready to accept any method of compelling the ignorant and the conservative to technical improvement. The increase of scientific knowledge had made them better aware of their ignorance, more conscious of the difficulties of their work. They had less pride in their own achievements, less self-sufficiency. They saw that state inspection could only enforce on others the methods which they themselves devised, that laws could hamper little men who must be consulted in their making.

In 1842, to quiet the persistent demands of Lord Ashley and his friends, a royal commission was appointed to investigate the conditions of the employment of women and children underground. The north took little notice of its sittings, hardened as it was by custom to a state which horrified the stranger.

It was mildly surprised at "the universal feeling of abhorrence and disgust" to which the terrible exposure of the cruelties of industry gave rise. In smug complacency it applauded such parts of Lord Ashley's speech as the acknowledgment that in the north need for his interference was by comparison small. Yet even in the northern coal-field, "which stood out in almost every respect in very favourable contrast with other districts," children of five and six were commonly employed in places where they were "compelled to pass through avenues not so good as a common sewer, quite as wet, and often more contracted." "It is not possible," said Lord Ashley, when he presented his report to the Commons, "it is not possible for any man, if he have but a heart in his bosom, to read the details of this awful document without a combined feeling of shame, terror, and indignation"[1].

Perhaps the coal-owners were silenced by the public Horror. Perhaps those from the north felt almost qualified to join in it. At any rate they were at first uncertain whether to suffer the interference of the law. It seemed probable that the regulations which were proposed would weigh most heavily on their competitors. Buddle, who was sent down to watch the progress of Lord Ashley's bill, was for a time on the side of reform. Suddenly benevolent neutrality turned into whole-hearted opposition. It was the suggested appointment of inspectors, to compel obedience to the act, which brought the change.

[1] House of Commons, June 7th, 1842.

Where one inspector came others were certain to follow. In the upper house Lord Londonderry fought the bill at every stage.

The commissioners had collected· evidence from artful girls, and ignorant boys, putting questions which suggested their answer....It was more important that lads should be taught their future occupation than that they should learn to read and write....He would say of the coal-owners that there was no set of men in the world who did more justice to the men employed by them[1].

But though Buddle primed him with facts his opposition failed to delay the progress of the bill, and the reply to the commissioners' report which the coal trade issued had no better effect. They claimed that the system of ventilation in use in the north was "the best in the world, and that their treatment of the children was not so gross as the commissioners alleged." The blame for the employment of very young boys they threw on the parents, who deceived the managers by making false statements to them about the age of their children. The small boys were not allowed to put, they were given a door to mind. They seldom stayed at work more than ten hours, never more than twelve. Their loneliness was relieved by the frequent passing of the putters, and "they beguiled the time in fond and childish amusements, cutting sticks, making models of wagons and windmills, drawing figures with chalk, modelling in clay"[2]. But state interference was inevitable. The employ-

[1] House of Lords, June 24th, 1842.
[2] *Reply of Coal Trade to Commissioners' Report* (Annexed to House of Lords' Report, June 24th, 1842).

ment underground of women, and of boys under ten, was forbidden. Lord Londonderry threatened that he would obey the law to the letter. It made no mention of active assistance to the inspectors. He would say to them "you may go down the pit how you like, and when you are down you may remain there!"[1]. The only result of his outburst was the insertion of a clause to compel the owners to give every facility to the inspectors in the performances of their duties.

The sub-commissioner deputed to report on the Tyne coal-field was by good fortune an unusually active man. While his colleague in Durham was content to collect such evidence as readily offered itself, the statements of owners and viewers and the stories of a comparatively small number of children, John Ridley Leifchild, working in Northumberland, set himself to produce a description of the pit-life unequalled at any time in its wealth of detail. To this day strangers find difficulty in understanding the language of the north-country, though now men who chat with one another in the broadest dialect can as a rule make use of a less mysterious tongue. But before the spread of education, and the mixing of the people which has followed increased ease of movement, the dialect was almost a foreign language, especially to a man ignorant of the technical terms his enquiry was certain to provoke. Especially was it hard to fathom the meaning of children, possessed of so small a vocabulary that "hurt his

[1] House of Lords, Aug. 1st, 1842.

arm" was discovered to mean a broken bone. Leifchild, unwilling to employ an interpreter, for some months devoted himself to study so that he might himself "translate the evidence"[1]. Moreover, he descended twelve pits "selected for diversity"[2]. One he inspected a short time after an explosion.

The deep-rooted jealousy the men had of their employers, "their assumption as a truth, amply justified by experience, that the masters could have no desire to benefit them"[3], made the enquiry still more difficult. The men thought that its only object was the imposition of some new tax. They would not themselves readily give evidence. They "instigated their children to rudeness, and imposed on them silence"[4]. As the commissioner found "for a stranger to read the mind of a pitman circuitous approach, and no small tact, are required"[5]. He was inclined to suspect that the stupidity of the bigger boys was a little assumed. All the managers had warned him of their tendency to deceit and he could get little from them beyond "a sweeping condemnation of their task, and the insufficiency of the remuneration." Of impartial evidence there was almost none. Among the residents of the outside districts "rarely did curiosity so far overcome the idea of danger as to induce them to descend a pit"[6]. The mining villages were remote and repulsive, the concealment of their inhabitants "equivalent to a temporary burial"[7]. And

[1] J. R. Leifchild, *Children's Employment Commission*, p. 514.
[2] *Ibid.* p. 519.   [3] *Ibid.* p. 515.
[4] *Ibid.* p. 515.   [5] *Ibid.* p. 515.
[6] *Ibid.* p. 520   [7] *Ibid.* p. 520.

because the life of the boys above ground "was of so short duration, as barely to be sufficient for the ordinary exigencies of life"[1] even when conversation at last became practicable there was small opportunity for it.

In the north there was no story of moral degradation to add to the terrible recital of physical hardship. There were no women in the pits. In his youth one man at Cramlington "had put with a woman" but that was years before, and even then it was a "rare case in the district." The pitmen not only kept their wives out of the pits, they denied them any outside occupation, holding that the care of their houses, their families and their men was work sufficient[2]. The strike of 1832 had made an end of truck, for little as it had flourished in the north, among the older men there were unhappy memories of the bad bread of the days of "ticketted corn"[3]. The butty system, under which the men are engaged by one of themselves, who has contracted to work a seam, was unknown. So too was the employment of pauper apprentices. There was a striking absence of that worst of all evils, petty tyranny, and a uniform level of wages and hours which made oppressive abnormalities uncommon. It was a result of the size of the pits and of the much maligned custom of the yearly bond. Every man and boy was engaged directly by the manager, whose authority was maintained by a well-ordered system of officials almost

---

[1] *Children's Employment Commission*, p. 514.
[2] *Ibid.* pp. 136, 519.　　　　　[3] *Ibid.* p. 627.

all of whom were promoted from among the more skilful, reliable, and educated men. The lowest grade, the deputy overmen, who watched the general progress of the work, had charge also of the discipline of the mine, and on their care its safety often depended. The systematic delegation of authority had brought a freedom from accident which was the envy of other districts.

Such abuse as existed was chiefly due to the extreme youth of the boys and the nature of their tasks. Perhaps because minute attention to drainage was not necessary for safety the workings were often wet and muddy, so much so that the putters passed in their journeys through places knee-deep in water. But it had dawned on the more intelligent owners that bad, low roads and the employment of very young children were alike poor economy. As a rule, the bigger the mine the better the lot of the miners.

Leifchild soon found that it was not safe to rely too much on the evidence of the viewers. Boys had sworn to him that at times they strained at their tubs, on the inclines, till blood gushed from their nostrils. They had shewn him the wounds on their backs where the low roofs had rubbed off the skin. Yet one viewer said of the putters' work that "it was healthy, and promoted perspiration"[1]. In contrast with the men, among whom there was almost unanimous agreement that twelve was young enough for pit work, even the most respectable viewers "willingly admitted that they employed boys of nine"[2]. Many

[1] *Children's Employment Commission*, p. 624.   [2] *Ibid.* p. 121.

swore that they had no children working below of
less than eight years. Leifchild found many of six,
and one of four and a half. It was true that on the
whole the blame lay with the parents, greedy for their
children's wage. They made excuse that the boys
refused to go to school and cried to be taken down
the pit. Poverty would have been a better excuse,
for almost all the very young children were members
of large families, sons of widows, or of idle and
drunken parents. Blind obedience to custom was
the chief reason. The parents had gone to work in
their infancy, they thought of no better lot for their
sons and it was commonly held that the sooner a
boy took to the pits the better workman he became.
Some definite act of interference was required to put
an end to what both masters and men agreed was
an unreasonable, unnecessary abuse. Unnecessary it
must have been, for neither owners nor parents seem
to have missed the labour of the children once it was
forbidden. It was not until later acts raised the
minimum age for employment from 10 to 13 that
murmurs began to be heard of a shortage of
boys.

It was no long time since starvation had driven
the farm labourers of the south to the potato diet
of the Irish peasant; no long time since death had
silenced Cobbett's roaring at the robbers who had
deprived the Englishman of the true right of man,
the right to eat bread and bacon at his meals. The
answers of the factory children had prepared the
commissioners for sordid tales of starvation. It was

a pleasant surprise to find that the pit-lad's readiest answer was that "he had as much to eat as he wanted." His "coffee, plenty of bread, and sometimes a bit of kitchen"[1] may seem poor fare enough but to the commissioners the viewers' tales of "potatoes, and bacon, fresh meat, tea, sugar, and coffee"[2] were ample proof of good living. In those days it was perilously near extravagant luxury for a labouring man to have his belly stretched, however simple the filling. And though the pitman himself was not content with his wage—had he not the memory of more prosperous days—his pay was enormous when contrasted with the few shillings a week of the farm labourer. The tenpence a day which the boys could earn from the age of six was good encouragement for the rearing of large families, true as it might be that "pit-lads eat a more than other lads, a vast"[3]. And if the men were at times irregularly employed there was none of that hopeless starvation common in the trades where machinery was steadily displacing labour. In fact, the source of the prosperity which has always been attributed to the miner is that there has been a steady, uninterrupted growth in the number of men to whom their calling offers employment. Never yet have the pitmen felt the pinch of a permanent contraction of mining activity.

What the commissioners found in the north was

---

[1] *Children's Employment Commission*, pp. 577 *et seq*.
[2] *Ibid.* p. 134, and comments on luxurious diet.
[3] *Ibid.* p. 618.

not a system of deliberate oppression but a system worked with too little attention to minor abuse. Nominally the boys worked a shift of twelve hours, and in a well-managed pit this time was seldom exceeded. But the great majority of the lads had at some time or other "worked double shift," staying below twenty-four hours. Several had worked three shifts, and one claimed to have been kept below on one occasion forty-eight hours. Either an official took a boy with him to carry his instruments, or a putter stayed to take the place of a lad in the next shift who had failed to appear. The extra work was not disliked. It is an old custom of the pits that a man keeps for his own use all money which he receives in excess of his normal wage. An extra shift was rather a favour than a grievance.

But twelve hours, which meant almost fourteen from home, was a long day for boys of eight. They were awakened by their mothers, fed, and sent off to the pits. They returned exhausted, to be washed and put to bed. It was the regret of more than one manager that they could not be kept from wasting their time in play "to the manifest abridgment of their natural rest"[1]. Often they were too tired to eat their meals. Their minds were enfeebled by the long hours; they had neither the will nor the ability to learn. What education they had acquired they lost as soon as they went down the pit. The mother of one little lad, who at six years and a half had been at work half a year, said that often when she

[1] *Children's Employment Commission*, p. 110.

awoke him he rubbed his eyes and complained that he had only just laid down to sleep. Yet his father "intended, when he got a little more hardened to the pit, to send him to the night school, and stop an hour off his sleep"[1]. It is not surprising that schoolmasters thought the pit-boys dull, and that "a vacant stare, and a heedless—I don't know—" was too often the answer to Leifchild's questioning. The owner's picture of the trapper passing his hours "in fond and [2]childish amusements" accords badly with the memory that Geordy Black had of his childhood:

When aw was a bairn, carried on my fether's back,
He wad tyek me away te the pit,
An gettin i' the cage, an gannin doon belaw,
Was eneuf to myek a yungster tyek a fit.
To sit an keep a door, midst darkness and gloom
Ay, mony an hoor by mysel,
An hear the awful shots that rummelled throo the pit,
And lumps o roondy coal cum doon pell mell[3].

That was the trapper's life. He rose at two, and went to work. All day he sat in his "neuk" in the darkness, the string of his door in his hand. Sometimes a kindly hewer would give him a candle to cheer his loneliness. More often a putter would find him asleep, and enraged by having to open the door himself, would fall on him and beat him. Sometimes he would stray from his post, to play with a near-by lad. On Sundays he went to the Ranters' school and

---

[1] *Children's Employment Commission*, pp. 17 and 584.

[2] *Reply of Coal Trade to Commissioners' Report* (see above, p. 88).

[3] "Geordy Black" (Rowland Harrison, 1841) in J. Wilson's *A Choice Collection of Tyneside Songs*.

learned to read A–B, ab. After a year or two as a
trapper the lad became a driver. Mechanical haulage
was only just coming into use. "Sets" of tubs were
hauled to the shaft by horses "urged at speed through
the sinuosities of the workings, to their continual dis-
figurement and destruction"[1]. The control of these
horses "not seldom unruly, not rarely plagued with
viciousness" "was entrusted to the merest children"[2].
In the eyes of the other lads, and in fact of every
class from the viewers downward, the driver's was
an easy life for though he drove as much as thirty
miles a day he "rode" all the time. His hours were
the usual twelve, exceeded at times by staying to
attend to the horse, for a few maintained some feeling
of kindness despite the brutal disregard, all too common, of everything but work. But his was almost
the most dangerous task in the mine. Hardly a
driver was examined who had not met with a fairly
serious accident. Either he had been kicked, or he
had been crushed between his tubs and the roof.
Most often he had been run over, after falling from
the small projection which was his insecure seat on
the tubs. It was not state protection but mechanical
improvement which lightened the lot of the driver.
Within a few years of the sitting of the commission
mechanical haulage began to replace horses in the
main roads.

Unless he was classed as a weakling and put to
such odd jobs about the mine as greasing tub wheels

[1] Matthias Dunn, *Winning and Working of Collieries*, p. 27.
[2] *Children's Employment Commission*, p. 523.

w   7

the driver in time became a putter. His work was to attend on the hewers, bringing them empty tubs and taking the full ones back to the "flat" where the driver waited with his horse. Like his father, every quarter the putter "put in his cavil," that is, drew lots for a fresh working-place. He was paid by the journey, at a rate which varied with the steepness of the slope, and the length of each trip. It was as putters that most of the lads were engaged. As a rule they worked in pairs. If they were "half-marrows," boys of the same size, they shared the work and the wage equally, taking turns to push the tub and to draw it with the "teams," short cords attached as handles to the front. A bigger lad worked as a "headsman," always pushing, assisted by a "foal," a small boy who always drew. These small boys were ill-used and overworked, driven on as they were by the oaths and blows of their bigger comrades. When a lad came to his full size he worked alone, hoping for the time when he would be bound as a hewer. Often his wage was as high as that of a man. In fact all "the putters, to increase their wages, frequently worked, regardless of fatigue, to utter exhaustion." Leifchild was not prepared to believe that all the blame for this harmful exertion rested on the boys. Not only did the system of payment by output offer temptations from which they should have been guarded but refusal to share in the blind competition to obtain a high wage was sure to bring a lad into disfavour. One boy, for sitting down to eat his "bait," was fined by the manager and warned never to waste his time in such a manner again[1]. The putters were not driven solely by the desire for money: they were urged on by the hewers, who would endure no delays in the removal of their tubs. They "worked as if they were engaged in a sea fight"[2], making the pause at each end of their journey as short as possible.

All the putters were agreed that their work was too hard, and to the surprise of the commissioners many of them said they would prefer to work less, even if they should lose pay by the change. They complained of aches in their arms and legs, and, when they had to pass through badly ventilated places, in their heads also. They strained themselves by putting overthrown tubs back on the rails. They fought their way up inclines, and struggled down slopes where the full tub threatened to break away and run them down. Despite the leather shields which they wore on their backs, and the patches stitched on their shirts, they rubbed themselves sore in the low places, and the sharp corners of the tubs took the skin from their shoulders. In wet places, where the mud came over the shoe-tops, and the water rose at times to their knees, the stones rubbed the skin off their feet. In the mornings

> It was, ne doubt, a cooen seet,
> Te see them hirplin cross the floor,
> Wi anklets shawed, and scather'd feet,
> Wi' salve and ointment plaistered o'er[3].

[1] *Children's Employment Commission*, p. 162.
[2] *Ibid.* p. 127.
[3] Thomas Wilson, *The Pitman's Pay*, p. 33.

While boys were tempted by high wages, and manly ambition, to attempt tasks far beyond their strength, too little attention was paid to the condition of the roads. The viewers drove the main roads three to four feet high, but the constant closing of the roof and the floor was not fought with any regularity. Sharp rises appeared on once regular inclines, deep puddles in level floors, nor was it until the place became almost impassable, and the work threatened to stop, that the shifters came to make the necessary repairs. Here again it was not legislation which improved the lot of the boys. Once before they had shared in the benefit of a mechanical improvement. "We put on the bare thill," said one old man, to shew by contrast how easy was the life of the boys of this later generation, and the putters had good cause to thank the man

> That furst invented metal plates[1]

for had

> wor bits o yammering yeps,
> That wowl about wor barrow way,
> Te slave and drudge like langsyne cheps,
> They wad'nt worsel out a day[2].

Now further improvement was on the way. For the viewers had discovered that Shetland ponies made better putters than small boys. Bigger tubs were made, more in keeping with the ponies' strength. The roads were made higher and more care spent on their repair. Where the ponies could not go, and in many places they went right up to the face, hand-

[1] *The Pitman's Pay*, p. 44.   [2] *Ibid.* p. 43.

putters were still required. But small boys could not move the big tubs. By degrees the age of the lads rose until now the putter is no longer a child but a strong young man. But boys they once were, and boys in name they still remain, to the confusion of the unenlightened stranger.

After the passing of the act which prohibited the underground employment of women and small children it was less common for small boys to work a twelve-hour day, at an age which we now deem too small for the hard labour of the school. But the act was badly enforced. In 1862 a journalist on a visit to the pits saw many boys "who on enquiry said they were ten" of the truth of whose answer he was justly suspicious. Until the Education Act compelled him to go to school the pit-lad knew little of the pleasures of infancy. The school registers did what several acts of parliament had attempted in vain, when they made impossible callous parental deception. But the restraint on the employment of the boys was not an unmixed benefit to them. In the old, unregulated days there had been so many children that many of them worked but half the week. But the Education Act, which imposed a minimum age of 13, so diminished the supply of boys, that such persistent idleness became unknown. Worse still, it caused so great a shortage of boys that to shorten their hours seemed impossible, for there was no hope of recruiting a second shift. Until the miners were assured an eight-hour day by act of parliament the north lay open to the reproach that the boys worked three or four hours a day longer than did their fathers.

The government shewed little wisdom when it appointed Simon Tremenheere to be their first inspector. It was impossible for any man, unaided, to exercise close supervision over the whole island. But Tremenheere was employed in more errands than the protection of miners' children. He seems to have been the chosen expert on the working classes, their education, and the improvement of their moral state. Of his first visit to the north the men made indignant protest that no whisper reached them until the issue of the report. His single source of information seems to have been the after-dinner conversation of the owners, composed as it was of the well-worn strictures on the extravagance of the pitmen, the conventional picture of their prosperity, and the regret that so excellent a body of men should be so prone to combination and so open to the persuasions of dishonest self-seeking demagogues. He seems to have been one of those evangelical philanthropists whose ideal of industry was the paternal employer, to whom the little girls were to bob, and the little boys touch their fore-lock. His main concern was that the children should attend Sunday school and their parents read "improving books" which should persuade them to contentment with their divinely appointed lot. He was full of admiration for the work of the Consett Iron Company, which "by the most legitimate means of scrupulously enlightened management" maintained "so thorough a mastery of their own works" that "no Chartist, no delegate, could succeed"[1]. It is to be doubted whether he had ever made a trip to their collieries and coke-ovens, where Irish immigrant labour found a ready welcome, and where low wages were the rule. His great contrast was Earsdon, a "plague-spot" which nothing but political economy could cure, such political economy as the S.P.C.K. tracts made plain for every man's understanding. He was less troubled by the open evasion of the act it was his duty to enforce—an evasion so general that in 1852 he made it an argument against advancing the minimum age to 12—than by the spread of pernicious literature. He recorded with horror that in one week a shop in Newcastle sold 1726 copies of nine different "Chartist and infidel newspapers," 600 copies of a Chartist paper, 1656 copies of newspapers "of an immoral nature, hostile to the existing state"[2], and of its four religious and moral newspapers, only 888 copies. He was an earnest advocate of increased education, but he thought the boys might be sufficiently improved by attendance at school on the days the pits were idle, and at nights. At first he testified to his fidelity to the Church as by Law established by constant assertions that the Ranter preachers were the strength of the union. Later, he changed his mind, perhaps persuaded of the benefit of Methodism among a people whom the church had so long neglected. He found that the delegates were young men, popular, fluent, and of

---

[1] Tremenheere's *Report*, 1849, p. 6.
[2] *Ibid.* 1851.

no religion, who terrified their less violent fellows into actions of which in their hearts they disapproved.

The chief value of his report, rendered irregularly until 1858, is its record of continued educational improvement. The employers were losing their fears that education would rob the pitmen of their skill and add to their stubborn indiscipline. They built schools in the hope that they might prove a counter to union influence. It was an age when the Government proposed to call on the church, as the most effective enemy of Chartism. Among working men there was an immense spread of "superficial knowledge" which led ignorant men to read Plato's *Republic*, fascinated by its communist doctrines[1]. There was an alarming increase of infidelity and socialism. But in 1854 Tremenheere had lost a little of his fear. He had conversed with two of the union leaders—mentioned by name, with the honourable affix of Mr—and had been surprised to find them possessed of a keener desire for education than his own[2]. But the need for his enquiries was gone. Since 1851 a new kind of inspector had been at work, Her Majesty's Inspectors of Mines.

For in 1850 the first Mines Regulation Act had been passed. It did little beyond appoint inspectors, but how eagerly these inspectors were awaited was shewn by the popular discontent at the delay in their appointment. From the first the Government chose their men well. The inspector for the northern district, Matthias Dunn, was a well-known mine

[1] Tremenheere's *Report*, 1852.   [2] *Ibid.* 1854.

manager of wide interests, who had long been an
advocate of state supervision. The new inspectors
confined their energies to technical enquiry, and it
was rare that their suggestions were resented. In
1856 the northern coal-field was given a second
inspector, Atkinson, an engineer even less open
to criticism than his somewhat dogmatic superior.
Scientific enquiry and legal action had for ever replaced reliance on paternal philanthropy. The need
had gone of appeal to sentiments of humanity. Henceforth the miners' demands were to have the ear of
political ambition.

Thus in 1850 three of the desires of the early
philanthropists had been attained, state inspection,
state regulation, and public registration of mine surveys. One only remained, the provision of support
for the injured.

It too came, and in a form which would have
received the approval of the Sunderland Society.
Lord Londonderry continued to assert his belief that
to maintain the sufferers was a duty incumbent on
the owners, that "in proportion as the collier devotes
his labour and incurs the risk of the mine for the
benefit of his employer, so is the latter in common
duty, honesty, and charity bound to provide for those
bereft of their protector"[1]. The stout-hearted old
soldier, whose opposition had twice destroyed the
union, justified his economic belief by his actions, and
kept his high place in the respect of the men. But
"the new-fangled doctrine" was not to the tastes of

[1] *Durham Chronicle* (Letter).

many of the owners. Quietly a Provident Society was formed. Membership was voluntary; there was a subscription from the men, a contribution from the owners. To the support of the society was enlisted the more stable element of unionism. In 1862 there were several notable disasters. The newspapers, while raising subscriptions, did not fail to recommend the Provident Society to the men's notice. From that time it became one of the firmest institutions in the north.

CHAPTER VI

THE THIRD UNION

T'HOUGH in the strike of 1844 the second union received its death-blow, it was to be a very long time dying. Next year the competition of the Midland collieries destroyed the harmony of the northern coal-trade. The system of allotment of contracts by which for over two hundred years high prices had been maintained in the London market was abandoned, and a fierce fight began for foothold which ruined many of the smaller collieries. In innocent simplicity the stout free-trade journals of the north bewailed the destruction of a monopoly which had been so profitable to their patrons. Unrestricted trade had never been of permanent benefit to the consumer, said the *Durham Chronicle*, a stout advocate of Corn Law Repeal[1]. The owners' quarrels brought temporary prosperity to the pitmen. Stout union men were no longer driven from colliery to colliery in a hopeless search for work: managers anxious for high output could not afford to turn good workmen away for a principle[2]. But though high wages and steady work helped to silence the complaints of the men, the feeble remnant of union survived the prosperity. In secret the old delegates continued to spread their teaching.

[1] *Durham Chronicle*, July 31st, 1846.
[2] R. Fynes, *The Miners of Northumberland and Durham*, p. 117.

When Slingsby Duncombe introduced his first "Mines Regulation" Bill, he was furnished with as thorough a record of disaster as Jude and Roberts could compile[1]. The men even dared to sign a petition asking parliament to undertake their protection.

In 1849 there was a series of local strikes, provoking new interest in union sufficient to encourage the leaders to call a secret delegate meeting. The men were uneasy. They suspected that the introduction of big tubs was in part an attempt to diminish their wages. For the size of the tubs was steadily growing, as improvements were made in the system of underground transport, and to conservative pitmen it was little use to plead that "the high character of the owners was in itself a guarantee that no advantage would be taken of the change"[2]. Threats of a strike were so common that the temporary disunion of the owners came to an end, and the men's complaints died away[3]. In 1851, when the seamen of the northern ports struck, the pitmen joined with their ancient enemies in demonstrations at Sunderland and Newcastle. At a huge meeting on the Town Moor, after the sailors' wrongs had been recited, Martin Jude read out a list of the miners' demands. They wished to be paid by weight, not measure. They wanted an eight-hour day for the boys. And they asked for a monthly inspection of the pits[4]. The magnitude of

[1] R. Fynes, *The Miners of Northumberland and Durham*, p. 121.   [2] *Durham Chronicle*, Nov. 9th, 1849.
[3] R. Fynes, *The Miners of Northumberland and Durham*, p. 138.
[4] *Durham Chronicle*, Oct. 19th, Nov. 10th, 1851.

the demands suggests that Jude's authority was slipping away. They were pious hopes, not suggestions for practical reforms, while the rider, that ponies and big tubs should be prohibited, was a mere appeal to ignorant conservatism. The men said that the big tubs interfered with the ventilation. There was no hint that they really feared a wage reduction.

Next year there were rumours of a general revival of union[1]. Perhaps it was memory of the poor response of the men to the efforts of the agitators which moved Fynes to record "in that year the union might be said to be at an end"[2]. But if the union was dead the idea of union was not. There were whispers that along the Wear valley the men were still banded together, and wherever a local grievance ended in a hasty strike at the first sign of war the men sent for their old leaders and refounded the local lodge. Each year there was a meeting on Black Fell to discuss the expected terms of the bindings[3]. In 1854 13,000 signatures were collected to a petition for better inspection, and at Christmas the Seaham men came out on strike. Though Martin Jude was allowed to arbitrate the men refused to accept his award[4]. They were evicted, and in the confusion a dying child was turned into the street. When the black-legs arrived the strikers fell on them and drove them away, bursting down doors and windows to reach them in

[1] *Durham Chronicle*, Oct. 31st, 1852.
[2] R. Fynes, *The Miners of Northumberland and Durham*, p. 139.
[3] *Durham Chronicle*, Aug. 26th, 1853, April 7th, 1854.
[4] *Ibid.* Dec. 22nd, 1854, Jan., Feb. 1855.

the houses to which they fled. The strike closed with
a long list of arrests for riot, and the prisoners again
sought the aid of Mr Roberts. Seaham was not the
only colliery which struck in protest against the insufficiency of wages. At Hetton 3000 men lay idle
for nine weeks in a vain attempt to stave off a reduction[1].

Next year (1855), on both sides of the Tyne, there
was sudden resistance. Its failure in Northumberland
had a result greater than that of many a small success
for "the minds of all thinking men began to turn to
union"[2]. Wages had fallen so low that there was less
to lose by a fight than by submission. A strike at
Seghill gave the signal for action. The manager,
knowing that further wage reductions were impossible,
made an attempt to raise the proportion of "round"
among the coal. Every man was given a rake, and
to every two men there was a riddle, in the use of
which the men wasted time spared grudgingly from
the hewing. Suddenly, at an hour's notice, they
struck. It was in the face of the warnings of a newly-
formed Methodist class, yet its members were chosen
for punishment. One man was arrested at the bed-
side of his dying wife[3]. It was in vain that the strikers
protested against the selection, telling the manager
that he had punished the wrong man. His reply
shews the spirit of the quarrel. "I know that. That
is why I have put them in prison. It is no use putting

[1] *Durham Chronicle*, June 15th, 1855.
[2] R. Fynes, *The Miners of Northumberland and Durham*,
p. 183.
[3] Ramsay Guthrie, *Black Dyke* (a semi-historical novel).

them in who cannot feel." In the words of the pre-
amble to the rules of the third union "the time had
arrived when the miners were called in the spirit of
love and friendship to unite, and be able to with-
stand the daily oppressions which were heaped upon
them"[1].

It was no easy task for the men to unite. The
lodges could not hire rooms for their meetings: even
the inns were afraid to receive them. As soon as a
leader appeared he was dismissed and "there never
was, at any colliery, men wanting who for a smile
from the master would betray their fellow-men"[2].
But union was the more difficult now that there were
rivals in the field. One, "The Miners' Provident
Association," was a society which was making a
successful attempt to provide relief for the victims
of mine disaster. Founded in 1859, it had a very
uncertain life for three years, until the Hartley
disaster awoke the pitmen to the dangers of their
life. A beam of the pumping engine broke and a huge
mass of iron plunged down the shaft, carrying with
it masonry and brattice alike. The single shaft was
so completely choked that a volunteer band of sinkers,
working day and night, were unable to win through
to the men below before the whole pit's crew had
perished. Enormous crowds assembled at the pit-
head to watch the progress of the work. The whole
country shared in an anxiety which changed into

[1] "Rules of the Miners' Union," *The Newcastle (Weekly)
Chronicle*, Feb. 15th, 1863.
[2] R. Fynes, *The Miners of Northumberland and Durham*,
p. 181.

sorrow as hope was gradually abandoned of reaching
the imprisoned men in time[1]. Two hundred and
fourteen miners, the manhood of an entire village,
perished, and though an ample subscription was
raised to relieve the sufferers, owners, pitmen, and
public alike were convinced of the need for some
provision more certain than casual charity. It was
not right that the advertisement of disaster should
be needed to provoke public sympathy, that the
family of the man killed in some petty, daily mishap
should starve while the Hartley widow enjoyed a
pension large enough to tempt the bigamous ad-
venturer. A burst of new enthusiasm, a rush of
members, assured the continuance of the "Provident."

From its earliest days it had refused to mix in
trade disputes. From the first it had enjoyed the
support of some owners. Yet it was looked on by
many with suspicion. If it incurred the distrust of
some owners it was not strange that to many of
the pitmen the "Provident" seemed a revival of
union. For in outward form it was very similar;
there were delegates, meetings, petitions, levies, and
officials; there were funds, accounts, and weekly
benefits. Moreover, a new evangel was being preached,
as a solution of all industrial trouble. The followers
of Robert Owen, the Christian Socialists, the weavers
of Lancashire, all raised their voices in the cry for
co-operation. There were distributive stores in plenty
among the ship-builders of the Tyne. There had been
experiments in production among the craftsmen of

[1] *Durham Chronicle*, Jan. 24th, 1862.

Newcastle. In 1861, at Cramlington, a co-operative distributive store was opened, the first of its kind in a mining village[1]. £20 was subscribed, a committee elected, and a stock of groceries of the simplest kind bought. Fear and suspicion almost ruined the venture. The men were afraid that the committee would abscond, the committee that thieves would break in and steal the stock. All through the first night watchers sat on guard over the store, but its immediate success cleared away all doubts. Each week the orders doubled, and at the end of the first quarter there was a profit of £38. 15s. 11d. to be divided, or almost 10s. a member. Soon every pit-village had its store. The Methodist congregations furnished men for the management, men of known probity. The saving effected by the store was not the only object of the co-operators. Cash payments rescued the pit-wives from the debts at the village grocers, and for "the first time the pitman escaped from the bands of credit." Within a few years, to own the pits in which they worked was a very general ambition among the pitmen.

But the elements of union began to collect again. It was seen that there was room for a trade society even among men who belonged to a store and sub-scribed to an insurance fund. In later years the store was often to be the strike larder, and the knowledge that he was in "The Provident" to hearten the miner to spend his savings in a strike. The new union had

[1] R. Fynes, *The Miners of Northumberland and Durham*, p. 183.

w   8

little connection with its predecessor. Roberts had taken himself to Lancashire, there again to play the part of the workman's champion. Jude was allowed to die in obscurity. The delegates came no longer to his tap-room, but met at the Victoria Hotel[1]. Since the great strike yearly bindings had been rare. The men worked as a rule under monthly agreements, but gradually in Durham the old system was revived, and in 1862 the owners gave notice that in Northumberland too they intended to re-introduce the bond. The new generation would have none of it. What their fathers had thought security they called slavery, and they had no wish to sink to the low condition of their southern neighbours. On Christmas Day 4000 men met at Harton, under the banners of '44. The third union had come to the birth[2].

In January, 1863, the delegates held their first meeting. Despite their fears that instant dismissal would follow disclosure of their names, they resolved to send a full report to the newspapers. The new leaders wished to make an end of the secrecy which had brought union into disfavour. To support the expected martyrs a "Victim Fund"[3] was established, but next month the name was removed. The men, indignant, had promised to stand so stoutly by their leaders that they had no fear of desertion. Towards the end of the year there were several strikes, marred here and there by riots. The Durham men asked to

[1] *Newcastle (Weekly) Chronicle*, Jan. 1863.
[2] R. Fynes, *The Miners of Northumberland and Durham*, p. 206.
[3] *Newcastle (Weekly) Chronicle*, Jan. and Feb. 1863.

be allowed to join and 15,000 recruits were at once enrolled[1]. In October a strike began, which wrecked the young association[2].

Mr Love, the owner of the colliery where the strike commenced, had in his youth been a pitman. In 1831 he was carried home shoulder high from a union meeting. In 1832 he promised to extend his credit to the utmost, to help the strikers. For he had left the pits, and set up in a small general shop. A preacher on the Plan of the New Connexion Methodists, fame and fortune came to him together. He married the daughter of a prosperous timber merchant, and again changed his trade. As a speculative builder—on one contract for colliery houses he made a profit of £10 a house, a return of over 30 per cent.—he was rapidly amassing wealth, when he was ruined by a bank failure. Nothing daunted, he took to the timber trade, as a dealer in pit props. Three years later, in 1840, he bought the Brancepeth Colliery. It was a white elephant, notorious for its high working costs and poor returns. He built coke ovens, sent no more coal to the market, and soon a steady profit gave witness to his foresight.

All his life Mr Love was a well-respected, highly religious man, living in Durham and delighting in simple hospitality. He found his main enjoyment in Methodism, and made foreign missions his particular care. In his later days he was very generous, building

---

[1] R. Fynes, *The Miners of Northumberland and Durham*, pp. 219–223.

[2] *Durham Chronicle*, Sept. 18th, 1863.

schools and chapels, and in one year he gave no less than £73,000 to his church. But in October, 1863, his pitmen struck. For twenty years, they said, they had groaned under an ever-increasing harshness. They were not taught by union to strike; they united with that intention.

The support offered them by all classes is ample proof of the truth of their story of grievance. It was the first strike in which the newspapers were entirely on the side of the men. Managers spoke from their platforms and owners contributed to their relief. That Mr Love's business actions were in sharp contrast to the piety of his private life is in no way remarkable. He belonged to a school which had well learned the lesson, to hide from the right hand what its left hand did. John Bright opposed the Factory Acts. Cotton manufacturers raised funds to free the negro slaves. There is no doubt that Mr Love, active Methodist as he was, laid the foundations of the fortune which allowed him to be lavish in charity by a system of management so callously commercial that it passed unnoticed into absolute robbery.

The men were paid for every tub sent full to the surface. Unless the coal was level with the top they were fined, and if they were fined the tub was confiscated, no pay being given for the hewing. The banksmen were given a small commission for every tub which they rejected. Few of the hewers earned more than 36s. a fortnight and there were many with a wage as low as 22s. The men shewed pay-notes which proved that from everyone some five to ten tubs were confiscated each "pay." It was said openly that Mr Love made £5000 a year from coal for the hewing of which he paid not a farthing, and the estimate was never questioned. Fines were exacted at every colliery, and though always unpopular, they were not often opposed. It was apparent that the working cost was increased by a high proportion of poorly filled tubs, for putters' wages were paid not on the weight of the coal they moved but on the number of their journeys. But at Love's collieries the fines were impossibly large. The seams were low, the roads but three feet high, yet the tubs were expected to come to bank "Level Full." It was not possible to heap up the coal at the face, for it was knocked off when the tubs stuck in the low places. The long journey was certain to shake the coal closer together. In compensation, the men invented a practice known as "Rocking the Tubs." Before a tub was given to the putter the man who had hewn it shook it violently up and down. At times he used a pitprop as a lever. More often he sought the assistance of his neighbour. Some men actually crawled under the tubs and lifted them on their backs. But no rocking could equal the shakings on the ways. Only by chance did the tubs reach the shaft level full. The banksman was able to impose as many fines as he wished. There was a further grievance. Each year, though the hewing price remained the same, the tubs quietly increased in size. Starting at $8\frac{1}{2}$ cwt. they were now approaching ten.

When the union was formed a new grievance came

to embitter the relations of Mr Love and his men. The story of his youthful enthusiasm accorded as little with the actions of his mature years as did his religious zeal with his callous management. One man was "turned-off" for giving a travelling lecturer a bed; another dismissed on an unproved charge that he read the *Miner's Advocate* and preached union to the Irishmen. Mr Love had learned thirty years before how great a help was credit to striking pitmen. In his pit-villages most of the small tradesmen were his tenants. In any case, they worshipped at the chapel where he preached. He stopped credit more effectually than had Lord Londonderry, feudal magnate though Love might call him, in Radical scorn.

Men were arrested, bailed, and released. Evictions began without delay, plainly as a counter-move to the strike, for the houses stood empty and it was weeks before the black-legs appeared. In the cold rain of a December day women and children were turned into the streets to shelter under the rude tents which the men made out of tables, and blankets, and the old four-poster beds. The union came promptly to their support. Pits levied themselves, each man paying from 1s. to 3s. 3d. a fortnight. The newspapers, friendly from the first, opened a subscription list. The vicar wrote appealing for relief. His curate turned a chapel of ease into a dormitory. The Catholic priest came to the help of his flock. Mr Love at once stopped their allowance of coal. The strike spread to the other pits in the Brancepeth group.

The men asked to be paid by weight. When their request was refused they offered to fill six sample tubs and thus ascertain what was their fair content after the jolting of the journey. That offer too was rejected. Other grievances were dragged into the fight. It was alleged, with some show of truth, that in Mr Love's pits there was small chance of promotion. All the smaller official positions were filled with friends and relations of the owner. The bad sanitation of the villages, the lack of schools, the absence of encouragement to self-improvement were all in turn the subject of comment. Mr Love wrote letters of defence at which the local newspapers jeered. He wrote to the *Times*, to find that even the London editors were on the side of the men. He said that the fines were distributed in charity, but no man had heard of it, and when the existence of a secret fund was proved it was remarked that very little of the money went to pitmen who were not Methodists. In any case the charitable spending of the fines did not excuse the harshness of their exaction, and if the owner did not profit by them he profited by the freely hewn coal.

His figures of wages were not accepted with the respect usually accorded to the owners' statements. There were always a few places in a pit where exceptional wages could be earned, said the *Newcastle Chronicle*. Reporters, attracted by the encampment in the stubble fields, were shewn a notice on the chapel door of a missionary meeting at which Mr Love would take the chair. They did not fail to note the strange comparison. Nor did they forget the motto on the strikers' banner: "He that oppresseth the poor, reproacheth his maker." It was a shrewd blow at a Bible Christian. At a public meeting in Newcastle a manager spoke in support of the strike, saying that "rocking the tubs" was a practice unknown at other collieries. When Mr Love published an advertisement offering good pay and houses to men willing to work it was placed next an article, descriptive of those same houses.

Hovels, built back to back, with gardens overlaid with clinkers, with no privies, sties in which it was impossible for the inhabitants to maintain the ordinary decencies of life.

Black-leg labour was imported and the pits began to work again. Sample tubs were filled, and a new standard offered to the men. They refused it: they would not trust the honesty of the officials who had made the test. They wished to be allowed to fill the tubs themselves, or better still, to send six rocked tubs to bank, empty them, fill them again, and so give ocular proof of the impositions from which they had suffered. But as Mr Love gave way the character of the strike changed. So many wild charges had been made, such grave irregularities attributed to either side, that neither party could obtain credit for its statements. More and more plainly the real issue emerged, union or no union. Other collieries were fired by the example of Brancepeth, and came out on strike. The public support began to diminish, the newspapers to repent of an enthusiasm, unprecedented, and almost impossible to explain. Even the men had the cause of union less at heart than the desire for an increased wage. They began to desert, and sign the proffered bond. In January the strike was at an end. The men had made an end of extortion. They had slightly improved their condition. "Rocking the Tubs" was stopped for ever. But Mr Love had broken the union[1].

While Northumberland had remained quiet there had been another serious strike in Durham. There was the same soreness at the falling wage, the same dislike for the steady increase in the size of the tubs, the same tale of harsh management. The strike, which occurred at Spennymoor, was actually to compel the dismissal of the overman, Parker. The pitmen said he was incompetent. Plainly he was a bully. He had sent men to work where the ventilation was insufficient. He had put others into places where a fall was imminent. When they had made protest he had laughed at their caution, saying that if the roof came down they could be got out in a few hours. The actual cause of the strike was a quarrel with some putters. Some accident blocked the roads, but he refused to allow them permission to "ride," that is, ascend the shaft. They entered the cage and were drawn away. When it reached the furnace outlet, where hot air, smoke, and gas poured out of the flue into the shaft, Parker signalled to the engineman to stop, reverse

---

[1] R. Fynes, *The Miners of Northumberland and Durham*, p. 226; *The Durham Chronicle*, Oct. 1863–Jan. 1864; *The Newcastle (Weekly) Chronicle*, Oct. 1863–Jan. 1864.

his engine, and lower away. When the boys reached the bottom again, Parker greeted them with oaths and threats. His final "Aw'll scumfish ye" they took to be a proof that their partial suffocation, caused by the delay in the shaft, had been deliberate[1]. But their story never received the attention so freely given to that of Mr Love's rebellious men. It was seen to be an excuse for a strike, rather than a cause of resistance.

But both strikes mark a change in public opinion. There was no more scornful comment on the delusions of union, the deceit of those designing men known as delegates, the dangers of combination. In the *Newcastle Chronicle* there was even an appreciative article in explanation of the rules of the Miners' Association. What harm could come from a union which had published so restrained a definition of its objects as "the protection of our labour, and the preservation of our lives"? What condemnation could be pronounced on leaders who wrote "the committee would demurely advise the miners to avoid what are termed strikes, certain that in almost every instance they have been the bane, the curse, the ruin of the miners," and who urged the men to arbitration? In the whole northern coal-field "the strike had a salutary effect, the managers became much less stringent in the enforcement of confiscation." But the men of those collieries, accepting the benefit of union, yet deserted its ranks, driven out by the im-

---

[1] R. Fynes, *The Miners of Northumberland and Durham*, p. 232; *Durham Chronicle*, Nov. 27th, 1863.

position of strike levies. As Crawford, an early president of the Northumberland miners, and the founder of the first lasting union in Durham, very plainly expressed it:

the Willington strike gave union its death-blow. In its original constitution the fatal mistake had been made, in imposing too small a subscription, $\frac{1}{2}d.$ a pay. As a result frequent levies were necessary. Of the 15,000 new members who joined from Durham, 14,000 were at once on strike.

In 1864 2000 men met on Framwellgate Moor to consider whether resistance should be made to the Yearly Bond. The smallness of the attendance was an admission of the defeat of the union, the conduct of the meeting a plain proof. There was no set programme. The proposals of the speakers were not well received. Hints of a strike were received with loud shouts of dissent. "De'il a strike, that would ne'er benefit us," cried the men, though they bore triumphant a small model of two men rocking a tub. Nor were they in favour of the alternative. "Restriction. Destruction you mean," said one of the speakers[1]. The wage was too low for the men to covenant to earn less. As colliery after colliery in Durham signed the bond the men of Northumberland lost faith in their neighbours. They admitted that the retreat was not a proper subject for blame, that the Durham men had long been subject to a harder yoke. But their own masters had formed a union to resist strikes. Prepare to fight they must, and they were better

[1] *Durham Chronicle*, Feb. 12th, 1864.

without costly and helpless allies. At a delegate
meeting, in 1864, Thomas Burt, then a young man
of twenty-two, proposed a secession. If it was the
formal end of the Third Union, it was the beginning
of the present "Northumberland Miners' Mutual Confident Association"[1].

[1] R. Fynes, *The Miners of Northumberland and Durham*,
p. 247.

CHAPTER VII

RECOGNITION

WHEN the Durham men consented to be rebound it seemed that union was for a third
time dead. It was hard to believe that a boy of
twenty-two could succeed where Jude and Hepburn
had failed, or that industry and perseverance could
triumph where enthusiasm had so often been defeated.
The Northumberland Miners' Mutual Confident Association could claim almost a hundred years of life.
It chooses to pay tribute to the genius of Burt by
dating its foundation to June, 1864, the month of
the famous secession. Crawford might deny that the
old union had been killed by the dissension of its
leaders, but dissensions there had been[1], and it was
Burt's resolution which gave the men confidence to
lay the axe to the roots and make a new beginning
where a compromise would have meant a still more
disastrous failure. With the older leaders the policy
of limited outlook had seldom found favour. Their
delight was in numerical strength, and constant opposition. Strikes, restriction, legal action were tried
in turn, nor did any discovery of the bluntness of
their weapons deter them from the battle. The
policy of the new leaders was the quiet acquisition
of strength in a small district. Strikes were to be

[1] *Newcastle (Weekly) Chronicle*, June 18th, 1864.

avoided at all costs. A high subscription was to
be at once the means of building up a fund and
a test of the firmness of the members. Too often
in the past had the unions been destroyed by popularity. Men joined in a fit of enthusiasm or of rage.
They had put nothing into the fund; they at once
became dependent on it. It was lucky if the disappointment of their untutored expectations did not
disgust them for ever with union. The aim of the
new association was to win recognition from the
owners by making plain the mutual advantage of
agreement and good will.

The first step was to reduce expenses. Sheldon, the
agent, was asked to seek work. The miners were not
dissatisfied with his efforts, but they feared that they
could no longer pay him. It is a witness to the
difference in spirit in Northumberland that he at
once found work at Cowpen, though in Durham the
known union men still found every pit closed to
them. They became hawkers of tea or managers of
the new stores, tiding over bad times until a union
could be formed again. Crawford, later to be the
maker of a strong union in Durham, was for a time
secretary to the Northumberland Society. To keep
alive the idea of combination he wrote a series of
letters to the Newcastle newspapers[1]. There were two
improvements suggested, a reduction in the length
of the boys' day and a change in the hour at which
the hewers went to work. At two o'clock the first

---

[1] *Newcastle* (*Weekly*) *Chronicle*, June 25th, 1864, and for
some weeks.

shift descended the shaft, and there was little excuse for maintaining a custom which was little more than a ridiculous survival. Perhaps Crawford remembered the "derisive laughter" which had greeted his speech at a Miners' Conference held at Leeds the year before. Starting with the popular demand for shorter hours he had made a proposal ridiculous in the ears of men unacquainted with the two-shift system of the northern pits. A ten-hour day for the boys seemed to them too long, where the men worked six.

But Crawford's faith in the future was not strong enough to support him in what seemed a hopeless task. Next year he resigned, to take an offered post as the manager of the Blythe Co-operative Store, and Burt took charge of the union. Almost at once, with but £23 in the funds, he was called on to conduct the most bitter and prolonged strike which Northumberland has ever known. At Cramlington, an extensive colliery, five villages stood side by side, each at its own pit-head[1]. For some time the men had made no resistance to a fall in their wage, though it continued until they received but 4s. a day, in a district where 5s. and 6s. was the rule[2]. Only at one pit, West Cramlington, was this passive policy despised. There the men had struck twenty-three times in twenty-two years. Suddenly they struck again, some 600 of them, and the strike spread to the other villages. For sixteen weeks the pits lay idle, then,

[1] R. Fynes, *The Miners of Northumberland and Durham*, pp. 248–253.
[2] *Newcastle (Weekly) Chronicle*, Nov. 25th, 1865.

after an attempt at arbitration, the owners gave notice to the men to leave their houses. The bailiffs appeared, hawkers and beggars who had long been known in the district. One was an Irish ballad singer who had for years lived on the charity of the pit-wives. For a time the men stood quiet while the bailiffs, known in every later strike as candymen, carried the furniture into the street. Then some boys released the colliery horses from a neighbouring field, and drove them galloping through the streets[1]. A party of stout lads barricaded the door of a house. A wordy dispute quickened into a fierce battle, and a shower of stones drove the evicting party away.

The police seized the leaders of the riot, but with threat of battle the pitmen obtained their release. For a week the evictions were suspended, then the candymen appeared again, with a much stronger escort of police. Again there was a riot, and it was not until a force of soldiers was sent that the owners were able to turn out the families which remained. Shelter was soon found for the women. The young men were advised to emigrate, the older ones to seek work in other collieries. The mechanics struck, and they too were evicted. The rioters, whom the pitmen had bailed at the cost of £200, were tried, and three were sent to prison. In December, when the strike was entering its sixth month, 300 strangers appeared in the village[2]. Some were Dorset farm labourers,

[1] David Addy, "Dusty Diamonds" (*True Tales from Pit Life*).
[2] *Durham Chronicle*, Dec. 8th, 1865.

but the majority were tin-miners from Cornwall, whom an agent had enticed from their homes by a promise of high wages. They were given pit clothes and under the direction of the officials they started to hew. Almost at once the union persuaded a hundred of them to return. For some of the strangers were union men, unwilling to be used as strike breakers even amongst "foreigners." A fortnight later a hundred more Cornishmen appeared, bringing with them their wives and their children[1].

A few of the strikers returned to work, lured by the promise of a deputy's place with "its upstannen wage, and the dooble hoose in Quality Raa[2]." But it was that most obstinate of all strikes, a strike against a falling standard of life, and the married men were its leaders. For over a year it continued, until every one of the strikers had found other work. It cost the union some £4000, but the drain on the funds proved an unexpected source of strength. For, with a strike levy of 1s. 6d. a week, there was a rush of new members anxious to help in the struggle. There could be no doubt of their good will when they joined to contribute so heavy a share of their wages. All the local patriotism of the north was aroused by the coming of the "Cornishers." They were foreigners, dark haired, dark eyed, wearing duck jackets and trousers in the place of the shorts and the pit flannels. They spoke a language hard to understand. Their wives,

[1] R. Fynes, *The Miners of Northumberland and Durham*.
[2] David Addy, "Dusty Diamonds"; R. Fynes, *The Miners of Northumberland and Durham*, p. 253.

said the Northumberland women, were little better than gypsies, with their gold ear-rings, and their sallow skins. They could not bake their own bread, that simple test in the north of good house-keeping. Yet they could make pasties far beyond the skill of the pit-wives, whose cooking, good as it is, is limited in its range. The men set to work to whitewash the houses, that they might a little resemble the cottages they had left behind. They had none of that feeling, still strong in the north, that a man has amply performed his share of the marriage compact when he has handed over to his wife the bulk of his earnings. They did not shame to help their wives to wash, or even to cook. They lived as strangers in their village, as one by one the old hands came back to the pit which was their home. At every excuse there were fights. The children were sent to different schools, though it meant a daily walk of several miles. Three years later a man who was fined for selling beer without a licence pleaded that the Cornishmen dared not go into the public houses. Not until the children married did the hatred die down. The store, the pride of Cramlington, had been closed to the strangers. So had the chapels. There was to be many a battle at Co-operative committee meetings, when some Cornishman became the son-in-law of an old member. And in the class meetings of the Methodists there was many a struggle with the conscience which reminded its owner that a black-leg had a soul to be saved, if indeed, he had not already felt the joy of conversion.

At first the pitmen stoutly maintained their belief

that the strangers could not acquire the skill necessary for hewing. But they learned fast, and they had
much to teach in return, in stone-work, and timbering,
and the use of the heavy hand drills. Some years
later, when there was a fresh influx of strangers, a
speaker at a meeting of protest was interrupted by
shouts that the Cornishers were as good men as those
they had supplanted. But if the owners won it was
at a high price. Before the strike good workmen
had earned but £2. 15s. a fortnight, less a sum which
reached at times 9s., for that collection of small dues
known as off-takes, rent, doctor, powder, and a dozen
other items whose uncertainty was long a subject of
complaint. In the new year the Cornishmen were
earning £3. 5s. 9d., yet they had to be hauled into the
courts to keep them to their bargain[1], while the men
who went back to the pits were paid 9d. a tub, or
1½d. more than they had demanded. Meantime, the
removal of the surplus labour from the West made
it possible for the tin-miners to start a strike, watched
with glee by the pitmen, who saw in it a revenge on
the Cornish mine-owners.

Next year at Blythe, where the miners assembled
for what was to become an annual pic-nic, Burt was
able to tell them that though the enthusiasm had
died down there were still 3000 men in the union,
and that despite the heavy strike expense the fund
had reached £1000. By the end of 1867 the fund had
more than doubled, and in March, 1868, it had doubled
again. There were at this date 4577 members, and

[1] *Newcastle (Weekly) Chronicle*, April 21st, 1866.

£4305 in the funds. Moreover, a small increase in wages had been obtained, without even the threat of a strike[1]. But such peace could not be expected to last. At Seaton Delaval the old grievance of fines and confiscations appeared again. In six months the hewers were fined £500, and of the tubs which they hewed a tenth was confiscated. Instead of a strike Burt ordered a demonstration. The whole of the members of the union assembled at Seaton, 5000 of them, marching from their special trains with bands and banners. "Wisdom is better than strength, nevertheless the wisdom of the poor man is despised, and his words not heard"[2] said one. Its words were prophetic. Months later the grievance was still unabated. Burt openly said that it was maintained in the hope of provoking a strike and bringing the union to ruin. The persistence of the quarrel can better be explained by the men's dislike of the manager. He it was who told the commission on popular education that the long hours of the boys were so little detrimental to their health that "they ran about like hares when they left the pits." If they ran, said the men, they ran to get back to bed.

In 1870 there was a strike at Backworth over the difficulty of hewing. The men said that the seams were so hard that the wage current in the district was insufficient for the seams they worked. They struck: quietly they submitted to eviction. A few strangers appeared, this time from Derbyshire, and

---

[1] *Newcastle (Weekly) Chronicle*, June 13th, 1868.
[2] *Ibid.* Sept. 5th, Oct. 10th, 1868.

the matter was settled by compromise[1]. The wages
were left at the old level, but it was agreed that the
men were not to be sent again into the hard places.
At the reckoning day that year the fund was found
to have reached £6500, and prosperity brought a
new tone of confidence into the speeches[2]. The Mines
Regulation Bill was being fought through the Commons, and after a few words of thanks for the industrial peace of the past year Burt sketched a plan
of campaign for the immediate future. "A miner's
life," said he, "is as valuable as that of a bishop,"
and in the Mines Bill several important amendments
were necessary. If the parliament wished to make
a practical reform it should extend the vote to the
pitman, and listen to his opinion on matters which
so closely affected his life. Another year passed without trouble. Thirty thousand people attended the
annual demonstration, which seemed to have become
a county holiday. This time the subject of complaint
was the duration of the miner's life. While the
agricultural labourer could expect to attain the age
of 47 the average life of the miner was as little
as 27 years. It was partly the fault of the poor
housing, for if the new cottages were a credit to the
owners most of the old ones were only fit for stables.
But the union leaders made further suggestion. They
wished that the law would take the pit-boy under
its protection as it had done the lad in the factory.
The one had his day fixed, the other worked from

[1] *Newcastle (Weekly) Chronicle*, May 21st, June 4th, 1870.
[2] *Ibid.* June 18th, 1870.

4 a.m. to 6 p.m., and there was no good reason why even that time should not be exceeded. Meantime a practical argument was advanced for a change in the hour at which the men started work. Two in the morning was the traditional time, and on Monday many of the pitmen were absent. It was hinted that not all the absentees were idle, or drunken, but that many a man who used his week-end to visit his friends remained deaf to the early caller[1].

By his consistency, skill, and moderation Burt at last persuaded the owners that it was better to deal with a disciplined body of pitmen under his command than to continue to oppose the union in the hope of bringing back the old anarchy. At Newcastle a meeting was arranged between the Steam Coal Association and the union leaders, and by peaceful agreement two important reforms were quietly made. The time of the beginning of the shift was changed to 4 a.m., though its duration remained unchanged. On the demand for a reduction in the boys' hours agreement was less easy. At first the men asked for a reduction from 12 to 10. In the end 11 was accepted[2].

Next year saw the amazing spectacle of a coal-owner building a hall as a meeting-place for the local lodge of the union. In his opening speech he declared that it was for their use alike in times of agreement and of difference. It was better to have strike meetings in a public hall than in a public-house. Meantime Burt began his first battle with the mal-

[1] *Newcastle (Weekly) Chronicle*, July 27th, 1871
[2] *Ibid*. Dec. 9th, 1871.

contents in the union. The feeling spread among the ignorant that the sudden change in the owners' attitude was compelled by the consciousness of the strength of their opponents. Not every man shared Burt's desire for moderation and peace; there were many who thought that a timely threat would win a better share in the new prosperity which so plainly promised. In the local newspapers anonymous letters began to appear attacking a union secretary who was so high in the owners' good graces. When one lodge proposed that his wage should rise with the rising wages of the pitmen, there were angry protests that the agent received enough for his easy life. In the end Burt was compelled to turn and defend himself[1]. After an attack on that worst of all tyrants, the working man, Burt laid down the conditions on which he was prepared to continue in his office. He was to be protected from attack. If his wage remained unchanged he was to be allowed the liberty of thinking himself underpaid. And, said he,

I shall at all times claim the liberty of speaking as I think on every question. I will not consent to become the mere tool and mouthpiece of any man or body of men. What I am convinced is right, that will I ever advocate to the best of my ability[2]. What I am convinced is wrong, that I shall ever oppose, whether it be popular or unpopular.

At the gala, held in June, he was loudly cheered. There were 9000 men in the union, and £11,000 in the funds[3]. There had been no strike, but in April

[1] R. Fynes, *The Miners of Northumberland and Durham*, p. 255
[2] *Newcastle (Weekly) Chronicle*, April 13th, 1872.
[3] *Ibid*. June 15th, 1872.

there had been a meeting with the owners of so
formal a nature that the union could boast at last
that it had attained a share in the conduct of the
coal-trade. Ten demands the men had made; seven
of them the owners at once conceded. And in the
later months of the year the owners, after prolonged
discussion, allowed the justice of the demand for a
wage increase of 20 per cent. Alone in England the
Northern miners had not been induced by high wages
to reduce their output[1]. The union was formally asked
to exert its influence to maintain this desirable industry, and to check, by every persuasion in its
power, idleness, and unwarranted stoppages.

APPENDIX

The Ten Demands

(1) The coal should be filled as it was won, and the
small no longer separated from the round.

> Agreed, but the price to be reduced 1*d*. a ton.

(2) Equal prices to be paid for working in the whole,
and the broken.

> No. The broken (*i.e.*, the district already partly won)
> was easier to work, and it produced more small coal,
> for which the full market price was never obtained.

(3) The practice of "nicking" was to be discontinued, and
"shooting fast" allowed, *i.e.*, the men were to be allowed
to put in a charge, and shoot down the coal, with an undercut alone, and no vertical cut at the side of the block.

> No, for it shattered the coal, and reduced its value,
> making it less able to bear transport.

(4) A fortnightly agreement was to be allowed in the
place of the monthly contracts in vogue.

> Yes, but all notices were to be given at the "Pay."

---

[1] *Newcastle (Weekly) Chronicle*, July 20th, 1872.

(5) The 10 per cent. wage advance, just gained, should be given to the off-hand men also (*i.e.* not to the hewers alone).

> Yes. Most owners had done so from the first.

(6) The 10 per cent. advance was to be inserted in the agreements.

> Yes.

(7) Boys were not to work more than 9 hours on Saturdays.

> Yes.

(8) The system of paying putters by "Renk" (*i.e.* by results, on a scale governed by the length of their average journey) was to be re-established.

> Yes, but the precise length of the "renk" was first to be decided.

(9) Any doctor's certificate should be accepted, as an excuse for absence, and a warrant for the demand for "smart money" (*i.e.* weekly compensation for accident disability).

> Yes.

(10) Single men were to be given an allowance as lodging money, and an equivalent for the rent allowed to the married men.

> No.

(5), (6) and (7) were temporary matters.

(2), (4), (8) and (9) have remained in their essentials, thus decided.

(1) and (3) have more than once produced later trouble, but the owners' arguments have prevailed, for they are almost impossible to controvert.

(10) Remains as a recurring grievance among the young men. It receives small sympathy from the married, and there are few men who remain single after they become hewers. Moreover a high proportion of the young men live with their parents, not on a strict commercial footing, while their parents get either the "free house," or the allowance in lieu.

CHAPTER VIII

THE FRUITS OF EXAMPLE

IN Durham the union died, for there the yearly
bond, refused by the men north of the Tyne,
had been successfully re-imposed. Every April the
manager of each colliery read aloud to his assembled
men the terms of service for the coming year. The
bond which the men were required to sign was a
long document. It covered in a strange mixture of
legal and technical phrase both sides of a closely
printed sheet. It opened with a description of the
manner of working, and a statement of the hewing
and putting prices. Clause after clause followed until
no matter seemed to be left open for dispute. From
the demand that hewers should at need undertake
work of any kind the clauses turned to such trivialities
as the restraints on keeping dogs and pigeons in
colliery houses. In most cases the bond was read
in a hurried, unmeaning manner. Few of the men,
except those immediately surrounding the manager,
could hear his words. Even if he began in a loud
tone it was impossible to continue the monotonous
repetition in a voice at once audible and emphatic.
Often the reading was badly contrived with intent
to make unpleasant conditions unintelligible.

Year after year the men engaged themselves under
a contract the terms of which were almost unknown

to them. Many of them could neither read nor write, but it was rare that a request for a copy of the bond was given a favourable hearing. The first few sentences told them whether their wages were to remain unaltered, but the long series of fines and drawbacks was passed unregarded. At the famous Thornley trial the magistrates said that no man would make an agreement which he was plainly unable to fulfil. But the men willingly signed bonds, ignorant of the confiscatory fines and the penalties to which they had submitted themselves, and many a bond, cheerfully signed, produced a strike after a few weeks of trial. In some places the men accepted the invitation to sign "the same bond as last year," forgetting that many a small increase of pay had been granted of which the bond made no mention. Such a bond, when enforced by a new official, might change the whole conditions of their service, yet if the men struck they could make no good defence at their trial. In the face of their oath that some newly enforced condition was strange to the customs of the mine the manager could produce bonds in which the supposed innovation was plainly mentioned year after year.

Moreover until the bond was abolished united action by the men of the whole county was difficult, if not impossible. For a strike could only legally be called by refusing to sign the bond for the coming year. Yet in Durham as much as a month interposed between the signing of the first and the last bond, and in every strike there were men confronted by the dilemma that they must strike and break their contract, or work on and injure the cause of their comrades. Or, if the strike was commenced pit by pit, the strength of unanimous action was denied to the union.

It was not easy to persuade the men to refuse the bond. At the binding time the officials were wise enough to put on their most affable manner, and at many of the pits a friendship had grown up between the men and the manager which made it hard for them to resist his persuasions. Beer in abundance washed down any dislike of his proposals, and the offer of a guinea to the first man who signed the bond ensured a rush at the opening of the office door, a rush in which the drunken, the selfish, and the excited swept away the waverers, still revolving obnoxious conditions in their hesitating minds.

In Durham there were many factors tending to disunion. The collieries were newer than in Northumberland, the men less settled. There is steady complaint from the philanthropic that the habit of annual migration made social improvement impossible. The rate of wages was low when compared with that which obtained north of the Tyne, a proof, said many, that the work in the coking collieries required a smaller degree of strength and skill. But some blame for this difference must be attached to the Irish immigrants. They were strangers, possessed of a low standard of life. Their religion denied them the comradeship of the chapel, and of its adjunct the store. They lived in the worst and most insanitary houses. They remained in the most wretched poverty. They could not benefit from that curious association of ideas which confounded the spending of money with the vice upon which it was spent, as did the Methodist, who was apt to believe that narrow economy was in itself a virtue. If to the Irishman the wages seemed high, he spent them freely: whisky gave him more pleasure than a bank-book. As a result, the Irishmen surpassed the pitmen in the violence of their amusements. Every prizefight had its principals with Irish names, every pay night brought its crop of drunken brawls, faction fights, and religious riots. In later years it was with difficulty that the radical politicians of the north stilled with their home rule arguments the local outcry against the immigrants. When, in December 1864, a conference was called of the Miners' National Union but one man appeared from Durham, E. Rhymer, the delegate of the men of Spennymoor. He could see no hope of future union. "Ignorance, cowardice, and drunken habits" made the pitmen accept without resentment wages which fell as low as 2s. a day, and which never exceeded 4s. 6d.[1] Poverty, stupidity, and greed made them dependent on the wages of children who worked twelve, fourteen, and sixteen hours a day.

1866 was a year of growing prosperity. There were the usual meetings, held just before the bond expired, and the usual resolutions, calling for certain obvious reforms. But the demand for better sanitation in the miners' dwellings was given unusual prominence, and

[1] *Newcastle (Weekly) Chronicle*, Nov. 25th, 1865.

a hint of the Northumberland example appeared in the request for alteration in the hour of the fore-shift's descent. But in the enjoyment of "remuneration which would have seemed fabulous to their ancestors"[1] the Durham pitmen remained deaf to the advice of the Miners' National Union, that it was time for them to re-organize. Next year the prosperity began to fail, and the National Union tried again. It held its annual conference at Durham, thinking by this invasion to rouse the Durham men from their apathy[2]. But the failure of a spontaneous effort, earlier in the year, had left a stronger impression. In March the men of Shotton had struck, in protest against a wage reduction of 1s. a day, which they thought unwarranted by the bond they had so recently signed[3]. Six men were arrested, tried, and sent to prison for a month. Ten days later twelve more of the strikers were brought to the sessions at Castle Eden. They too went to prison: they asked for an adjournment, to give them time to obtain the help of Mr Roberts. It was denied them. A week later, when Mr Roberts had arrived, two more offenders presented themselves for trial. The bench adjourned the case for a week. The surrender of the men had been so unexpected that the owners had not retained a lawyer. It appeared that the men had been told by the viewer that the hewing prices would be those which had obtained the year before. They

---

[1] *Durham Chronicle*, Oct. 5th, 1866.
[2] *Newcastle (Weekly) Chronicle*, Nov. 16th, 1867.
[3] *Durham Chronicle*, March 3rd, April 17th, 1867.

had signed the bond and had found that their wages had fallen. But the sworn testimony of the men was of little weight when opposed by the written text of their own agreement. To free the prisoners the men consented to return to work. Mr Roberts had done little except launch a violent attack on the partiality of the bench. "The magistrates," said he, "were hand in hand with the coal-owners"[1].

Next year the men of Shotton struck again. They pretended they had no faith in the colliery doctor, and they asked to be allowed to choose another. There was a widespread impression, which had some appearance of truth, that the owners used the doctors' posts as convenient sinecures for their friends, who drew the money and sent, as their representatives, poorly-paid unqualified assistants. A friendly agreement settled this quarrel, but near at hand a new dispute arose. For some time distress had been rapidly increasing at the Castle Eden collieries, and at last the curate in charge had established a soup kitchen. He appealed to the owner, Mr Burdon, for help, which was denied him. There was a simple remedy for the distress, said Mr Burdon; the men should leave the colliery, or apply for poor relief[2]. A fierce correspondence began, the owner denying, the curate asserting, that he had made the statement. It was watched with the greater interest, because Burdon was the magistrate at whom most of Mr Roberts' remarks had been aimed.

[1] *Durham Chronicle*, Oct. 23rd, 1868.
[2] *Ibid*. March 5th, 1869, and several weeks.

At the binding there was a general wage reduction of 10 per cent.[1], and at Thornley, where the reduction was greater, the men struck a few days after signing the bond. Their leaders were brought before the Castle Eden bench and after a few minor alterations in the bond the men consented to return to work. In July a formidable strike began which was to have far-reaching results.

Burt might be opposed to a strike policy, but the Northumberland Union had been established by a strike. The Durham Miners' Association, from the first keenly desirous of peace, was founded in a bitter trade war. In 1869 the men of Monkwearmouth struck. They had signed a new bond in March, in May they were convinced that it was an unworkable agreement, and that the wages it assured them were insufficient to maintain their families. In those days the magistrates' courts were used as informal arbitration tribunals. The merits of a strike were decided by the trial of such leading men as the owners thought fit to prosecute for breach of contract. At the trial of the Monkwearmouth leaders two old opponents faced one another, Heckles the viewer, and Mr Roberts. For it was Heckles' economies which had provoked the strike. In the three years of his management wages had fallen 32 per cent., and while the case was still being heard the evictions began. And it was Roberts whom the pitmen brought to defend the prisoners. This time he did not repeat the success of

[1] *Durham Chronicle*, March 12th, 1869; *Newcastle (Weekly) Chronicle*, June 5th, 1869.

the Thornley case. The magistrates had seen the follv of intolerance. Mr Roberts began by saying he would make no formal defence, he had not read the bond. He was countered by an offer of a copy, and of immediate adjournment for a fortnight for its study. It was fine bombast to declare that "he was right glad of this case, the fourth estate would record it; he was working for posterity" but the men were not "prepared to establish in martyrdom the strength of their case" whatever their lawyer might assert. They cared little for posterity, and even less for martyrdom. Next week Roberts was offering "to do anything to save those poor men from imprisonment." In a last collision with Heckles the case ended. "At the cry that the poor only were suffering, one of their oppressors grinned. That grin was from ignorance, tobacco and drink." Heckles could afford to smile, as with every word Roberts made himself more ridiculous in the eyes of his clients. After this case the pitman's Attorney-General appeared no more in the north, and the newspapers spoke truth when they said that no one was sorry. For if he did not produce disturbance his coming was always the sign of unrest[1].

The strike killed the bond. In open court the owners' lawyer had said that it was time an end was made of a system which seemed to provoke more trouble than it pretended to prevent[2]. The men returned to work at the old prices of 1867. They

---

[1] *Newcastle (Weekly) Chronicle*, June 26th, 1869.

[2] *Ibid*. Sept. 9th, 1869.

had formed a union, and this much it had been able to win for them, but it was not strong enough to compel the re-employment of the leaders. One was established in a small shop, the other, Richardson, was made a permanent union agent at a weekly wage of £1. 18s. 3d.[1] The union steadily won recruits, when, in its growing strength, it was confronted by a familiar peril. The men of the north-east of the county had no sooner joined than they called a strike[2]. Richardson was unable to control them. It was felt that a man with some financial training would be a better agent than a simple pitman. Crawford's name was suggested. He was offered the post, and as soon as he was able to leave the Blythe Co-operative store he accepted it, to begin his life work, the firm foundation of the Durham Miners' Association[3].

In October letters from the new secretary began to appear in every local newspaper. They were mostly directed against the bond. "It had been the curse, the withering, blighting curse, of thousands of miners"[4]. Crawford was convinced of the wisdom of caution. He made ready to enforce a policy of rigid economy and of peace, but he was not wholly in sympathy with the ideas of his northern neighbour Burt. He was old enough to have some of the idealism of those early leaders, whose enthusiasm had directed the strikes of 1831 and 1832. As a boy he had shared in those strikes, and since that day "he had never

[1] *Durham Chronicle*, Oct. 20th, 1869. [2] *Ibid*. Oct. 1st, 1869.
[3] R. Fynes, *The Miners of Northumberland and Durham*, pp. 258–59.
[4] *Durham City and County News*, Aug. 1870, onwards.

flinched from the union cause." He was not so far
blinded by the philosophy of the Manchester radicals
as to lose the root idea which he shared with the
Owenite socialists that there was some fundamental
fallacy in the laws of a political economy which denied
to the poor man the right to a decent life. He relied
far more than Burt on emotional appeal, and the
violence of his language was perhaps the best weapon
for arousing the Durham men from their apathy. The
county was too far behind Northumberland for the
slow methods of Burt to be effective. Crawford saw
that his task was to build up a strong union before
the coming prosperity should shew signs of decay,
and to win, by threat if need be, a share in the conduct
of the coal-trade, for time did not allow of the slow
building up of confidence between master and man.

In the early months of 1870 the union grew rapidly.
Mass meetings were held to protest against the proposed Mines Regulation Act, and to pass resolutions
asking for the abolition of the bond. A delegate
meeting in January reported that there were then
2500 members[1]. A month later a thousand recruits
had been enrolled. But the size of the fund showed
how new was the strength of the union. There was
but £80 in the hands of the officials, and out of that
a grant was to be made for the support of the striking
miners of Yorkshire. Following the signing of the
bond in April there was a sudden decline in membership, for many of the abuses had been removed and
the prices offered were a little more generous. At

[1] *Durham Chronicle*, Jan. 21st, 1870.

Thornley the check-weigher was provided with a copy of the bond a fortnight before the binding day. Later he was given an attested copy for use in case of dispute[1]. At Tudhoe "the bond was read quite slowly and distinctly, so that all could hear," and the men were given an opportunity of discussing its conditions. But the Wearmouth men struck again. Since the fight of the year before they had worked on fortnightly agreements. They claimed that their wages were still 1s. 6d. a day less than the county average, but their success in resisting the reduction of the year before was used as an argument against their claim to share in the advance of 1870. Six hundred of them struck. Eviction soon drove back the weak-hearted, while strangers from Wolverhampton filled the places of the determined[2]. Work was quietly resumed on the manager's terms.

In June the Durham Union put its affairs in order. The county was divided into three districts and an agent appointed for each. Their weekly wage was fixed at £1. 5s. 6d., and their authority was increased by a new rule that any colliery which struck in an "unconstitutional manner" should be denied union aid[3]. In September there was a short strike at Sheriff Hill, provoked by a threat of wage reduction, and later in the year a disturbance arose at Thornley which lasted through the winter[4]. Of the half-yearly income £674, or more than half, was spent in these

[1] *Durham Chronicle*, March 4th, 1870.
[2] *Ibid*. April 15th, 22nd, 1870.   [3] *Ibid*. June 10th, 1870.
[4] *Ibid*. Sept. 16th, 1870.

disputes, and the membership fell from nearly 4000 to 1891[1]. At Brancepeth three men were given notice for "connecting themselves with, and advocating the principles of, the miners' union"[2]. The first excitement was over, and the apathy of the men was slowly discouraging the agents. "At the meetings, they were often insulted, and sometimes maltreated, by the men they had come to help"[3]. Crawford tried in vain to interest the county in the Thornley strike. It had been begun by the refusal of the manager to provide the hewers with a copy of the bond. In angry letters to a weekly newspaper, but recently established in Durham, Crawford expanded his text, that "any employer who thinks it beneath him to meet his workmen ought to think it beneath him to profit by their labour"[4].

Perhaps these letters had their effect. A successful meeting was held at Tantobie. Tommy Ramsay, a veteran of the three defeated unions, drew the men together. In the Miners' Hall at Durham there is a picture of this old warrior, who for years tramped from village to village, preaching the need for combination. There he stands, in his Sunday Blacks and his top hat, a roll of hand-bills in one hand, the "Corn-Crake of Union" in the other, that policeman's rattle which was used to attract the men from their houses and the inn parlours. Mostly he preached from the same text: "Lads, combine, and better

[1] *Newcastle (Weekly) Chronicle*, Dec. 10th, 1870.
[2] *Durham City and County News*, Dec. 9th, 1870.
[3] J. Wilson, *History of Durham Miners' Association*.
[4] *Durham City and County News*, April 14th, 1871.

your condition. When eggs are scarce, eggs are dear. When men are scarce, men are dear." His speeches, full of rough humour, were delivered in the broadest dialect of the pits. At this meeting he warned the men against the wiles of the officials. "I'll give thou a deputty's place, I'll give thou stonework. Thou's sittin' in thee own leet"[1]. It was by such dishonest promises that doubtful men were weaned from the union. And he brought out the unanswerable argument that the Northumberland men, who were united, had a wage 30 per cent. higher than was current south of the Tyne. Tommy Ramsay's creed was summed up in a speech which he delivered at a strange debate at Gateshead, at which Cowen had collected most of the workmen's leaders from the Tyneside. "Yor maisters hes nowt to dee wi yor wages." So long, said he, as men's labour was bought and sold, so long would strikes continue[2].

In August 7000 men assembled at Durham to hear a speaker whom the union had brought from Staffordshire, Willy Brown, the Midland miners' agent[3]. He provided them with a new text: "It's the big worker who brings prices down," and he taught them a new song, for at his meetings songs and speeches were mixed, in curious imitation of a Methodist revival. "Britons sons, though slaves ye be" was to be the Marseillaise of the revolt against the yearly bond. Meantime Crawford was preaching in every village

[1] *Durham City and County News*, June 9th. 1871.
[2] *Newcastle (Weekly) Chronicle*, Feb. 1st, 1868.
[3] *Durham City and County News*, Aug. 18th, 1871.

the doctrine of more money for less work. All his life he reserved his worst abuse for the public-house boaster, who to make good his pay-night vaunts, "on a Monday would hew coal till he vomited blood"[1]. By leaps and bounds the demand for coal grew, and work became so plentiful that pitmen were imported from both Lancashire and the Forest of Dean. Their coming was little resented, in fact the Gloucestershire men were praised as the best men who ever came to the north, and a curious intimacy began between the two coal-fields. In December a delegate meeting announced that there was £1200 in the funds, and that the membership, which had once sunk to 1616, was now over 10,000[2]. The bindings of 1872 were eagerly awaited. At every colliery meetings were called to protest against the system of the Yearly Bond. Preparations were beginning for a new struggle. Suddenly, in February, the coal-owners invited the Durham agents to a conference.

Ten delegates went to Newcastle, to speak for 20,000 miners. They were told that there was no desire to force on the men a new bond, that it was time a better system of hiring was devised, and that a reduction was made in the hours of work. "The most pleasant and amicable feeling prevailed on both sides." The owners professed a desire that their men should be given a share in the prosperity of the trade. An advance in wages, of 20 per cent., was freely granted. Fortnightly agreements were substituted

[1] *Durham City and County News*, Sept. 8th, 1871.
[2] *Ibid.* Dec. 8th, 1871.

for the bond. Within a month the wage advance was extended to all underground workers, and a smaller advance, of 12½ per cent., was given to the surface workers. All that was asked of the agents was that they would exert themselves to prevent idleness, and to reduce to a minimum the number of petty local strikes. News of this success brought 8000 men into the union, and almost at once the agents were called on to fulfil their share of the bargain. They condemned a hasty strike at Haswell. They refused to give strike pay to the men of Littleburn, who had rejected an award made by Crawford himself. Everywhere they preached against the doctrine of restriction, which the hewers advanced to justify their idleness. All the relief they allowed the men was the admission that it was no longer necessary to do a day and a half's work for a day's wages. But this revolution of opinion did not convert every one to the cause of union. A series of letters appeared in the newspapers which betrayed the hand of the old-fashioned coal-owner:

Is it not notorious that hundreds, nay thousands, of men have been compelled to join the union, through the systematic annoyance and ill-treatment to which they have been subjected, sullen looks, and taunting remarks, jeering cries of "twig him," clottings with clay and coal, refusals to descend the pit, or work with them, breaking their pick-shafts, hiding their clothes[1].

Much of the accusation was true, but these methods were preferable to the old brutal habit of assault, and infinitely preferable to the outrages, the strippings and beatings, the shots through the windows, which

[1] *Durham Chronicle*, April 19th, 1872.

had served as arguments against the black-legs of other years.

Slowly the union fought its way into public favour. A dispute at Seaham proved the sincerity of Crawford's protestation that he wished to work in harmony with the owners. In most of the pits there were two shifts of hewers; both descending in the morning, one at four and one at ten. The manager at Seaham wished to introduce a third shift, to descend in the afternoon, and work until almost midnight. Giving no notice to their agents the Seaham men, some 1500 in number, struck[1]. Remonstrance from Crawford and Ramsay was met by a vote of censure, and a threat to secede from the union. At last argument persuaded the men to allow the dispute to be settled peaceably[2]. Arbitrators, two from each side, went down the pit[3]. The men had advanced three objections to the manager's proposals. One was that a night shift made the pit unsafe, for it allowed no time for free ventilation. Examination proved that the contrary was the case, that a pit was in a better state when working continuously than when lying idle. Another was that they were hampered in their hewing by the off-hand men, the men to whom is entrusted the upkeep of the roads and of the air ways. So little was this true that it was not thought worthy of answer. The last objection was that if the time of coal-drawing was increased from

---

[1] *Durham Chronicle*, May 17th, 1872, and succeeding weeks.
[2] J. Wilson, *History of Durham Miners' Association*, p. 57.
[3] *Newcastle (Weekly) Chronicle*, June 15th, 1872.

ten to twenty hours, in the end the length of the working day would increase also. This the manager promised should never happen. False arithmetic analogy persuaded the men that if two shifts of men could keep the pit at work for ten hours it would require more than three shifts for a day of twenty hours. A short trial proved that instead of lengthening the hewer's day the addition of a third shift actually decreased it.

It was one of those quarrels common in the history of the coal trade, in which the men endeavoured to conceal by a host of technical complaints an objection which they feared would be ignored. The men disliked the night shift because it was an innovation which threatened to interfere with the settled habits of their life. With two shifts there was a time when all the hewers were out of the pit, with three, it was difficult for them all to meet together. It was the sacrifice of the free evening which was the root cause of the hostility to the proposal. But the arbitrators decided that exceptional circumstance at Seaham justified the introduction of the night shift. By no other method could the output be raised without addition to the standing costs of working. Provided that night shifts were used sparingly, the union was prepared to give them its approval. The miners' agents had well redeemed their promise to the owners that they would exert themselves to the utmost to increase output, and help to make hay as long as the sun of prosperity continued to shine[1].

[1] J. Wilson, *Hist. of D.M.A.* p. 66.

In June a great demonstration was held at Durham, the first of a series of festivals which continued un-interrupted until 1915. For a day the pits were laid idle. The shop-keeping citizens of Durham made protests. They feared that violence would accompany a huge invasion of pitmen. Some of them barricaded their windows, many of them fled the town. With bands and banners 40,000 pitmen marched to the race-course, accompanied by a crowd of women and children whose presence must have assured the timorous that no revolutionary violence was intended. The change of feeling which union had brought had its outward witness in the legends on the banners. £3000 had been spent on these symbols of union. One had on it a picture of Mr Macdonald, with the Mines Regulation Bill in his hand. One had a colliery horse, refusing to work more than eight hours a day. Some had the traditional device of union, the bundle of sticks, others, the "hand in hand" of fraternity. But on most were pictures of arbitration boards, with underneath messages of friendly invitation to the owners: "In the past we have been enemies; in the future let us be friends." The moderation of the speeches surprised the attending journalists, who had construed the rumour of the meeting into the threat of a general strike. But the behaviour of the pitmen surprised them even more. Only two of the huge crowd came in conflict with the police. The pitmen went quietly home, proud that so few of their number had lapsed into their good-natured sin of intoxication[1].

[1] *Durham Chronicle*, June 21st, 1872; J. Wilson, *Hist. of D.M.A.* pp. 61–63.

Following the meeting a new wage demand was made and a new advance conceded of 15 per cent. to the pitmen and 10 per cent. to the surface workers. But it was no easy task for the agents to keep the men constant in their peaceful resolution or to persuade them that the accession of strength provided no reason for its immediate use. In every newspaper letters from Crawford appeared exhorting the men not to hurry him in his quiet arguments with the owners, not to press too strongly for advance after advance, not to obscure by greed the justice of their demands. In September, speaking for 35,000 men, he asked for a further 15 per cent. The request was refused. The council of the union was not satisfied with his failure; 35 per cent. was the increase which they desired, and with it they demanded a decrease in hours. The owners, though they said that the new prosperity had encouraged idleness, and that the men were working but eight days a fortnight, were persuaded by this unrest to accede to Crawford's demand; the second 15 per cent. was granted[1]. Meantime the new Mines Regulation Act had come into force. Pamphlets from the union leaders advised the men of its purport, warned them against opposition to its provisions, and attempted to reduce a little their unduly high expectations. Crawford preached steadily against the doctrine of restriction of output, a doctrine at all times apt to become popular among coalminers. His words were an amplification of the wisdom of Burt. "The more the produce is restricted,

[1] *Durham Chronicle*, July 12th, 26th, 1872; J. Wilson, *Hist. of D.M.A.*, pp. 66, 71, 74.

the less the means are, at the command of the employers, wherewith to pay all classes of workmen "[1].
He had seen unions rise as quickly in the past, to
perish in miserable failure. He feared that the temper
of the men would ruin the work which he had almost
completed.

We have so far worked successfully, but that success
has been greatly, if not altogether, owing to the caution
and moderation we have exercised, the general reason-
ableness of our demands...having at all times a respect
for the rights, while we have tried to bring into active
operation the duties, of capital.

In 1867 the National Miners' Association had held
its missionary conference in Durham. In 1871 it
refused an application from Crawford, for the admission of his union to membership. Though there
were 16,000 men in the new Durham association, its
stability was not yet above suspicion. In 1872 the
conference was again held in Durham. At it Crawford
took his seat, as the representative of the strongest
union in the country. He could speak for 35,000 men,
or three times as many as did Burt, the secretary
of the model union of Northumberland. In 1869
men were being dismissed their work, for spreading
the principles of combination. In 1872, the union
had met in formal, friendly conference with the
masters. A joint committee had been formed to
settle disputes on pay, and hours, and conditions of
work, a committee to which men and management
alike appealed. It was so immediate a success that

[1] J. Wilson, *Hist. of D.M.A.* pp. 67, 79.

Northumberland, in flattering imitation, itself set up a similar committee. In 1874 the Durham agents proposed the building of a hall, as a memorial to Tommy Ramsay, who had died in the midst of the triumph of his life's work. There were 40,000 subscribing members, and £34,000 in the funds. Prosperity had founded the union; it was soon to be seen whether it could, with as firm hope and as good temper, face the poverty which the far-sighted had seen would surely come. It was to be seen whether the men in their strength would extend to the demands of the owners the patient hearing which had by the owners been granted to them in their weakness; whether the friendship of owners to union would be as great in strife, as it had been in alliance.

CHAPTER IX

ARBITRATION AND WAGE REDUCTION

FOR three years prices had been rising and wages following after them. Despite the stories of drunken folly and domestic extravagance and the loud outcry against the spread of gambling, on the whole the men had made good use of their new prosperity. But their new comfort was far more due to the steadiness of employment than to the high daily wage. They were by no means satisfied that they had shared fairly in the profits, and they were convinced of the justice of their demand for a further wage increase. They made no protest when in the autumn of 1873 the owners refused their application for an advance, but next spring, at the first hint of a reduction, they prepared to strike. For a time Crawford encouraged their desire for war, but when it became plain that the good times were over the tone of his circulars changed. The men of Yorkshire and Northumberland had submitted to a wage reduction. Were the miners of Durham to stand out, unsupported, and risk a lock-out on a falling market?[1] Labour could not yet hope for complete justice. Profits still claimed the lion's share of prosperity. But in three years wages had risen 58 per cent.[2] The

[1] J. Wilson, *Hist. of D.M.A.* pp. 87–95.
[2] *Durham Chronicle*, April 24th, 1874.

men should rest satisfied if with changing prices they could maintain a portion of this advance, and lift their wages for ever above the level of 1871. On their side the owners halved their original demand. A bargain was struck. The gross wage fell 10 per cent.[1]

At once there was a storm of protest. In Northumberland the reduction had been accepted quietly, and the men had lost but 10 per cent. of the wage of 1871. The Durham colliery mechanics, who had not shared equally in the recent advance, refused to share equally in a general reduction. The delegates of the larger collieries complained that the agents had acted in the face of the known wishes of the majority of the men. The only sanction for the bargain was the failure to obtain in the annual delegate meeting a two-thirds majority for a strike. But there was a defect in the constitution of this council. Large or small, the collieries had in it but one vote, and the delegates from the large collieries had all voted for a strike. For a week there was uproar. Every day brought its tale of local strikes, meetings, and disorderly protests. A champion was found to oppose Crawford, who was charged with betraying the cause of union, as he had betrayed it before when he left the Northumberland men in the midst of the Cramlington strike. But the agents stood firmly to their agreement. In speech and pamphlet Crawford overcame his opponents. He was more than a match for Pritchard, the leader of the malcontents. Grumbling,

[1] *Durham Chronicle*, May 1st, 1874.

the men returned to work. Only at Thornley did the strike persist[1].

There the year had begun with a dispute over the hewing price of a hard seam. The lodge, dissatisfied with the settlement, had led the agitation for a general strike. Now it found excuse for continued idleness in an alleged infringement of colliery custom. Though most of the Durham pits worked eleven days a fortnight there were some where the Northumberland custom was in use, and a five-day week the rule. Thornley claimed to be one of them. The union refused to pay strike allowance but the angry lodges levied themselves, as much to plague the agents as to oppose the owners. The strike continued until June, when by the eviction of their leaders the men were persuaded to submit their claim to impartial enquiry. The Thornley dispute is typical of the many in which the first grievance to hand has been pleaded as an excuse for a strike in time of wage dissatisfaction. In August the umpires decided that without doubt Thornley had always been in the eleven-day group[2].

At the annual pic-nic of the Northumberland miners Burt thanked the men for the loyalty which had persuaded a strong minority to submit to a wage reduction against which they had voted. Not only

---

[1] *Newcastle (Weekly) Chronicle*, May 2nd, 1874; *Durham Chronicle*, March 3rd, April 24th, May 1st to June 12th, 1874; J. Wilson, *Hist. of D.M.A.* pp. 95–98.

[2] J. Wilson, *Hist. of D.M.A.* p. 95; *Durham Chronicle*, April 24th, May 5th, 29th, June 5th, 12th, Sept. 25th, 1874.

had there been no open expression of discontent but the men were convinced at last "that a social millennium was not to be achieved by a restriction of labour"[1]. It was a polite phrase of thanks for a remarkable absence of reduced production, the usual manifestation of sulky ill-will. At the Durham gala the speakers found little to celebrate beyond the increase in the numerical strength of the union[2]. Meantime, the constitution of the annual council was amended. Lodges were given votes in proportion to their membership. When the owners sent a preliminary notice of an intended demand for further reduction the council returned plain defiance. So far were the men from offering submission that nothing would content them but an advance of 15 per cent. To avert a strike the dispute was submitted to a court of arbitration.

There were four judges, two well-known owners, and two nominees of the men. One was Thomas Burt. The other was Lloyd Jones, the fustian cutter, in his youth a disciple of Owen, in his maturity, agnostic though he was, a friend of the Christian Socialists, now, in his old age, as a journalist on the staff of Cowen's *Newcastle Chronicle*, about to begin the education of the miners in the belief that profit should be the reward of labour, not the monopoly of capital. Russell Gurney, the recorder of London, was named umpire. The case, the first of its kind in Durham, was opened in October. The umpire's de-

[1] *Newcastle (Weekly) Chronicle*, June 20th, 1874.
[2] *Durham Chronicle*, Aug. 24th, 1874.

cision was published in the first week of the next
month. In the discussion almost every argument of
later dispute arose. The procedure of the court became
decisive precedent for the future, its conclusions the
basis of every succeeding agreement. The owners
opened the battle with a demand for an immediate
gross reduction of 20 per cent. In 1871, in spite of
low wages, low material costs, and long hours, the
pits were being worked at a loss. In 1872 the owners
made an end of the yearly bond, and for the first
time became subject to the restraint of state interference. As a result of the Mines Regulation Act of
that year the hours of coal-drawing were reduced,
and the proportion of boys and off-hand men increased. A boom in the iron trade concealed the
effect of these changes. A sudden extension of the
markets, due to the increased use of steam in sea
transport, brought an unprecedented condition of
prosperity. Profits rose, wages were increased, and
though on the whole the high wages did not increase
idleness the daily output of each hewer fell by 14 per
cent. With 13 per cent. more hewers and 27 per cent.
more boys and off-hand men there was 6·7 per cent.
less coal raised. Labour costs rose 90 per cent., the
cost of materials 80 per cent. At times abnormally
high prices were obtained, but they brought profit
only to the dealers, for the pits sold their coal under
a system of long contracts. In April, 1874, the men
had accepted a reduction of 10 per cent. In the six
months which had elapsed since, there had been a
fall in price which would have justified the owners in

claiming a wage reduction of 28 per cent. They would not exact the uttermost farthing. They demanded an immediate reduction of 20 per cent.

Much to the surprise and pretended indignation of the owners Crawford at once asked for an adjournment. His case—he could not conceal it—was to be mainly destructive. For the men possessed little accurate information, and such figures as they had prepared were useless to refute statements based on statistics compiled only from the books of certain collieries which the owners had selected as representative. After some dispute, in which the owners' advocate jeered at the insufficiency of the men's preparation, an adjournment was granted, with a show of magnanimity. Crawford was at pains to make clear that it was not the accuracy of the figures which he wished to examine, but the effect of the selection. Next day the men came before the court, haggard from want of sleep, to appeal for a further adjournment. For 26 hours they had worked, six clerks assisting, and still their case was not finished. Without further objection, indeed, with sincere expression of sympathy, the request was granted.

Crawford opened his case in a tone of apology for his presumption in joining battle with the owners. On behalf of the men he acknowledged that capital must be allowed a fair remuneration. But he claimed that labour should share in profits, though it was willing to see its share diminish, except when the fall in profit was caused by reckless competition. He admitted that his figures, based as they were on the published prices of the markets, were of little value. They were little more than a guide to price movement. But until a better system could be devised, it seemed that price movement must control wage movement. The men refused to allow the wage they had received in past times to be used as a basis for the present agreement. The whole of their recent demands had not been granted, and it was notorious that the wage in 1871 was too small to maintain a decent standard of comfort. Costs incurred under the Mines Regulation Act were a burden imposed by the State. The men refused to accept any part of them. The owners must bear such costs themselves— they had some return, in the increased safety of their property—or thrust them on the consumer. The point from which all wage enquiry should start should be *cost of production*.

After a repetition that in the past wages had been insufficient, and that despite the depression selling prices were still high, and profits enormous, Crawford told of the discomfort, the danger, and the unhealthiness of the miner's occupation. In Durham more than half the men worked in seams less than 3 feet 6 inches in height. He returned to the central feature of his case, that the cost of living was too high to allow of return to the old wages. His speech concluded with a demand for the production of the colliery books, in disproof of his estimate of cost price, selling price, and profit.

The owners said, as they had said before, that the prices in the London market bore no relation to prices at the pit-head. They refused to admit that the high cost of living was a valid reason for withstanding a wage reduction. Like everything else, wages depended on "the inexorable laws of supply and demand." They contended that in mining, dependent as it was on manual labour, there was little hope of increasing output by reducing hours. They laughed at Crawford's story of ill-health. "We have long ago ceased to find marks of cramped bodies and distorted limbs. In no industry is there a finer body of men." It was an apt argument, to point to the miners' leaders, strong, healthy-looking men, in disproof of their own stories. The dangers of the trade were exaggerated. Mining had become so attractive an occupation that in the last three years 3000 new men had gone into the pits. But the owners reserved their fiercest opposition for the attempt to discover the profits of the trade, and the doctrine that in profit labour was entitled to a share. "That wages should follow profits, and of course losses, is a proposition so opposed to every law of political economy...so bewildering in the consequence it would entail" that the owners' advocate dared pursue his thought no further. Price movement alone could be allowed to measure wage demands.

After a little bickering on the length of the working week the case was closed. The arbitrators, who failed to agree, referred their dispute to the umpire. He made award that there should be such reduction as would leave wages 30 per cent. above the standard of 1872. It meant a loss of almost 9 per cent. on the gross wage. In the same month a similar arbitration in Northumberland had an almost exactly similar result. There, wages fell to 26 per cent. above the wage of 1871.

Except at Ashington there was no opposition to the awards. The men swallowed their resentment that unions, formed to better their condition, should take so prominent a part in wage reduction. By their willing submission to verdicts so unpopular they proved the sincerity of their desire to substitute arbitration for the old and brutal judge of trade dispute, strikes. The men had for ever refused to bear any part of the cost of State regulation of their industry. They had advanced, and the owners had rejected, the argument that wages should be maintained at a height which sufficed for a reasonable minimum of comfort. It was an argument which they themselves shrank from using, so terrifying was it in its logical consequence. On their part, the owners, by a resolute silence on the whole subject of costs and profits, had compelled the use of price movement as a measure of wages. As yet neither side had a developed theory of industry, while the men were hampered in argument by the inaccuracy of their statistics. The desire of both parties was to make peace, rather than to achieve justice. Discussion was at once closed, when it threatened to expose a fundamental difference of idea[1].

In Northumberland 1875 opened with a strike at

[1] *Report of the Durham Coal Trade Arbitration*, 1874. (In the Library of the Durham Miners' Association.)

Seghill[1], which cost the union nearly £3000. Bad times had made necessary the closing of an unprofitable seam, and the men struck against the attempt to discriminate in the dismissals. An old custom said that the last-joined hewers should be the first to go, and the victory of the men provided a clear precedent in its favour. Meantime, the owners had made a demand for a further wage reduction. The men in the hard coal districts were sufficiently afraid of their Welsh competitors to be ready to accept the demand, but, as the soft coal men pointed out, the wages in the soft coal districts were already less than were wages in Durham. After an offer to submit to a general reduction of 10 per cent. the Northumberland men allowed the dispute to be brought before an umpire. In March the umpire, Mr Rupert Kettle, made his award, which he explained in a long and carefully written document[2]. To make plain that the men's submission was not one of conviction, but consent, he recorded their main objections to the owners' case. They refused to accept the owners' assumption that the rate of profit current in 1871 was sacred, untouchable. They were not persuaded that selling price was the natural guide to wage movement. He recorded, as a fact sufficiently proved, the owners' statement that in 1875 twenty men were required to do a task which fourteen men had done in 1871. But, lest it should be thought

[1] *Newcastle (Weekly) Chronicle*, Jan. 9th, 1875; *Durham Chronicle*, Jan. 8th, 22nd, 29th, 1875.

[2] *Newcastle (Weekly) Chronicle*, March 20th, 1875; *Durham Chronicle*, Jan. 22nd, Feb. 5th, 1875.

that the fault for this decline in output rested wholly with the men, he devised an explanation which impartially divided the blame. In the late years of extravagant profits prices had lost all relation to working costs. Seams had been opened which at no other time would have paid, seams which could be worked only by a lavish use of labour. Some part of the owners' demand he warned the men it was necessary to concede, but to keep the decrease as low as possible the men must be prepared to submit to a general contraction of employment. He considered that a wage distinction between the hard and soft coal districts was essential. The hewers in the hard coal were to lose 10 per cent. of the wage of 1871, those in the soft, 12½ per cent. But in the general reduction he made many exceptions. All were to lose, but all were not deserving of equal loss. He excepted the stone-men, because their work was laborious, the deputies, because their work was responsible, the datal men, labourers working for a daily wage, *because their wages could not be brought below a minimum*. Underground men were not to suffer a reduction if their wage was less than 3s. 6d. a day, surface men, if they earned less than 3s. It was an admission of the principle, doubtfully advanced by the men, that wages should in part be based on the necessities of life, that price could not warrant reduction to the point of starvation[1].

The award had one unlooked-for consequence. The mechanics said that they too were entitled to special

[1] *Newcastle (Weekly) Chronicle*, Mar. 20th, May 17th, 1875.

exemption. They seceded and struck, and though eviction put an end to the strike, the new association of colliery mechanics remained, a union independent of the miners[1].

In Durham, where the owners demanded a further reduction, there was wide dissatisfaction. At Thornley, where one of the men had been discharged for exchanging his free coal for paint, the men struck, and with success[2]. At Wearmouth there was a second strike, to compel the dismissal of the 18 men who alone among the 1100 employed stoutly refused to join the union. The agents declared that a quarrel among the men gave no excuse for a war with the owners, and refused both strike pay and official support. But the sympathetic lodges again levied themselves, and the strike dragged on until the committee of the union was compelled to issue a circular of protest. A strike which continued in defiance of the union commands brought discredit on the union, and hindrance to the agents in their negotiations with the owners. The protest had its effect. The lodges withdrew their support, and the strike came to an end. The wage dispute, the initial cause of the disaffection, was about to be brought before a court of arbitration[3].

With novelty had disappeared hesitation. Both owners and men spoke in a more decided tone. Bunning, the secretary of the Durham Coal-Owners'

[1] *Durham Chronicle*, April 16th, 30th, 1875.
[2] *Ibid.* Feb. 19th, 1875.
[3] *Ibid.* Mar. 26th, April 9th, 1875.

Association, opened the employers' case. His hardest task was to check the stream of damaging admissions which came from the owners sitting in the court. He had realised more clearly than they the danger of the men's demand that in the fixing of wages account should be taken of the movement of profits.

His first premise was that high prices had compelled a widespread economy in the use of coal, which, by becoming permanent, had caused a definite contraction in the demand. He admitted that combination and restriction of output could for a time stimulate prices, but he claimed that a depression inevitably followed. In the past there had been many attempts at regulation, the chief result of which had been the excitement of popular feeling against the coal trade. Whatever might be the men's desires the owners had no intention of resorting again to an obsolete system in which restriction of output was combined with price control. The coal trade had one hope of salvation, a revival in the iron trade, which might be hastened by a reduction in the price of coal. To make possible such a reduction some economy in the cost of working was necessary, and the cause of the rise in working cost had been as much the decrease in hours as the increase in wages. The number of men in the pits had risen faster than had the output of coal. Each hewer was producing 13 per cent. less than he had done in 1871. Bunning was not allowed to state his case unchallenged. The umpire demanded a definite statement of the desired wage reduction, free from the obscurity of a comparison of hours and output.

Lloyd Jones, sitting as Crawford's companion, the second arbitrator for the men, kept up a continual stream of comment and question. He shewed that the rise in price had been in no way due to the wage increase, for wages had always followed prices. He questioned the wisdom of Bunning's theory, that to add to hours, and thus to output, could bring relief from the low prices of a glutted market. A former arbitration had established the fact that in 1871 the average pit-head profit was 4d. a ton. Bunning, for all his figures of increased costs, dare not suggest that his profits had yet fallen so low.

The men denied that their union had any policy of restriction. They countered the owners' figures with the assertion that the hours of very few men had been reduced. They would not accept the blame of the reduction in individual output. They contended that the existing price was not abnormal, but a return to the old level after a period of extraordinary inflation. There was no justice in the claim to lower wages when it had its origin in a desire to maintain unprecedented profits. It was said that the coal trade was suffering because of the stagnation in the iron trade. Yet firms like Messrs Bolkow Vaughan, which owned furnaces, coke ovens, and collieries, continued to pay dividends which ranged from 12 per cent. to 40 per cent., and to put by huge sums as a reserve fund. If their profits were not made out of iron, were they made out of coal? But the sting was in their final threat. If the owners continued to harp on the rise in working cost, the men would insist that profits, not prices, should be the measure of wage demands.

The umpire was alarmed. He intervened to remind the owners that both parties had promised, come what might, to arrange a settlement. He was persuaded that profits, not prices, provided the fairest measure of the owners' ability to maintain the wage, but he was willing, if the owners definitely refused information about their profits, to give judgment on the standard of price movement. His promise would have satisfied Bunning, but the owners had a greater desire for justice than had their secretary. To them the enquiry was more than an attempt to find a settlement. One owner gave a long list of items, which he said made up the tale of costs. Another offered an estimate of the proportion which these costs bore to each other. Bunning tried in vain to silence them, and to minimise the damage of the admissions by a claim that as wages and materials together made up more than three-quarters of the total working costs no saving could be made in other directions to off-set their rise. But enough had been said to suggest that the total working cost had risen 41 per cent. It was information eagerly received by the men. All Bunning could do was to divert the argument, until the case ended in a useless dispute about the number of men employed, and the irregularity of their attendance at work.

Some reduction in wage was necessary, if only to keep the peace in the coal trade, but the umpire could hardly have made it smaller than he did. Of the wage of 1871 the surface workers were to lose 4 per cent., the underground men 5 per cent. It was less than the men had offered in the preliminary negotiations. Lloyd Jones' insistence on the disclosure of profit had won the day for the union[1].

As the year wore on the frequency of local strikes shewed how nearly the patience of the men was exhausted, and how firm were the owners in their resolve to make no concessions. Thornley, always a storm centre, was quiet, for since May the colliery had been closed, to allow of repair of the damage done by a fire, but the men of Broomside were with difficulty persuaded to refer a grievance to arbitration. In Northumberland a permanent dispute as to the method of working was for a time settled by appeal to Mr Kettle. The men wished to blast the coal out of the solid, with no more than a simple undercut. The owners said that it shattered the coal and spoiled it for export. They asked the men to nick up the side of the seam, as well as undercut the bottom. Kettle was convinced by their proof that the side cut was necessary. "Shooting fast" he decided could only be adopted with the manager's permission[2]. The return to the old practice, locally abandoned during the season of unreasonable demand, brought a serious fall in wages.

In November the owners on both sides of the Tyne were compelled to make a fresh demand for a wage

[1] *Durham Coal Trade Arbitration*, 1875. (Book in Miners' Hall, Durham.)

[2] *Durham Chronicle*, Oct. 1st, 1875.

reduction. Only after earnest argument could the agents persuade the men to submit their case to arbitration. In February, 1876, the Northumberland award was published. The men lost, not the 20 per cent. which the owners demanded, but 8 per cent. of the wage of 1871. The respect for the standard of life was maintained. No part of the reduction was to fall on men whose earnings were less than 3s. a day. The men had relied on two arguments, that the fall in price was temporary, a periodic result of the winter freezing of the Baltic, and that the rise in working cost was due to the opening of unprofitable seams during the boom, a mistake which they ought not to remedy by a wage reduction. In the Durham arbitration Bunning repeated for the owners the same arguments he had used before, figures of high costs, falling prices, and reduced output, and suggested the same remedy, a cheapening of coal to stimulate the iron trade. The fall in the wage had made the issue more clear. It resolved itself into a simple choice. Did the men prefer underpayment, or unemployment? It made plain a fundamental difference in idea. Were wages the slave of prices, or could provision be made for an untouchable standard of life?

The altered spirit of the enquiry is shewn by Crawford's threat, that "if the workman was to be stripped naked by the laws of political economy, he might some day be forced to seek his protection outside those laws." He had departed far from his old tone of apology when he accused the iron masters of using up their coal stocks to produce a false depression during the hearing of the dispute. The owners protested against the bitterness of his attitude. They warned him that as long as the men continued to neglect their work at the week-end such absence would be used to discredit the story of domestic hardship. The umpire made award that wages should fall, for the underground men 7 per cent., for the surface workers 4 per cent.[1]

Both in Northumberland and Durham the umpires had suggested that some permanent tribunal should be appointed, for the discussion of wage claims, or that some system should be devised for the automatic movement of wages.

[1] *Durham Coal Trade Arbitration*, 1876.

CHAPTER X

A NEW WAY TO PEACE

THAT some change in the method of wage settlement was necessary the union leaders were well
persuaded. The constant arbitrations were a source
of expense and of trouble. They excited too keen
interest among the men, and provoked serious discontent. It was plain that by no system of peaceful
agreement could complete justice be obtained, and
that persistence in debate would in the end expose
the fundamental opposition of owners and men. The
steady refusal of the coal trade to accept any other
basis for wage demand than the movement of selling
price made plain that no concession would be made
to the men's desire for a revelation of profits. It was
easy to base a scale for wage calculation on price
movement. It was possible that under such a scale
alterations would be so frequent and so small as to
pass unnoticed. Arbitration was better than war but
it had brought none of the promised peace to the
coal-fields. If the panacea had been of little worth
there was yet hope of a salve for the ever-running
wound. A new system of wage settlement was devised,
that of the sliding scale, a system which had no
pretence to be other than a practical solution of a
permanent difficulty.

In June (1876) the Durham miners opened a hall

the foundations of which they had laid in times of prosperity. Trade was in a very gloomy condition. Many of the pits were working on short time, some had actually closed, despairing of being able to reduce working costs to a level which would allow the production of coal at the market price. The first council which met in the new hall was convened to consider a demand for a further general reduction[1]. It voted for a strike, but a general ballot reversed its decision. In a private circular the agents had bluntly told the men that the union funds were not strong enough to support a war. Early in the year Crawford had roughly rebuked the Ryhope men for allowing their putters to strike "at a time when the owners almost seek an occasion for quarrel"[2]. His judgment was not far at fault. The knowledge that the union funds were falling encouraged many of the more reactionary of the owners in their belief that the time had come to aim a final blow at combination. A bitter correspondence began between Crawford and Bunning, the owners' secretary, on the subject of local strikes[3]. The union was warned that if it remained unable to control its men the owners would resort to the old remedy against idleness, legal action. The news of the last arbitration had led to a secession in Durham. Many of the deputies—officials whose duties hardly removed them from the ranks of the workmen—had hitherto been members of the union. Now they resigned, enticed by a promise from the owners that

[1] *Durham Chronicle*, June 9th, 1876.
[2] *Records of Durham Miners' Association*, March 15th, 1876.
[3] *Records of Durham Miners' Association*, Oct. 10th, 1876.

they would be exempted from the reduction if they would form an association of their own. The owners professed a belief that it was bad for discipline for officials to be in the same union as the men. From the first Crawford held that their action was a direct attack on the strength of union, but so little able was he to face a struggle that he dared do no more than make angry protest. Strike was impossible with financial ruin so near at hand[1].

A better spirit obtained in Northumberland. There owners and men, afraid that the wage would bear no further reduction, began to seek relief in a fundamental change in the method of hewing payment. A joint deputation was sent to Wales to study the system there in use. In the autumn an arbitration, presided over by Judge Fairplay, took away a further 7 per cent. of the standard wage, and recommended the adoption of the Welsh system, by which payment was made only for the round coal produced. It was an award of which the vast majority of the men disapproved. The change, though quietly suffered, was never acceptable. Soon "Billy Fairplay" became the catchword of a most furious campaign of violent mob-oratory[2].

As the winter passed, and distress and discontent grew, both in Northumberland and Durham internal strife began to weaken the tottering unions. Wilkinson, the financial secretary of the Durham Miners' Association, charged the whole of the executive committee

[1] *Records of Durham Miners' Association*, Oct. 1876....
[2] *Newcastle (Weekly) Chronicle*, Oct. 22nd, 1876.

with personal extravagance. Without reason, and without sanction, the members had travelled to London to be present at the announcement of an arbitrator's award. The council suspended the offenders, and in a reconstituted committee the agents were given greater power, as a bar to the repetition of such extravagant folly[1]. The ousted committee-men were not easily silenced. They issued circulars. They excited the local lodges to revolt. Meantime a co-operative colliery, to which, inspired by the example of the unions, many of the miners of the north had subscribed their small savings, was compelled by bankruptcy to close down. In the main the cause of the failure was the prevalent trade depression, assisted by the steady rise in working costs. But the men were persuaded that they had been the victims of a cruel fraud, and that the seller had grossly overstated the output. Not only did the funds of the union suffer—Durham alone lost £15,000 —but many of the miners lost the whole of their life's savings[2]. Naturally the leaders, whose enthusiasm for co-operation had led them into the rash experiment, lost popularity, and Burt and his fellows made a second and even more costly mistake. A large sum from the funds of the Northumberland Association had been invested in an "Industrial Bank," another moribund offshoot of co-operative enterprise.

In March, 1877, the demand of the Durham owners for a further general reduction led to the adoption

---

[1] J. Wilson, *Hist. of D.M.A.* p. 114; *Records of D.M.A.* 1876, p. 111.
[2] *Durham Chronicle*, March 23rd, 1877.

of a sliding scale. The wage fell, $7\frac{1}{2}$ per cent. for the men underground, 6 per cent. for the workers on the surface. Further wage movement was to be governed by the fluctuation in the pit-head price of coal. A rise of 8*d*. per ton was to be followed by an increase in wages of 5 per cent. A fall was to bring a similar reduction. Surface wages were to move in jumps of 4 per cent. But the scale was less simple than this. All the probable prices were named, and there seemed to be no thought that 5*s*. 4*d*. a ton was too high a minimum. Later reductions below that figure were to make valueless the sliding scale[1].

Meantime the men were adopting a better defence against under-employment, emigration. For a time the union managed the departures, but, as Crawford said, "some poltroon fellows directly interested in getting emigrants grudged the loss of the commission"[2], and the agents abandoned the unprofitable and unpopular business of retailing passages. To satisfy the men that the rumours of the horror of the voyage were unfounded Crawford himself made a trip to America. Continuing its advice to the young men to try their fortune in America the union bravely attempted the duty of relieving the older men who remained. A "Relief Fund" was established, in part supported by grants from the general fund, in part upheld by a systematic levy on those fortunate enough to be still at work[3].

[1] *D.M.A. Records*, March 14th, 1877.
[2] *D.M.A. Records*, Handbill, June 26th, 1877; J. Wilson, *Hist. of D.M.A.* p. 133.
[3] J. Wilson, *Hist. of D.M.A.* p. 139.

If by alternate threat and persuasion Crawford was
able to keep the peace in Durham, in Northumberland a storm was fast rising. The system of payment
for the round coal alone produced among the pitmen
nothing but discontent, while, despite Kettle's award,
they were persistent in their demand to be allowed
to "blast out of the solid." When in April the owners
asked the exasperated men for a further wage reduction the men almost unanimously called for a strike.
Burt told them that they had a right to make their
own choice, and that the owners were deserving of
blame for a demand so extravagant, and an action
so hasty. But for the failure which he saw would be
the inevitable outcome of a strike he plainly warned
them that he would not take a particle of the blame[1].
At a mass meeting on the Newcastle Town Moor,
the union president, Bryson, was refused a hearing and
in the end driven off the platform by a shower of
stones. Willy Brown of Stafford, the quaint evangelist
of union who mixed prayer and song and economic
argument with his persuasions to peace and to union,
was asked to take the chair. He roundly accused the
meeting of cowardice and folly. Burt followed, to
warn the men that as they opposed arbitration, so
would they oppose their desired sliding scale as soon
as it authorised a wage reduction[2]. At every colliery
in the county there were similar excited and disorderly meetings. Alone among the union officials
Burt retained his prestige. Others might be stoned,

[1] *Newcastle (Weekly) Chronicle*, April 26th, 1877.
[2] *Ibid.* June 9th, 1877; *Durham Chronicle*, May 25th,
June 8th, 1877. For strike, 11,380; Against, 946.

and shouted down, but to his condemnations of their
folly the men always gave a ready hearing. They for-
bore to shame the miner whom they had sent to
Westminster, and to whom they had voted a salary
of £500 a year that he might worthily uphold his
new dignity as the miners' member for Morpeth.
His steady condemnation of violence had its effect.
The men had given the usual fortnight's notice of their
intention to cease work, but before the time expired
a strong majority in a general ballot authorised appeal
to arbitration. Bryson was re-elected president, and
a vote of confidence wiped away the memory of his
recent ill-treatment[1]. In August Herschell, the chosen
umpire, made his award[2]. Since the case of the owners
rested entirely on their statement that labour costs
had risen, a statement unsupported by any proof that
the total cost of production had increased, he refused
to make any change in the wage. But to give some
relief to the owners the men were recommended to
make two changes in their working practice. They
worked but five days a week. In future they were to
work every alternate Saturday, as in Durham. Delay
in the long journeys to the face was steadily reducing
the hours of actual work. They were to strive to
attain a minimum of six. The settlement was accepted.

In October the owners repeated their demand for
a wage reduction. To excuse the haste of their action
they asserted that the men had ignored the con-

[1] *Newcastle (Weekly) Chronicle*, July 14th, 1877.
[2] *Ibid*. Aug. 25th, Nov. 8th, 1877.

ditions of the recent award, and that in particular
they had made no effort to add to the length of their
working day.

By a majority of one the men instructed Burt to
appeal for arbitration. But the owners would not
bargain. They said that it was not a time for agreement, but for concession. For the funds of the union
were so low that a strike seemed impossible.

Yet at Christmas a strike began, a strike which
with some justice the men persisted in calling a lock-
out. A general appeal for support was sent to the
other unions, but in the eight weeks of their idleness
the men had little other support than their own
resolution. The utmost strike pay which the union
could afford was a sum of 3s. 4d. a week. There was
little disorder, though as the strike progressed the
demand of the men for a sliding scale grew louder
and more insistent. In principle the sliding scale was
acceptable to the owners, but the negotiations which
were begun broke down over the question of the wage
which was to be the standard. While the men asked
for 5s. 3d. a day the owners would offer no more than
5s., and they refused to entertain the suggestion of
arbitration. By local private agreements several of
the collieries were enticed back to work. In the south-
east of the county a new union was formed. At last
the weekly ballot failed to shew the required two-
thirds majority for the continuance of the strike.
Burt gave up the disputed threepence and hastened
to get the men back into the pits, so that he could
make an end of the threatening schism. As in Durham,

so in Northumberland, the miners had submitted to the insistence of the owners that prices, not profits, should be the measure of their wage[1].

If in Northumberland there was secession, in Durham there was dissension almost as dangerous. In August the men of Bearpark struck, to resist a local reduction. They refused to refer the matter to arbitration. They refused to sanction an agreement which their own agents framed, as a reasonable concession. Even eviction did not change their attitude, it but brought further discord, for a quarrel began between the young irreconcilables and the householders. In September, at a mass meeting, the Bearpark men attacked the whole policy of the union. They said that arbitration had become a farce, that in every case the owners asked for twice as much as they expected to get, sure that the umpire would halve their demands. They complained that local lodges were too much under the domination of the central executive of the union, which took too big a proportion of the weekly subscription for the general fund. And they attacked the inherent defect of the Joint Committee, to which pits were expected to carry their disputed demands. The Joint Committee was empowered, when it found the average wage in a pit differed too much from the average wage in the county, to recommend a local advance or reduction. But an astute manager was easily able to defeat the Joint Committee. He discharged the old men.

[1] *Durham Chronicle*, Jan., Feb., March, 1878; *Newcastle (Weekly) Chronicle*. same. especially Feb. 9th, 1878.

The wage of the young and vigorous hewers rose. He appealed for a local reduction, and in a pit where the working efficiency of the men was far above the average the wage sunk to the common level. But at last the conviction of thirty of their number for breach of contract persuaded the Bearpark men to submit to the decision of the Committee, whose short-comings they had so plainly exposed. This dispute was but one of many where a small alteration in wages suggested an examination of every possible grievance. The men demanded the dismissal of the black-legs. The owners persisted in their refusal to employ notorious local leaders. One minor strike dragged on for forty weeks[1].

The distress grew. In the spring of 1878 it was said that pits which had employed 4000 men were closed, while in the still busy pits seams had been abandoned which in the past had employed a further 1500 men. The relief levy, which had grown to 5d. a fortnight, did not meet a third of the liabilities of the fund which it was supposed to support. All respect for the county agreement seemed to be gone. Everywhere managers made a direct bargain with their men, getting a local reduction in wage in return for a promise to keep at work. The miners were puzzled by this depression in which prices fell, men were discharged, and the output steadily, if but slowly, rose. They began to appeal to the owners to stop the reckless competition which they thought

[1] *Durham Chronicle*, Aug. 8th, 31st, Sept. 7th, 14th, 21st, 1878.

was hastening ruin. They wished to return to the old system of output restriction, to make an end of the glut, and so force prices back to their old level[1]. In May the union allowed the hours of coal-drawing to be increased to eleven. It was an attempt to relieve the owners by enabling them to make a fuller use of their machinery. In September the agents were compelled to abolish the relief fund. It had drained away the funds, it threatened the numerical strength of the union, for the men were deserting to avoid the heavy subscription. The constitution of the old National Association, to which both north-country unions were affiliated, was amended. It was to exist only for the inexpensive object of promoting trade legislation. In October the decline in the union strength became so serious that their agents asked the Durham men to make a definite stand against "the carelessness which has taken hold of the country." Without coercion, without intimidation, they were to try to prevent further desertions and to persuade the weak-hearted to come back to the fold. In November all the workmen's associations in the Durham colliery districts joined in a single federation. Cokemen, enginemen, mechanics and miners were for the future to act together. It was the last stage in a desperate fight for existence[2].

In Durham the period of trial of the sliding scale agreement was at an end. The executive was em-powered to discuss with the owners the conditions

---

[1] *D M.A. Records*, May 27th, 1878.
[2] *Ibid.* 1878–9.

of its re-establishment. The one demand which the owners made was that the basis wage should be reduced by 20 per cent. Long ago the decline in coal prices had made inoperative the whole sliding scale agreement. They wished to restore the accord between wages and prices. The men refused the demand, and suggested that the whole matter should be decided by a formal arbitration. When they found that their proposal was not likely to be considered, they prepared for a strike[1].

Crawford saw the folly of their decision. In speech and circular he sounded a note of frantic warning.

At this juncture to attempt to strike would be suicidal. On every hand you can count men unemployed by hundreds.... The abstract principles of trades unionism will not fill the bellies of the hungry. In two years the union had spent on local strikes £100,000 and there was not a single strike which had not signally failed. A strike meant destruction[2].

But the men were not to be persuaded. Three years' insistence on the virtues of arbitration could not be offset by a warning in time of expected calamity. It might be useless, pernicious, and dangerous to talk of abstract rights, as their leaders said, but the men were determined[3]. The owners were to accept arbitration, or prepare for a strike.

In the second week of March, 1879, the strike began. The agents issued a solemn warning against

[1] *Durham Chronicle*, March 7th, 14th, 1879, and succeeding weeks.
[2] *Durham Miners' Association Records*, March 10th, 1879.
[3] *Ibid.* March 17th, 1879.

resort to violence: "Let nothing induce you to pursue a course which at all times is to be deplored, and which at this juncture would be aggravated into heinous crime." It was a warning scrupulously obeyed. Both sides appealed to the public. The men contended that the strike had been forced on them by the masters, whose deliberate intent it was to wreck the union. They admitted the need for wage reduction, but not the owners' right to unquestioned power to fix its amount. The fight, said they, was for the continued existence of the system of wage agreement. At the final conference the masters had bluntly refused to consider every claim put forward by the men. Bunning tried to silence the men's cry that they were striking for a principle by offering to submit the dispute to arbitration if the men would accept an immediate reduction of 10 per cent. But 10 per cent. was the whole of the reduction which the men were willing to grant and the full extent of the loss they expected from an arbitrator's award, seeing that the original demand of the owners had been for 20 per cent. and that the wage statements of the two parties accorded ill one with the other. Only 200 of them voted for a return to work on Bunning's terms, and even the women supported them in their decision, saying that life on coffee and bread could not be made more wretched by a short starvation[1].

[1] *D.M.A. Records*, March, April, May, 1879; *Durham Chronicle*, same period, especially March 14th. April 25th, ballot for strike to continue, 22,633; against, 224.

In May the men came near to victory. Public opinion was firmly ranged on their side. Many of the owners were not in sympathy with the policy of their association. Seventeen had voted in favour of referring the dispute to arbitration. One held an enquiry in his own collieries which convinced him that the necessary reduction was but 6½ per cent. In June the owners offered to refer the whole question of reduction to a committee which should consist of an equal number of nominees of both contending parties. It was, said the newspapers, arbitration in all but name. By a huge majority the men accepted the offer. A week later Bradshaw, the County Court judge, who sat as umpire, made his award. The standard wage of the underground men was reduced 8¾ per cent., that of the surface men 6¾ per cent. The award was not popular but the men were glad to get back to work, and the owners seemed willing to accept it when it was made clear that a further and more formal enquiry was to follow. Late that month a court was assembled to make that final decision, which was to authorise, and extend at need, the grant of Judge Bradshaw. A chairman worthy of the importance of the occasion was chosen, Lord Derby[1].

The dignity of the new president and his ignorance of the local conditions of the northern coal-field justified the advocates in an unusually full statement of their arguments and their demands. Starting from 1871 a thorough description was given of the change

[1] *Durham Chronicle*, May 2nd, 9th, 16th, 1879. Ballot for Committee, 18,446; for strike, 6,362; *D.M.A. Records*.

in working conditions. It was the old story of high wages, high material costs, and low output; of the good fortune of the men with their short hours, their free houses, their coal and their gardens. Then came a new grievance, the failure of the sliding scale. Within a few months of its acceptance the price of coal had sunk below the lowest figure named in the schedule. But the men, firmly clinging to the letter of the agreement, would not allow their wages to follow at the pre-determined rate. Once wages had reached the indicated minimum, there they were preserved. As a result a great depression had come over the coal trade. Fifty-two pits had been closed, and in many more local wage reductions alone enabled work to be continued. The men themselves had suggested this wholesale evasion of the sliding scale. Pit by pit, with the knowledge, even with the tacit approval, of the union, they had struck bargains with their managers. It was time that the existence of these local reductions was honestly admitted, that they were incorporated in the formal county average.

The men disputed the accuracy of the owners' figures. They opposed the use in argument of the tale of housing improvement. Such improvement was necessary. Had it not been made, it would have been ordered by the local sanitary authority. In many villages there were still houses unfit for human habitation. Were the men to pay, by a reduction of their wage, for the rebuilding of these hovels? Houses were as necessary a part of original capital costs as were winding engines. Lloyd Jones, again sitting as

Crawford's companion, again intruded his uncomfortable observations. To increase the length of the shift, said he, would rather increase unemployment than reduce working costs. The hewers were paid according to their output. Surely it could matter little to the owners whether for the hewing of a given quantity they paid one man or two? And despite the short shift it could not be disputed that man for man the Durham miners produced more than did their rivals in any other district. For the depression the men would take no responsibility. The blame rested on the owners alone. They had provoked it by their wild competition. In the hope of huge profits they had rapidly increased the potential output of their pits. The increased output had resulted in the fall in price which always accompanied a glut. The owners should bear the burden of their own folly. Moreover, it was to be remembered that there was a definite limit to the relief which reduction in wages could give. It was an economic law, as "inexorable" as the law of supply and demand, that the wages of the workman should suffice for his support.

The owners were a little taken aback at the boldness and persistence of the men, and the excellence of the information which enabled them to expose the inconsistency and untruth of the figures with which they had in the past been overwhelmed. Lloyd Jones had been too clever for them. Unguarded reply to the cross-examination which had been the feature of his two previous cases had furnished the men with much valuable information, insignificant as it had appeared when item by item it had been divulged. Lord Derby, after momentary alarm at the hint of a minimum wage, leaned more and more to the side of the men. His award, published at the end of July, took away from the men but $1\frac{1}{4}$ per cent. of the basis wage. The sum of the two reductions which it authorised was 10 per cent., the exact amount which the men had offered to accept in the negotiations which preceded the strike. At the same time hints were made that no further relief was to be expected from wage reduction. Two sources, as yet untapped, were indicated, the salaries of the officials, and the rents of the royalty owners[1].

Many of the men were not far-sighted enough to understand the extent of their victory. There were many district meetings of protest at the outcome of the arbitration which they had fought so hard to obtain. In October a new Sliding Scale was devised. Based on the recent agreements, it was free from the defect of the scale which had proved of so little use. There was no limit fixed to the movement of wages: there was an end of the minimum. "All parties were agreed in this, for they had seen the evil which had arisen in the two years of its existence."

The strike had saved the union. Deserters re-joined to help in the fight. Waverers were cheered by the proof that submission was not for ever to be the policy of the agents. And to the owners the strike was a warning not to persist in their campaign of

[1] *Durham Coal-Trade Arbitration*, July 1879. (*D.M.A. Records*, Miners' Hall, Durham.)

destruction. Crawford gave them plain warning that persistence in opposition would produce its legacy of hate, and that the men would repay with interest a malevolence which pursued them in their weakness.

In five years of constant wage reduction the whole of the advances won in the years of prosperity had disappeared. The savings of those good times had been spent. The inrush of new men had been offset by recent emigration. The union funds, built up by so steady a refusal to strike, had in both Northumberland and Durham been wasted in philanthropy, which the men now felt had but saved the owners from an increase in the poor rate. In one year, 1878, the Durham men spent £54,000 in the relief of unemployment. Then, in both counties, an impoverished union had been driven by unbearable demands into strikes. Yet in both counties, despite poverty, desertions, loss of funds, and widespread unemployment, union had survived.

It was enough. In 1880 the price of coal began to rise. Better than that, the demand increased until the markets began to absorb the swollen output. It meant a return to steady employment, a boon infinitely more precious than a small increase in the daily wage. In the period of distress the men had clung to their right to share in the conduct of the coal trade. For the next forty years joint committees, arbitration boards, sliding scales, were to satisfy their ambitions. With the better will, that their leaders were convinced of its folly, they had sacrificed the principle of the standard of life. They had given up their claim to a share in the profits of their trade. In exchange they had obtained unquestioned recognition of their union, a recognition which grew until men and owners felt and admitted a perfect equality in negotiation.

CHAPTER XI

POLITICAL TRIUMPHS

BUNNING was right. It was a revival in the iron trade which was required to restore prosperity to the collieries. But it was Bessemer's steel discoveries, not the cheapening of coal, which made an end of the pitman's starvation. In the early months of 1880 pit after pit re-opened, unemployment diminished, and the working fortnight rose from seven days to the full eleven. In the soft coal districts, for whose product there was an ever-increasing demand, there followed a decade of peace broken only by local bickerings. It was the foundation of the union leaders' regard for the sliding scale. They admitted that as a system of wage assessment it did not secure for the men full justice, but they were persuaded that it had the merit of averting strife, and the poverty consequent on war. And since wages more nearly approached certain cost it brought a new steadiness to trade, for the owners were encouraged by its existence to make long contracts. But the sliding scale was not the only cause of the strange quiet. Owners and men alike were exhausted by the long depression, afraid by any rash move to imperil the return of prosperity.

In Durham the deputy dispute was allowed to

remain unsettled for over two years. The union made no protest when it saw that the owners were resolved to encourage the new union of seceding officials. On their side the owners wisely ignored a half-hearted attempt to enforce a system of restriction of output, which finally collapsed through the refusal of the older men to limit their already insufficient wage. There was the same patient goodwill in Northumberland. There, in the pits where the lamp was used, a small advance in wage was granted. But the men's demand for a rent allowance where no free house was available was bluntly refused a hearing. The weary tolerance of the men is shewn plainly by their attitude to the sliding scale. They disliked it, they criticised it, but they did not insist on its abolition. They were puzzled by the new and strange prosperity, in which demand steadily rose, while prices and wages remained at their old low level, but they did not revive their old claim for a share in the profits, plain as it might be that this claim alone could justify a new wage demand. They grumbled, but endured, and when their grumbling was at its loudest a return of the depression swept away the perplexing prosperity.

As in the Chartist days the interest of the men was distracted by politics. By fighting their claim through every court of appeal the miners resident in the boroughs had established their right to vote. Though they paid neither rent nor rates the value in unclaimed wage of their "free house" entitled some of the miners to be ranked among the voting householders. The legality of their claim, and the injustice of the

owners' attempts to oppose it, were for some years
the subject of fierce discussion. Adverse decisions by
revising barristers were eagerly noted, as plain illus-
tration of the defects of a property basis for a modern
democracy. In the north there was but one borough
with a high proportion of pitmen householders, the
Tory borough of Morpeth. In 1874 Burt, the secretary
of the Northumberland miners, a hewer to whom a
still distrusted combination of workmen paid an allegiance which marked him as a dangerous demagogue, stood for the seat as a Radical. The Tories
worked their hardest to enlist social feeling against
so vulgar an intruder. Many of the Liberals found
the concrete outcome of reform an unpleasant shock
to their polite democratic enthusiasm. But the
miners outvoted the respectable tradesmen and for
the next forty years Burt sat in the House of Commons as a member of the advanced wing of the
Liberal party. Many a miners' union sent a grant to
help to pay his election expenses. His own association voted him a yearly salary of £500. Soon in both
counties an agitation was begun for the removal of
the legal anomaly which gave to one man the full
rights of active citizenship but denied them to his
neighbour who lived on the far side of an arbitrary
boundary. Meetings were held at which the union
agents forgot their industrial hopes in their political
zeal. "County Franchise Associations" almost co-
extensive with the unions were formed.

In 1885 the extended franchise was won, and at
once three more miners' members were elected. Two,

Crawford and Wilson of Durham, were union officials, but in Northumberland Wansbeck sent Fenwick straight from the coal-face to Westminster, paying him, though he held no rank in the union, the salary they had offered to their secretary.

While Burt stood alone his strength of character, his moderation, his simple pride in the honour with which the men had rewarded his labours, concealed all political difference. Even in the strike of 1878, when the men were starving and the union funds were exhausted, the suggestion was indignantly refused that they should withhold for a time his salary. If they were idle, his work at Westminster was still continuing. But when the number of miners' candidates grew, and it was seen that they were all to be of the same formal Liberal opinion, difference appeared. Until the county franchise was won the men were well content to see politics thrust trade matters from the place of honour at the annual galas. Bradlaugh, long the most popular speaker in the north, was always well received. His obscure birth, his early life, his fluent speech, and the injustice against which he struggled combined to win him the friendship of the pitmen. The majority shared his political views. Some few, especially in Northumberland, were attracted by his materialistic philosophy.

But when radical miners' agents began to advocate Home Rule with all the vigour and fervour which they had once expended on the union cause there were some protests. Not every miner could convince himself that Home Rule was a labour question, and that the Land League was a kind of trade society. The influx of the Irish black-legs, ignorant, violent, improvident, drunken, priest-attended, had not yet been forgotten. Nor was it forgotten that stout north-country pitmen had been driven to America by the wage competition of these strangers, and that in the recent trade depression the high number of surplus pitmen had compelled the adoption of a system of unemployment relief which had almost ruined the union. It was a common saying that prosperity would not return to the north until every Scotchman went home, bearing two Irishmen on his back. And, jeer at him as his leaders might, the Conservative working man stuck firmly to his political faith, the more so as foreign policy was of absorbing interest. Not every miner was captured by the cry of "Peace, Retrenchment, and Reform," nor convinced of the unwisdom of Disraeli's imperial schemes. The desertion of General Gordon caused none the less feeling in Northumberland because Burt was an admirer of Mr Gladstone, and a member of the party which had given his action countenance. At the first election Mr Wilson lost his seat, though his constituency was almost wholly devoted to mining.

Though by their insistence on the need for improved inspection, and by their steady demand for a new Mines Act, the miners' members well earned their salaries, even their trade legislation did not meet with unqualified approval. Burt made his first important step as a member of parliament when he elected to support the Employers' Liability Act. His first taste of public criticism was given him by Bryson, the president of the Northumberland Miners' Association. For the presidential speech at the Northumberland Gala of 1880 voiced the fear of the old pitmen that with the gain of a legal right to compensation they would lose the old, unquestioned payment of "smart money," the weekly five shillings which had been given from time immemorial to every injured miner[1]. There were many union men who said they wanted no legal protection, now that their strength added the power to strike to the old power of complaint. Burt replied that at the root of such criticism lay nothing but ignorance and local selfishness, for there were many miners in England to whom both strikes and smart money were alike unknown. The Durham miners passed a vote of indignant censure on Bryson. The Northumberland men refused next year to re-elect him to his office. He joined with Fynes, another rejected stalwart of the old times and the old opinions, in steady protest against this mistaken policy of political activity.

Perhaps his cry did not remain entirely unheard. In 1887 the wisdom of heavy political expense was hotly questioned. The miners, then engaged in a strike which had begun in defiance of Burt's warnings, voted that the parliamentary salaries of their members should be discontinued. A delegate meeting reversed the decision, on the excuse that it had been made in a momentary fit of ill-temper. Burt was not content with such grudging hire. Next year he brought the

[1] *Newcastle (Weekly) Chronicle*, June 24th, 1880.

whole matter up again. He said that in his judgment
the wisest policy for every miners' member was to
continue "cordially and earnestly to work with the
radicals"[1], and by a narrow majority his salary was
restored to him. The size of the adverse vote was
witness to the feeling, common in both Northumberland and Durham, that it would be better for the
miners' agents to subordinate politics to trade
matters.

The early miners' members were insistent in their
cry that they did not represent the miners alone. As
"working men members" they claimed to speak for
every class in the country, though from a stand-
point which differed from that hitherto adopted. To
them Home Rule, Free Trade, and foreign policy, and
every other essential of the Liberal programme, came
before such minor matters as hours and wages. Trade
legislation was a kind of private business. It had in
view the interests of a class, temporarily, perhaps,
deserving of unusual attention by reason of its
numbers and of its long neglect. But it was a material
change when the miners' members were to work *with*
the Radical party: before, they had been within it.
The distinction was a hint that the miners were not
willing to be swept into the existing political system,
there to have their views stretched on the bed of
party allegiance. The miners' agents might be blind,
in their Radical pride, to the fact that the party of
their choice was fundamentally averse to the ill-
defined political aspirations of their supporters, but

[1] *Newcastle (Weekly) Chronicle*, March 17th, 1888.

Lloyd Jones, who had done the men such good service in the arbitrations, had a clearer vision. In 1885 he stood for Chester-le-Street as an independent "Miners' Candidate." A bargain with the Liberal party, which assured the agents safe tenure of their own seats, compelled them, at the same time, to give their help to Joicey, a coal-owner, and the official Liberal candidate. Lloyd Jones was defeated though many of the miners supported him, and the quarrels which the election provoked hastened his death. The fact that this Welsh fustian cutter, who had become in his later days an independent journalist, received several thousand votes should have warned the Liberals that reverence for Mr Gladstone was not the whole of the miners' political creed. For Lloyd Jones was to the end of his life an opponent of those social and economic ideas based on the individual, utilitarian philosophy of which the Radicals were perhaps the most logical exponents. He had been one of the first disciples of Robert Owen; to the end of his life he clung to the ideal of the co-operative community, and preferred corporate development to unrestricted individual progress. It was not strange that in 1887, when the disciples of Marx first appeared in the north, that they should have found a field prepared for the harvest.

In that year delegates from the London dockers addressed meeting after meeting in the north in support of their claim that the state should possess itself of the means of production. In one Northumberland pit-village, 8000 men gave them an enthusiastic vote of support. At the annual gala the speakers were interrupted by cries unmistakably inspired by the new belligerent socialism, and two years later Henry George, the advocate of land nationalisation, appeared on the platform. Before long the men of both counties were demanding the abolition of royalty rents. More and more the new cry for economic change took the place of the old Radical political enthusiasm until in the north the formal Liberals saw their alliance with the miners broken by what they were pleased to call ingratitude. Nor did national politics alone attract the newly enfranchised pitmen. As soon as a measure of local government was given them they prepared to take full advantage of it. At its formation a quarter of the Durham County Council was composed of miners' nominees, and before many years that proportion was exceeded.

At the same time there was an unprecedented and perhaps unequalled awakening of interest in education. In the middle of the century the adult miner painfully learned to read in the hall of some Methodist Sunday School. In 1883 the University Extension Lectures were given the official support of the Durham Miners' Association. At union meetings, in the union circulars, the advantages of study were urged upon the miners. Over a thousand men attended the lectures given that winter, losing wages, and paying fines for shifts missed to learn elementary science, history, and political economy. The local secretary of the movement paid a high tribute to the intelligence of his new pupils, to their straightforwardness of speech, and their appreciative attention. Many of them had read the works of John Stuart Mill, and all of them seemed ripe for a scheme of education of a more advanced order than that provided by the elementary schools[1]. The local newspapers devoted whole pages to articles on mining science, law and history, even to subjects more abstract such as economics and philosophy. The fierce battles which raged in their columns shewed that much of this new information was eagerly received, much thoroughly digested. In particular the belief of Lloyd Jones that over-production was the cause of all the mysterious poverty was called in question. He wished to control output. He hoped to put a stop to the reckless competition of the capitalists by a system of organised restriction. His articles in the *Newcastle (Weekly) Chronicle* produced many a champion eager to confute his economic heresy by exposition of Burt's text that to produce less was a mistaken policy if it were dictated by a hope of adding to the workman's share. Political interest and secular education dealt heavy blows to the old enthusiasm for Methodist religion. Economic law was quoted where once the Sermon on the Mount had sufficed. On the union banners party cries replaced the Bible texts. The young men began to aspire for success more worldly than that witnessed by a place on the connexion plan.

[1] *Newcastle (Weekly) Chronicle*, March 31st, 1883.

CHAPTER XII

THE PETTY TROUBLES OF PEACE

1880 was an uneventful year. In Northumberland, under the terms of the sliding scale, there was a last wage reduction[1], but in both counties, by the end of the year, a small general advance was made, while in the meantime the whole of the local reductions had been everywhere returned. Best of all steady work encouraged the pit-wives to resume their old habits of generous housekeeping. A mark of the returning prosperity was the announcement in February by the Durham Miners' Association that its funds had so far improved as to allow of return to the higher scale of financial benefits. The relief fund and the strike had brought bankruptcy so near that only the adoption of a rigid system of economy had averted a complete suspension of payments. In turn three matters demanded the attention of the agents, a cokemen's strike, an owners' protest, and the unsettled deputies' question. The strike was settled within a week of its beginning[2]: the owners' protest was answered almost as rapidly. In January the Durham Miners' Council, a full gathering of delegates from every lodge, had passed a resolution that no hewer should get coal when his day's output seemed

[1] *Newcastle (Weekly) Chronicle*, Jan. 17th, 1880.
[2] *Durham Chronicle*, March 5th, 9th, 1880.

sufficient to assure him a wage of 4s. 2d.[1] In March
the owners stumbled on definite proof of the existence
of this policy. There was a short strike at Hetton
which in the end was referred to the Joint Committee.
There it was admitted in evidence that for some time
a partial restriction had been in operation, of which
the motive was desire to maintain a tonnage rate
slightly above that at which the county average wage
could be earned. Several other disputes revealed a
similar evasion of the understanding that the men
were to work to the best of their ability. Suspicion
grew that the restriction was not, as in the past, local
defiance of the agents' orders, and in the end a
definite notice was found at Seaham that "next week
restriction would begin according to rule." Bunning,
the owners' secretary, sent a copy of the notice to
Crawford, with a remark that such a rule, if in existence, was a breach of the sliding scale agreement. The
agents warned the men of his action, and advised them
to order the withdrawal of the February resolution[2].
They did so, and, as Wilson, later the union secretary, said, "thus ended the only county attempt to enforce uniformity of piece work. It ended as all such
attempts will end. Human nature is too strong for
such arrangements"[3]. Meantime several small matters hindered the settlement of the deputies' dispute.

There was a short and successful strike at Wood-
lands, against the imposition of a local reduction, a

---

[1] *D.M.A. Records*, Jan. 17th, Feb. 14th, 1880.
[2] *Ibid*. March 25th, 1880.
[3] J. Wilson, *The Hist. of the D.M.A.* p. 169.

strike at Bearpark, to check the employment of non-unionists[1]. There had been friction over an attempt by the men to employ the official method of coercion, refusal to "ride" with the black-legs, that is, to descend the shaft in their company. The strike had the usual indecisive result, for both manager and men had never expected it to be fought to a definite and logical conclusion. A disaster at Seaham provoked a much more bitter quarrel.

The pit, admittedly well-managed, was wrecked in September by a mysterious explosion, and 164 men were killed. Before the rescue party could recover the bodies a fire broke out, and it was decided to isolate the seam, where many of them lay, with airtight stoppings. Years before a similar action had provoked a strike, for the men then thought that their comrades had been too easily abandoned, but on this occasion there was little outcry. The men seemed ready to resume work, for though a few in terror decided to abandon the pits they were newcomers to whom five years before the high wages had been an irresistible bait. But the cause of the disaster was hotly disputed. The coroner's jury said that there was no sign of gas in the pit, but that the explosion had begun in an atmosphere thick with coal dust. Almost all the older men refused to accept this theory. Blasting, said they, was the origin of every mysterious occurrence: dust was harmless, as by experience they well knew[2]. Meantime the agents were busy over a

[1] *Durham Chronicle*, July 16th, Oct. 1st, 1880.
[2] *Ibid.* Sept. 17th, 1880.

strike at South Moor[1]. The owners, who were not members of the owners' association, refused to accept an award by which an umpire had authorised a slight reduction in the hours of colliery mechanics. The Durham Federation, that close alliance of all the local unions of colliery workers, brought out every man employed in the pit. Almost at once the owners found a sufficient number of black-legs to enable them to restart work. They evicted the strikers, ignoring the protests of the union, which six weeks later was compelled to declare the strike at an end and to remove the strikers to other villages. The most violent circulars on the cruelty of the evictions failed to arouse any general enthusiasm. The strike, from the first ill-supported, ended in failure more than usually complete[2].

Suddenly, at Christmas, when the Seaham pit had been roughly repaired, the hewers refused to return to work[3]. They said that it was a breach of all colliery custom and a blatant disrespect of the dead to hew coal while there were bodies in a pit. For a time the trouble was overlooked. It was thought that the men would soon tire of their unprofitable mourning and that the strike would come to an end. Again the attention of the agents was claimed by other matters. In the new year the question of the inequality of the deputies' wage was settled by arbitration. Early in February, 1881, the umpire, John

---

[1] *D.M.A. Records*, Oct., Nov. 13th, 1880.
[2] *Durham Chronicle*, Nov. 19th, Dec. 3rd, 1880.
[3] *Ibid.* Dec. 17th, 1880.

Hinde Palmer, made award that the wage difference between the two classes, the union and the non-union men, should be removed[1]. The owners' position was untenable. There was reason in their claim that it was bad for discipline for officials to be members of a society primarily intended for the men. There was even some truth in the allegation that local lodges had censured deputies for too zealous performance of their duties, and had forbidden them to work the full number of shifts. But neither of these matters provided argument for the creation of a difference in wage between the deputy who remained in the union, and the deputy who withdrew. It was, in truth, a bribe to induce desertion from the union. The award was not well received, for the owners made a foolish quibble on its right interpretation. Not until May, when Hinde Palmer restated his judgment, was the matter finally settled. It seemed that the owners' action was dictated by an obstructive petulance, the outcome of the failure of their scheme for accident insurance. They had asked the men to confer with them, in the hope of arranging some system of compensation which would satisfy the provisions of the new Employers' Liability Act. It was suggested that the "Provident" could be made the basis of a comprehensive insurance society, contribution to which should be obligatory on owners and men. But the miners' agents said that in spirit "Contracting Out" was an evasion of the law. Their desire was not money

[1] *D.M.A. Records*, Aug. 16th, 1880; March 1881. *Deputy Arbitration*. (Book, Miners' Hall, Durham.)

compensation, but increased safety. Their support had been given to the Act, when it came before parliament, in the hope that increased pecuniary liability for accident would compel the owners to more thorough precaution in working. They were not moved by a threat to discontinue the payment of "smart money." "Smart money," they said, was no charitable concession, but a definite part of the wage[1].

In the midst of these arguments they discovered that the Seaham strike was still continuing. The agents knew that the burning seam would be kept sealed for several more months. They were not convinced of the wisdom of the strike, but they agreed that it would be unnecessary harshness to deny the Seaham men strike allowance. They hoped that soon an end would be made of the protracted mourning, but in February the strike was still continuing, though the men had spent their savings and the women and children were beginning to suffer from privation[2]. The union grant of £750 a week was wholly insufficient for the needs of the strikers, to each of whom it brought but 10s. a week. An appeal was made for a lodge levy, but its success did not bring complete relief, and starvation soon had its usual fellow, violence. Towards the end of the month a series of fierce riots, arising out of an attack on some black-legs, disturbed the peace of the village. To persuade the men that their persistence was ridiculous the

[1] *D.M.A. Records*, Dec. 1880. *Durham Chronicle*, Dec. 3rd, 17th, 31st, 1880.
[2] *Durham Chronicle*, Feb. 4th, 18th, 1881.

owners brought together several notable engineers, who agreed that it would be impossible for many months to reach the burning seam. It was of no avail, and to end the strike they were driven to threaten the men with eviction. The threat was enough: work was about to be resumed, when the manager refused to re-engage twenty-six men whom he accused of having been guilty of inexcusable outrage. Though later the number was reduced to eight it included most of the lodge officials, and on those terms the men refused to bargain. Crawford, thoroughly weary of the whole dispute, persuaded the manager to re-employ the marked men on condition that they gave a promise to resign as soon as the union could find them work elsewhere[1]. Work was started, but the promise was not fulfilled. Not until May, when eviction had actually been begun, was there an end to the strike[2].

After eighteen months of quiet prosperity a new depression began[3]. To check the unemployment two remedies were suggested, emigration, and restriction of output. Lloyd Jones' socialist sermons, in the *New-castle (Weekly) Chronicle*, closely copied by Crawford's monthly circular to the union lodges, blamed the owners for the threatened poverty, asserting that the reckless competition of capital always resulted in over-production, and glut. It was a doctrine which met steady contradiction, and Crawford in the end

---

[1] *Durham Chronicle*, March 4th, 11th, 25th, 1881.
[2] *Ibid.* May 13th, 1881.
[3] *Ibid.* Aug. 12th, 1881.

was put to silence[1]. As the year drew to a close there
was a slight trade revival, though it was too uncertain to check the stream of emigration. In 1881
as many as 3000 people left Durham for the United
States. But they did not take kindly to their new
home. In frequent letters they warned their friends
against the discomforts of the new country, the high
prices, the long hours, the disregard of safety, and
the fanatical opposition to union. As soon as they
could collect together their passage money many of
them returned.

Meantime the dislike of the sliding scale began to
make itself heard in every quarter. In April the
Northumberland men voted that their agreement
with the owners should be allowed to lapse, if the
rent allowance should still be refused. In June the
owners made partial surrender. Though at the existing
coal-price they asserted that no rent could be paid,
they offered to add a small, variable, allowance to
the sliding scale. Grudgingly their offer was accepted, and in October a small increase of $2\frac{1}{2}$ per
cent. brought hope for the new year. In Durham
1881 passed with no wage change whatever, and as
work grew slack agitation began again for a return
to the old principle of a minimum wage of about
5s. a day[2].

"It is no secret," said the *Durham Chronicle*, "that during
the whole of its existence the present sliding scale has
been steadily opposed by many of the men whose voices

[1] *D.M.A. Records*, Aug. and Sept. 1881.
[2] *D.M.A. Records*, Lodge Resolutions, 1881, late.

are never heard in trade dispute outside their lodge rooms"[1].

But the grumblings were silenced. The activities of the County Franchise Association—embarked at last on a definite campaign for the election of its chosen candidates—diverted the attention of the men from trade grievance to political ambition.

Meantime in the last week of December a strike began which was to ensure a sufficiency of incident for the next two years. Westoe, the lodge secretary of Ushaw Moor, was dismissed from the colliery for persistent absence, and for filling dirt among his coal[2]. The dismissal was but the outward sign of a widespread dissatisfaction. The owners said that the men had deliberately increased their lost time, at the moment some 23 per cent., as part of a general policy of restriction of output, and that the pit had come entirely under the control of the local union officials, who were men unfit for their responsible positions. The men complained of the general attitude of the manager: he was discourteous, overbearing, violent both in speech and action. In the hearing of Crawford he called the men "a set of lazy b....s"[3]. It was an indiscretion he was not allowed to forget.

Ushaw Moor was a colliery with an unusually high proportion of Irish Catholic pitmen, and race and religion soon added their prejudice to what became almost at once an unnecessarily bitter struggle. If the actions of the manager shewed that he lacked

[1] *Durham Chronicle*, Dec. 23rd, 1881.
[2] *Ibid*. Jan. 6th, 1882.   [3] *D.M.A. Records*, Jan. 1882.

both tact and self-control, time was to prove that the
men had chosen unworthy leaders, men not ashamed
of taking the lead in drunken brawls and more calculated violence. South Moor, which had struck on a
question of mechanics' hours, had been but ill-supported, but this new strike, which embraced every
one of the traditional hewers' quarrels, was judged
worthy of more generous interest. Mixed with the
hints that union and restriction were the main points
at issue were stories of the bullyings of a surly
manager, of fines for improper tub-filling, of interference with the right of the men to stay at their will
from work. By lodge levies the strike pay of 10s.
a week was raised to 16s., and carts sent round the
nearer collieries returned laden with bread[1]. In
January the first men were evicted. Father Fortin,
the village priest, offered the union his schools as a
dormitory for the women and children. The men
built themselves an encampment in the fields. In
February the evictions were completed[2], and the
daily parade of the strikers, a somewhat disorderly
march past the pit-head and the houses of the black-
legs, had become so much a routine that it had lost
its demonstrative value. Soon one of the men was
charged with a more direct act of intimidation, but
he escaped conviction. In revenge Robinson, the
manager, was summoned by the wife of the lodge
president for assault. He had pushed rudely by her
during the later evictions, but his action could hardly

---

[1] *Durham Chronicle*, Jan. 27th, 1882.
[2] *Ibid*. Feb. 3rd, 1882.

be construed into an assault. In March a mass meeting was held to enable the neighbouring lodges to have the cause of the dispute explained to them. The wage figures given by the owners were flatly contradicted. The dismissal in turn of such deputies as were members of the miners' union seemed proof sufficient that Robinson was a reactionary, determined at all points to oppose the men. And, in regular monthly circulars, Crawford continued to repeat the story of the insult to his dignity. If the manager dared to use foul language in his presence it was certain that on less formal occasions his behaviour was unbearable[1].

The owners replied by charging several of the women with intimidation. They escaped with a strong lecture from the magistrates. Then three men were arrested on a charge of wounding a black-leg. Westoe and Lee, the lodge secretary and president, were the two leading offenders. At first bail was refused them, but at the trial they made a successful defence, proving an alibi, and compelling the black-leg to admit that he had returned home drunk and bleeding, but ignorant that an assault had been committed on him. Father Fortin began to take a more prominent part in the strike. He complained that the colliery policeman had ejected him from houses to which he was making a priestly visit, and that several similar discourtesies had been offered him. Robinson, the manager, had used "unrepeatable language" about Irishmen in general, and the teacher in the Catholic

[1] *D.M.A. Records*, March and April Circular, 1882.

schools had been unable to obtain a house. The Methodist under-officials made immediate reply. It was the Catholics who owned all the land in the parish, and they had set the fashion of religious intolerance by refusing to sell any to the Methodists as a site for a chapel[1].

Meantime the number of black-legs was steadily increasing. In April thirty hewers appeared from South Staffordshire[2]. The union met them and persuaded them to return, though it seemed probable that the visit had been designed simply as a drain on the funds. About the same time one of the black-legs was assaulted and his skull beaten in. A drunken miner from Brancepeth was his actual assailant, but a group of strikers from Ushaw Moor watched the murder, and made no effort at interference. Only the actual criminal was hanged, and perhaps it was the accident that a fence-rail studded with nails lay ready to his hand which turned his assault into a serious crime. Both sides increased the violence of their methods. In June a striker, who in the presence of the manager and the chief owner of the colliery had made a savage assault on a deserter, was sent to prison for three months[3]. But within a few days both the owner and the manager were successfully charged with a similar crime. A second time Robinson was fined. He had overwhelmed a chance met striker with abuse, and then, unprovoked, had knocked him

[1] *Durham Chronicle*, March 17th, 24th, 31st, 1882.
[2] *Ibid.* April 14th, 1882.
[3] *Ibid.* June 9th, 1882.

down. A black-leg who stabbed a striker was sent to prison for six months, saved from a longer sentence by his plea that the crime was committed under apprehension of personal danger[1]. Twice more Robinson was successfully prosecuted, once for destroying a public footbridge which was a convenient short-cut for the men into the village, and once for discharging fire-arms on the highway. He had "protected" himself from a hooting mob by firing a revolver towards the leaders.

Such trivialities suggested to the county that the strike had ceased to serve a useful purpose. In September the lodges began to question the wisdom of its continuance. They sent delegates to investigate the truth of the owners' claim that the pit was in full work. But Crawford's wrath made sure that the strike would continue. "Never in the whole of my twenty years experience of negotiations," said he, "have I met with such discourtesy, nor known such unfair demands from the men, as Robinson has made"[2]. Christmas brought plain proof that normal life had returned to the colliery. The black-legs made a presentation to one of the overmen. In the strikers' encampment a rival ceremony was held. Father Fortin, for his stout support of the union, was given a gold watch and chain[3]. In February, 1883, the manager resigned. He was given a handsome testimonial, and the vicar led the speeches, paying tribute

---

[1] *Durham Chronicle*, July 21st, 1882.
[2] *Ibid.* Sept. 15th, 1882.
[3] *Ibid.* Dec. 8th, 15th, 1882.

to his long, successful, and generous management. But the hope that the departure of the manager would make an end of the strike were soon disappointed. Its object had long been forgotten. It seemed to have become a struggle with little more meaning than the faction fights of an Irish town. The strikers had come to prefer the daily march past the colliery, and the weekly meeting of protest, to the hope of a return to work. The rough life of the bivouac drove them to the comfort of the inn-parlour. There drunken debate led to argument, argument to defiance, defiance to quarrels. In April Lee, the lodge president, was fined for an assault on a soldier who happened to be visiting a friend in the village. He ventured into the inn where Lee sat drinking, and an argument ended in a fight[1]. In June half-a-dozen strikers were sent to jail for a similar disturbance[2]. Early in the autumn the Lords of the Privy Council ordered the priest to return his schools to their proper use[3]. Already he had lost the grant from the education rate, though the union funds made good the deficiency. Now the women left their dormitory to shelter themselves with such friends as were able to receive them. Meantime the men remained in their encampment. In November Crawford resolved to make an end of the strike. Once his advice was rejected by the union council, but in December he laid the matter before the whole county. A circular recited the facts of the defeat, that the pit was in full work, the colliery

[1] *Durham Chronicle*, April 20th, 1883.
[2] *Ibid*. June 15th, 1883.   [3] *Ibid*. Aug. 24th, 1883.

houses full, the evicted men scattered over the whole coal-field. A quarrel with the manager had begun the strike, but long ago the manager had departed. An end must be made of so purposeless a struggle. The strikers could be supported, as "sacrificed men" victims to the owners' resentment, until such time as they could obtain work[1]. It was enough. A vote brought the strike to an end. It had lasted two years. It had cost the union £5707. 3s. 6½d. The money had purchased nothing but ridiculous defeat.

Ushaw Moor was not the only centre of unrest. In the same two years, on the single question of the employment of non-unionists, there were half-a-dozen local strikes. Such strikes as a rule were begun with little intention of forcing new members into the union. Their design was to reclaim those members who from carelessness or too narrow economy allowed their subscriptions to fall into arrear. To remind them of their fallen status here and there a lodge put into practice the rule which forbade union men to descend the shaft in company with a black-leg. After a short strike the deserters returned to their allegiance, perhaps bringing with them a few of the men who had always shrunk from the payment of the subscription. Such strikes were not directed against the owners, and as a rule they received little encouragement from the union head-quarters, for the agents knew that the decline in a lodge membership was usually the fault of an inefficient secretary, or a general neglect of union exhortations to good-fellowship and enthusiasm.

[1] *D.M.A. Records*, Dec. 29th, 1883.

In addition there were several strikes among the putters. Perhaps because an unusual number of young men had gone with the emigrants, perhaps because of a slow change in working practice, there were many signs of a shortage of putters. In particular the hewers made steady complaint that the practice was on the increase of taking them from their proper work to put. As a consequence of this shortage the average age of the putters rose. Many of them were young men of twenty, some of them were married, fathers and the heads of households. Strikes among these young men, technically still known as boys, became every year more common, and they were the more serious because they were as a rule lightly begun, with little appeal to authority, and little respect for rule and formality. The old safeguard, that the putters were under the control of their parents, became yearly of less value.

Meantime a new development of union strength turned every local dispute into a serious danger. At Auckland Park the sudden resignation of eight deputies from the union became the cause of a strike. The lodge refused to work with these deserters until they paid the whole of the arrears of subscription which they had incurred. To settle the dispute the manager discharged the offenders, and sent them back to hew. He had been in no way concerned in the strike, but he was seriously alarmed by the discovery of an agreement between the whole of the Bolkow Vaughan collieries to join in any strike which involved one of the lodges[1]. In the same manner a

[1] *Durham Chronicle*, May 12th, 1882.

strike at Brandon was hastily compromised, at the discovery of a similar agreement among the men employed by Messrs Straker and Love, the owners of the affected colliery[1]. This readiness of groups of pits to combine for mutual action over trivial matters was a spontaneous outcome of a new consciousness of strength. It had neither the sanction nor the encouragement of the agents, who indeed a little distrusted this tendency to devolution, and local independence.

In August, 1882, local strikes had become so numerous and so troublesome that Crawford felt compelled to issue a circular of warning and protest[2]. Their continuance, said he, would imperil the agreement with the owners, and the existence of some agreement was essential to peace. But though most of the men were prepared to accept his views on the necessity for good relations with the owners, many of them were convinced that the agreement under which they were working was bad in detail. In February the council had decided that an advance of 20 per cent. in the basis wage was a necessary preliminary to a renewal of the sliding scale. They were offered an increase of $2\frac{1}{2}$ per cent. By the insistence of the agents they were persuaded to accept this unsatisfactory bargain, made the more acceptable by the addition of a further temporary advance of $3\frac{3}{4}$ per cent. In May a new sliding scale had come into force[3]. But though Crawford was at pains to explain

---

[1] *Durham Chronicle*, Aug. 11th, 1882.
[2] *D.M.A. Records*, Aug. 1882.
[3] Sliding Scale Agreement, April 29th, 1882.

that the scale contained no provision for a minimum wage, he could not destroy the men's desire for a return to the device which had been tried, if with little success, some six years before. A new depression warned the men that their hopes of a wage increase under the new scale were doomed to disappointment. Alternately they began to ask for the fixing of a new minimum, or for a return to the old policy of output restriction, concealed under the demand for more holidays, shorter hours, and a five-day week.

In Northumberland, though local strikes were less frequent, there was much widespread discontent. There was the same dissatisfaction with the sliding scale, the same recurrence of lodge resolutions for a change in the basis wage, the same reply by the agents that the scale, though imperfect, was the best method yet devised of wage settlement, and that the owners could not be bullied into granting an increase. It was admitted that of late the county had been more fortunate in its competition with Wales. The owners, assured by the sliding scale of continued peace, able, moreover, to reckon on a stable wage, had begun to underbid their rivals in the foreign markets. Meantime a festival of union diverted the men from speculation, to memories of past triumphs. On Christmas Day, 1882, a great gala was held at Blythe to celebrate the twentieth anniversary of the foundation of the union[1]. All the veterans of the pioneer combinations were assembled, fifteen who had fought with Hepburn, nineteen who had stood

[1] *Newcastle (Weekly) Chronicle*, Dec. 30th, 1882.

by Jude. There were still five of the "Apostles" alive who had journeyed in vain to London to collect funds for the strike of 1844. Many of them spoke from the platform. They had been driven from the pits, and compelled, as one of them remarked, "to better their situations." Now the leaders of union did not need to tramp from door to door, and beg their bread: they sat at Westminster, governors of the nation. Few words were needed to emphasise so plain an object lesson on the benefits of union. It was a broad hint that leaders who had achieved so much were still worthy of the confidence of the men. When the sliding scale agreement expired, by a small majority the union authorised its renewal. In March 1883 the particulars of the new scale were made public. There was no great change in the basis wage. In fact, the scale was almost a repetition of the old one, with its plain statement that there was to be no limit, upwards or downwards, to wage movement[1].

[1] *Newcastle (Weekly) Chronicle*, March 17th, 1883. J. C. Munro, *Sliding Scales in the Coal Industry* (1885).

CHAPTER XIII

SLIDING SCALES AND A STRIKE

IT was known to the men that the cost of coal production was falling. The unprofitable seams, opened in the years of crazy prosperity, were by this time all abandoned. Low price had compelled attention to working practice, redundant men had been dismissed, and a harsh if necessary economy had reduced the numbers of the old and feeble hewers. Since 1879 the output of the individual hewer had been steadily rising[1]. It was natural that the more thinking men should be convinced that, even with the continuance of low prices, a wage increase might justly be demanded. Moreover, the more intelligent saw a fundamental defect in the sliding scale, that it enabled the owners to quote low prices in their competition for contracts. Here was a system in which the wage was conditioned by the price, yet it offered temptation for a continued price reduction! They began to search for a remedy which should more nearly reach the root of their poverty.

In the autumn of 1882 a general conference of the Miners' National Association met in Leeds. This National Association was a kind of loose federation by which the miners' unions of the whole country

[1] *Reports* of H.M. Inspectors of Mines, 1879, 1880, 1881, 1882.

kept themselves reminded of their common industrial desires. It had no control over its members. It had no fund. A small grant was made by each affiliated union to pay necessary expenses, mostly incurred by promoting legislation. Most of its officials held high place in the two north-country unions, which in those days were unrivalled in financial strength, organisation, stability, and firm purpose. To its meetings delegates were welcome, whether their unions were weak or strong. Side by side with Burt and Crawford, who could speak for three-quarters of the miners of the north, sat unknown men, sent by the scattered enthusiasts of the Midland collieries, where but 10 per cent. of the miners had heard of combination. Yet they spoke with an equal voice, and the delegate who appeared and claimed a seat, though in his district union was still unknown, had a vote as weighty as Crawford himself, for all his 30,000 men. Ignoring its own futility this conference passed resolutions, calling for a general strike and a definite policy of restriction of output. Burt, the president, exposed the folly of the proceedings, but soon both he and Crawford were engaged in the difficult task of explaining to their own supporters the reasons for their refusal to abide by the "majority vote" of the National Conference[1]. For its schemes were in accord with the desires of many of the hewers in the north.

It was at the moment when Lloyd Jones was most insistent on his doctrine that over-production was the cause of the depressions which came so regularly

[1] *D.M.A. Records*, March 1883.

to rob the miner of his prosperity[1]. Burt was opposed
to the whole principle of restriction and the Northumberland men were content to be guided by his wisdom,
but Crawford was less easily convinced that Lloyd
Jones was a preacher of economic heresy. He opposed
immediate resort to restriction, chiefly because its
enforcement seemed impossible. Perhaps some day,
when thorough organisation should give the miner
strength commensurate with his latent powers, control of production would come, to end poverty and
unemployment alike. It was his belief that "as men
get wiser they will not go on working for ever for
somebody else, but will claim and obtain a much
greater share of the wealth which they themselves
produce"[2]. He had learned enough of the new
Marxian creed, or the old socialist doctrine, to promise his men

that the doctrine which teaches the entire subservience
of labour to capital,...and that the laws of supply and
demand shall determine whether the workman shall be
fairly fed and clothed, or starved and ill-clothed, shall
at all times have my most strenuous opposition[3].

But as he well knew the time for action was not yet,
and at last he persuaded the Durham men also of
the impossibility of raising the price of coal by interference with its supply.

When the lodges saw that their demands for a
wage advance, or a new attempt at restriction, inevitably incurred his opposition, they began to cloak

---

[1] *Newcastle (Weekly) Chronicle*, 1882–83.
[2] *D.M.A. Records*, May 1881.   [3] *Ibid.* Oct. 1880.

their desires under repeated requests that the hours of work should be reduced, that Saturday labour should be discontinued, and that the time of coal-drawing should be fixed at ten hours, instead of the eleven which was the general rule. In May 1883 these requests were embodied in the formal list of demands which it had become the practice to present once a quarter to the owners[1]. Other desired improvements had a less involved origin. As the extent of the workings increased the necessity for the introduction of a payment for the journey from the shaft to the face became more and more apparent, and there was no principle involved in the demand for a higher rent allowance, fewer extra shifts, and a more definite scale of wages for the boys. Most of these requests were made in hope rather than expectation and there was no great dissatisfaction when they were refused, especially when in September the boys' wage scale was revised[2]. In the autumn the dislike of the sliding scale could no longer be concealed. Lodges began again to send to the general council of the union the old resolutions, asking for its abolition, for a general wage advance, or for the insertion in the agreement of a clause which should sanction a minimum below which wages could not fall[3].

When the owners made reply that the low price of coal did not permit of wage concessions, an attack began on the royalty system. Strangely enough it

[1] *D.M.A. Records*, May 1883.   [2] *Ibid.* Sept. 1883.
[3] *Ibid.* Oct., Nov., 1883.

was the outcome of a series of colliery disasters. In February, 1882, seventy-three men were killed at Trimdon Grange. In April, fifty more lost their lives in three less notable explosions. Most of the victims were members of the " Provident," which had not yet recovered from the expense of the Seaham disaster. It was threatened with financial exhaustion, for in three years, in addition to its regular daily expenses, it had incurred unexpected liabilities amounting to over £42,000. It dared not raise the subscriptions, sixpence a fortnight was as much as the men could well pay, for they had their union subscription also, the occasional levies, the dues of their friendly society, and probably some payment to their chapel fund. Since the passing of the Employers' Liability Act most of the owners had withdrawn their former subscriptions. There seemed but one untapped source of revenue, the rents of the royalty owners. Suggestions became common that a definite tax should be levied on royalties for the relief of the widows and orphans. It was a hint to the men, so long dissatisfied with their low wages. They began to reply to wage demands by asking the owners to seek relief rather from their wealthy landlords than from their hewers.

When in the spring of 1884 the Durham sliding scale agreement expired, the men could not be persuaded to renew it. The owners warned them that a new depression was about to begin, and that only by immediate tender could they secure contracts sufficient to keep their pits at work. They asked that any new agreement should be made for three years, not the customary two, and as an additional security they suggested that it should include three new conditions. The first was that the miners' association should pay damages for illegal strikes, and for cases of refusal to submit demands to the judgment of the County Joint Committee. The second was that men who lived in colliery houses should pay a fine for every day of inexcusable absence. The third was that there should be a distinct understanding that the manager could employ whom he wished[1]. It was the indiscipline in the union which caused the owners to make these requests[1]. There was little fault to find with its general policy, but there were many lodges which shewed their discontent by the adoption of an aggressive attitude, which restricted the number of shifts their members could work, and censured the deputies for too zealous performance of their duties. Crawford was in favour of some concession. He had been deeply impressed by the general feeling of gloom which had prevailed at a recent conference of the Miners' National Association. Every delegate had made report of the coming of hard times. But until the men had experienced the depression they could not be convinced of the need for submission. In March, 1884, a general council of the Durham Association was convened, to consider what should be the reply of the union to the owners' policy of closing pits and dismissing men[2]. It was generally thought that this timorous economy had been adopted to drive

---

[1] *D.M.A. Records*, Dec. 1883.
[2] *Ibid.* March 22nd, 1884.

the men into a renewal of the sliding scale agreement. Resolutions were brought forward, and eagerly carried, that until the owners offered some explanation of their actions the men should restrict their output, and proceed to a general vote as a threat of a strike. Though the number of men unemployed was increasing, and though many were getting work only by offering to pay their own rent, in April the council was still full of suspicion. As a necessary preliminary to the discussion of a new wage agreement it demanded that all the pits should be reopened. In May the agents warned the men of the folly of continued blindness. The time had gone for delay. The owners had made a demand "for a substantial reduction of wages," a demand which they were prepared to enforce. Lodges which had begun to ask for unemployment relief could no longer refuse to believe that a new period of depression had begun[1]. The warning was enough. In June a new sliding scale was devised, and two months later, in accordance with its terms, the first reduction was made[2].

The security of the sliding scale brought a little relief. The owners hastened to secure the contracts of which they had spoken, hoping, if not for profit, for the occupation which was less costly than idleness. The progress of the depression was a little checked, and the men convinced at last of its existence. In the autumn the union set aside £2000 from its general fund, as a nucleus for a new unemployment relief

[1] *D.M.A. Records*, May 20th, 1884.
[2] *Ibid*. June 16th, 1884.

fund, and the "Relief Levy" was reimposed. During the remaining months of the winter almost the only dispute in Durham was over the attempted settlement of an agreed age at which lads should commence to hew. In the past it had been eighteen, but with widespread unemployment and a mysterious decrease in the supply of putters it had crept up to twenty-one. There were several evils resulting from this change. The lads became more unmanageable. The older ones, convinced that they were fit to hew, made incessant complaint, if indeed by steady indiscipline they did not attempt to obtain promotion. Putters, who for a time had been allowed to hew, continued to descend with the fore-shift, not two hours later as was the general custom. It was a dangerous increase in the already excessive length of the putters' day. And an intermediate class came into existence, "Hewing Putters," lads who hewed, but who ranked as putters, for they did such putting as was required. They worked the full putters' day, ten hours, a dangerous infringement of the hewers' traditional short shift. They received neither house nor coals, a distinct breach of the wage agreement[1].

In the past, seasons of trade depression had always been, at any rate in their early stages, devoid of incident, though they soon provoked attacks on the royalty system, and in Durham demands for a revival of the policy of restriction. This one was unusually quiet. The grant of the county franchise, and the opening of the election campaigns of Crawford,

[1] *D.M.A. Records*, Oct. and Nov. 1884.

Wilson, and Fenwick, completely absorbed the men's attention. There was some expectation that the increase in the number of miners' candidates would encourage them to forsake the Liberal party. That Burt was a convinced Liberal the men were aware, and they were well content that he should keep to his allegiance, but it was hoped that the others would stand more distinctly as "labour" men. They were disappointed. Crawford made plain explanation of his creed:

It was not possible for the rich man to understand the poor man's needs. The working man was necessary to legislate for the working man. But the chasm which divided the rich from the poor must be bridged over, and the working man must do it. He must do it not by trenching on the interests of other classes, but by devising more equitable means of distribution of the wealth produced by the newer and easier methods[1].

He was to be no root-and-branch reformer of existing evils, but a watchman to prevent the growth of other and worse evils in the future.

The peace was not unbroken; such quiet has never been attained. In 1885 there was a short, successful, strike at Tudhoe, because one man had begun to hew eight hours instead of the customary seven[2]. In June a series of strikes began in the Bolkow Vaughan collieries[3]. Their causes were paltry, in the main they were putters' disputes begun in a moment of irritation. But when several of the strikers were success-

[1] *D.M.A. Records*. National Union Circular, "Working Men's Representatives," 1884.

[2] *Durham Chronicle*, March 27th, 1885.

[3] *Ibid*. June 19th, 26th, 1885.

fully sued for damages the men held a meeting of
protest at the attitude of the agents. The officials
had time enough to spend over parliamentary elections, but little, said the men, for matters which
came within their union duties. Yet the whole county
had been lately given a plain lesson in the benefit
of unicn. The Thornley colliery, seat of old discontent,
was laid in, and the company which owned it declared
bankrupt. To secure the payment of such wages as
were due to the men the union made·legal seizure
of the colliery property. Only prompt and decisive
action saved the men the loss of their fortnight's wage.

Next year there was the same tale of formal wage
reduction under the terms of the sliding scale, of
growing unemployment, and of universal short time.
The owners resorted to every device by which in the
past they had evaded the general agreements. Men
were warned that at the county rate the pit in which
they worked would be compelled to close. It was
hinted that a local reduction alone could avert inevitable unemployment. As a rule an illegal bargain
was struck between the men and the manager, and
the pit worked on. At South Medomsley, where for
fifty years there had been no dispute, a change in
the management was followed by a strike[1]. The new
manager asked the men for a local reduction. Either
his demand was too blunt or he had not yet won the
men's confidence, for they struck at once. Already,
they declared, they were earning much less than the
county average, yet it had been hinted to them that

[1] *Durham Chronicle*, Jan. 8th, 1886.

if they would leave the union they would be assured of an eleven-day fortnight. There were the inevitable evictions. Soon there was the first charge of intimidation, defeated, not as in the old days by appeal to the rights of man, but by legal argument. But intimidation there must have been, for almost at once the black-legs promised to leave. A snowball attack on the few men who remained at work developed into a dangerous riot, but the only two men against whom violence could be proved were strangers, one a hawker, the other a smith. There was more trouble at the evictions, for the men obeyed the orders of the union " to stay in the houses till they were pitched out." In April the front of the manager's house was damaged by a mysterious explosion, for which the men indignantly denied responsibility. The strike failed, as that at Ushaw Moor had failed. The pit was filled with black-legs, and no general protest could be made, for South Medomsley was not under the control of the owners' association[1].

At Castle Eden the men struck, to enforce a local wage demand. Ninety of them were successfully sued for damages, and the strike was quietly settled[2]. At Hebburn a half-hearted attempt was made to resist a reduction, but in most collieries the wages continued to fall, though the universal evasion of the county agreement did not in any way check the growth of the depression[3]. Again unemployment relief became a serious burden on the union funds.

---

[1] *Durham Chronicle*, Jan. to July, 1886.
[2] *Ibid.* Sept. 1st, 1886.   [3] *Ibid.* Dec. 31st, 1886.

Exhortations to economy were succeeded by plain warning that nothing but a reduction in the scale of benefits could save the union from financial ruin. Yet at no time, as the agents deplored, had there been so many fraudulent appeals for help, or so little reluctance to seek union support. In 1887 two disputes began which still further depleted the funds[1]. Seaham, apparently, was resolved on a strike. Its first excuse was the friction which arose out of a refusal to "ride" with the non-unionists. Next, it refused to agree to the introduction of a night-shift, suggested as the only relief possible where wages could no longer be reduced. And along the Tyneside, at Usworth and the Felling, a dispute which threatened to involve 1700 men was averted only to break out again in the autumn.

It was not remarkable that there should be unrest in the north of Durham, for over the river a county strike was in progress. Smaller numbers and superior organisation, perhaps, too, the higher character of the men and the more dominant personality of their leader Burt, had kept Northumberland quiet, though its wage reductions were as frequent, and its unemployment the worse, for it was less stoutly fought by a union more careful of its funds. Yet there was widefelt dissatisfaction. The dispute over the refusal of the rent allowance was still remembered. The outcry against royalties was as loud. In fact at one time the men had joined in suggesting that if prices dominated wages, so they should control rents, and that land-

[1] *Durham Chronicle*, Jan. 14th, 28th, 1887, and some weeks.

lords should share with the men in the benefits of
a sliding scale. When, in the winter of 1886, the
sliding scale agreement expired and the owners demanded a reduction of 15 per cent. in the basis wage
as an essential condition to its revival, the men
refused the demand, and by a large majority gave
warning of their intention to strike[1]. The owners
modified their demand, they would be content with
a reduction of $12\frac{1}{2}$ per cent.; but this offer too was
refused, and in the last week of January the notices
were allowed to expire[2]. The men said that it was
no strike but a lock-out, a refusal of the owners to
employ them at the old terms. Morley, the member
of Parliament for Newcastle, interposed to suggest
that a reduction of 10 per cent. would be acceptable
to both parties. He was told that his interference
was both unasked and unwelcome[3]. The union officials,
who knew that the depression was certain to increase,
had little hope of staving off the reduction, and in
speech and circular continued to oppose the strike
policy. Irregular meetings among the men warned
them of the danger of over-insistence. The memory
still remained of the secession during the last county
strike. It was useless preaching submission to men
who were united in a demand for an advance of
20 per cent. "They had been getting a little bacon
for breakfast, and the children got the fat. With the
proposed reduction there would be neither bacon,

[1] *Newcastle (Weekly) Chronicle,* Jan. 1887.
[2] *Ibid.* Jan. 27th, 1887.
[3] *Ibid.* Feb. 5th, 1887.

nor fat "[1]. Here was no intention of surrender, because of a fall in the market price.

In February the whole of the officers of the union resigned:

Even if our self-respect allowed us to accept the un-merited censure which is being heaped upon us, we would still be powerless to help you without the assurance of your confidence....Mistakes we have made, as we are men. But we have nothing to apologise for[2].

The step, a last desperate defence against internal dissension, brought the malcontents to their senses. If they disliked the policy of Burt and his friends they had no alternative policy to suggest, and no leaders to maintain the formless opposition. As the funds of the association sank, it was compelled to issue a general appeal for assistance. It had recently spent nearly £10,000 on unemployment relief, during the depressions inevitable in an export trade subject to violent fluctuation. But the general poverty of the Tyne valley weighed as heavily on the shipyards as on the coal mines. There was no local union able to give the pitmen much relief, and it has always been hard for the miner to convince his immediate neighbours of his poverty, a fact too often forgotten in assertion of under-payment. Even in the union there were many who hinted that the funds would not have been so low but for the recent political extravagance. In vain Burt pointed out that the stories of the high wage of the Northumberland miners were gross exag-

---

[1] *Durham Chronicle*, Feb. 11th, 1887.
[2] *Newcastle* (*Weekly*) *Chronicle*, Feb. 5th, 1887.

gerations, and that in truth the average wage of the pit-man was less than £1 a week, taking the year as a whole together with its frequent periods of irregular work[1]. In six weeks the appeal produced only £903. Only from allied miners' unions did any substantial assistance come. Durham sent a heavy grant from its general fund and imposed a strike levy, but even neighbourly charity failed to raise the strike pay above 3s. a week[2].

Pride was a good substitute for supplies, and the men continued to refuse in turn the offers of the owners, and the proposals of the agents. By the end of the eighth week of the strike, when the poverty of the men drove many from their homes, the owners began to change their tone. They resolved to take advantage of the men's apparent defeat to pursue the quarrel to a definite conclusion. The change was not unnoticed by the general public. The strike subscription rose to £5882, though there was a great deal of resentment at the refusal of the union to help in the relief of men who, though not members, were taking a part in the strike. In April, though the delegates were in favour of negotiation, and the owners were offering to open the pits to all men who would accept the $12\frac{1}{2}$ per cent. reduction, the men still continued on strike. The wage committee of the union, a permanent body which conducted the periodic negotiations with the owners, resigned, saying that its services were not required[3]. By the appoint-

---

[1] *Newcastle (Weekly) Chronicle*, Feb. 1887.
[2] *D.M.A. Records*, Jan., Feb., 1887.
[3] *Newcastle (Weekly) Chronicle*, April 9th, 1887.

ment of a new one the men shewed their desire ultimately to effect a settlement, but still they continued
to refuse their agents' advice, and to entrust the
negotiations to the committee they had appointed.
Burt went from colliery to colliery telling the men
that the reduction was inevitable, and that concession and negotiation alone could make an end of the
dispute. In May the men abandoned their inflexible
attitude, entrusted the decision of the dispute to the
new wage committee, and made no protest when it
at once accepted the owners' terms[1]. The strike had
lasted seventeen weeks. It had done little but waste
the union funds. At the annual gala there could be
found but two subjects for self-congratulation; among
12,000 men there had not been a single desertion and
in seventeen weeks not a single breach of the peace[2].
The north as a whole seemed almost ignorant that
a strike was in progress.

At the gala Burt was received with the usual
cheers, but Fynes, who year after year appeared to
celebrate the success of the association he claimed to
have founded, was shouted down. By his steady
opposition to the strike he had lost all his popularity.
His doctrine of arbitration seemed to the men an
outworn creed. Even Fenwick found it hard to get
a hearing, and the cries of interruption had a new
and strange inspiration. The London dockers had
seen in the strike an opportunity for the spread of
their new doctrines of state ownership. At Horton

---

[1] *Newcastle (Weekly) Chronicle*, May 28th, 1887.
[2] *Ibid.* Aug. 6th, 1887.

their missionaries had received an almost unanimous vote of support, and in other collieries they had been well received[1]. When the feeling caused by the strike died down the popularity of the new gospel died also, but there were some remaining to whom the dockers had brought a new enlightenment. Moreover the strike had taught the men that, strong as their local union might be, it was powerless against the owners, at any rate in a falling market. It had shewn that adherence to the policy of their leaders brought reductions, and that at a time when work was irregular, and unemployment general. Even if the revolutionary proposals of the socialists found little support the ground was well prepared for the aggressive doctrines of the new general union, the "Miners' Federation of Great Britain."

[1] *Newcastle* (*Weekly*) *Chronicle*, April 16th, 1887.

CHAPTER XIV

A NEW QUARREL AND A CALAMITY

TEN years of failure and trade depression had disgusted the men of the north with their own efforts. Great as might be their local strength it seemed a puny weapon against the owners' persistence. The union leaders had come to prefer any course, arbitration, agreement, even simple submission, to the risk of a strike. They were persuaded that demand and supply fixed the market price of coal. They were content by sliding scales to secure for the men a wage which moved up and down with that price. Hope of further progress seemed dead, the purpose of union was no longer apparent. In their despair the men heard of a new union, a stronger alliance of the scattered associations of the country, the Miners' Federation of Great Britain, a body with a new wage doctrine, and a new and aggressive policy. If Burt and his fellows were convinced that wages must follow prices in their ceaseless movement, the Miners' Federation demanded a wage which should be a standing charge on industry, a controlling factor in price, a wage sufficient for all the normal needs of life. If local strikes had no history of success there was still hope that a general strike might be more fortunate. In both Northumberland and Durham the men began to hope for alliance with this new Federation.

In 1887 a general miners' conference, held at Edinburgh, took a step which for twenty years was to stand in the way of a national miners' alliance. It resolved to begin a campaign for a legal eight-hour day[1]. The decision meant the isolation of the northern coal-field from every other mining district. In both Northumberland and Durham an eight-hour day seemed impossible. In no way could it accord with the local system of work, with its minute subdivision of labour and its multiplication of shifts. There were in most pits two sets of hewers. The fore-shift descended the shaft at 4 a.m., and worked until it was relieved; the back-shift went down at 10 a.m., worked until about 4 p.m., and emerged at the pit-head half an hour later. The average day of the hewer, from bank to bank, was roughly seven hours, and of that some five and a half hours were spent in coal getting. The rest of the time was spent in the descent of the shaft, and in the long walk to the face[2].

To every hundred hewers there were, in 1890, some thirty-two shifters and stone-men, men who went down the pit in the evening to drive new roads, and repair the airways and to make ready the pit for the work of the next day. They too were within the limits imposed by the new bill, for they worked a shift of eight hours. It was the third class of workers, the "off-hand" men and boys, whom the bill promised to benefit. They were engaged for the most part in the transport of coal. They went down two hours

[1] J. Wilson, *Hist. of D.M.A.* p. 199.
[2] *D.M.A. Records*, Nov. 1887—March 1888.

later than did the fore-shift, and ascended immediately before the back-shift, being below some ten or eleven hours. There were about ninety-four of this third class employed to every hundred hewers. If they were given an eight-hour day, said both owners and men, the continuance of the two-shift system would be impossible. There were three suggested plans. The pits might work but one shift, of eight hours. It was plain that this course would diminish the output, throw many men out of employment, add enormously to the cost of production by leaving the machinery idle two-thirds of the day, and, as a last and most disastrous consequence, increase the length of the hewers' day. Two equal shifts might be worked, of eight hours each. That would increase the output, throw more coal on a market already subject to periodic glut, and add to the hewers' day. Moreover, so great was the shortage of boys that it was feared the staff for this second shift could not be provided. The third plan, which twenty years later was eventually adopted, was that three shifts of hewers should descend in turn, and be waited on by two shifts of boys. Though this plan overcame the two great difficulties, lack of pit room, and shortage of boy labour, though it kept the disproportion between off-hand men and coal getters, and barely increased the length of the hewers' day, it was open to grave objection. It made necessary an increase in the hours of coal-drawing, and as a result allowed of an increase in output, a notable defect in the eyes of men who were still apt to blame over-production for every fall in wage. And by introducing a shift which worked in the evening, it made necessary a change in the social and domestic life of an intensely conservative class. The eight-hour day has been in no sense a boon to the pit-wives, for at no time can the oven stand idle. Meals must begin at two in the morning. They are not well ended until midnight.

Even this solution did not remove from the north the reproach that the boys work longer than do the men, nor did it end entirely the contrast between the hewer, with his short day and high wage, and the unskilled labourer, working steadily, if more slowly, for a longer time, yet with less reward.

Burt and Crawford began a resolute opposition to the new demand. Excuse for an apparently selfish attitude there was plenty. Though the boys worked longer than did their fathers they did not work so hard. Many of them were boys only in name, young strong men in reality. It was better for them to work a few hours longer each day when they were young than on their promotion to a hewer's place to be compelled to an eight-hour day. Elaborate arithmetical proof was given of the eventual sacrifice of leisure the change would entail. Fear of unemployment and increased output, conservative opposition to change, hatred for the name "eight hours," alarming in its sound to a class which had not for fifty years worked more than seven, were all in turn invoked. The old traditional doctrine for which Bryson and Fynes had been despised was brought from its obscurity. Union effort was better than appeal to the law. If the other districts would organise as well as Northumberland and Durham had done, the need for political action would disappear. That one blot on the northern system remained, could not be denied. By the machinery of gradual change and mutual agreement, which had perfected the two-shift system, and had made the northern hewer the envy of Welsh and Midland colliers, the hours of the boys would be reduced. Meantime, they were willing victims to a system which held out so great rewards for sacrifice[1].

It was this question which kept the northern pit-men outside the Miners' Federation. It was this fear of an addition to the hewers' shift which upheld Burt and Crawford and Wilson in their opposition to the minimum wage. For much as the men might desire it, much as they might dislike sliding scales, conciliation boards, and the whole machinery of compromise, they could not swallow the bitter coat of the golden pill. Both within and without the counties the two questions, firmly if unnecessarily joined together, of the eight-hour day and the minimum wage, produced endless discord. In parliament Burt and Wilson fought the growing host of labour members. At home they strove ceaselessly to conceal an endless war. The off-hand men were in favour of the new legislation, from which they alone would clearly benefit. As the pits developed they grew more nearly to equal the hewers in numbers and importance, especially when the coal-cutter began to oust the pick from its pride of place. In some of the bigger, newer, pits—

[1] *D.M.A. Records*, Jan. 1888.

Ashington, Wearmouth, and Harton—a three-shift system had already been introduced. The men of these collieries, always foremost in union action, had less to lose by the change. They said that if an eight-hour day was the only bar to national union, the price to be paid for strength to fight in the battle for the minimum wage, it should be no longer opposed. But for over twenty years the older men, the hewers in the two-shift pits, and the leaders who disliked the aggressive policy of the Miners' Federation, formed a majority sufficient to preserve the independence of the two northern unions. For a generation Burt and Wilson stood in the way of the Eight Hour Act. Only when the Federation followed their advice, and set its own house in order, only when the northern coal-field lost its supremacy in output and practice, and the Welsh and Midland unions began to bulk larger in the public eye than those of the Tyne, was the bargain struck. Northumberland and Durham entered the Federation, the Eight Hour Act was passed, and two years later the minimum wage itself received parliamentary sanction.

In 1887, as an immediate result of the Northumberland strike, the men refused to renew the salaries of the members they had sent to parliament. A delegate meeting, convened in November, reversed the decision of the August ballot, saying that the vote had been taken when the men were enraged at their defeat[1].

[1] *Newcastle (Weekly) Chronicle*, Feb. 25th, Aug. 14th, 1888. *Durham Chronicle*, Aug. 23rd, 1887.

But by a large majority the same meeting resolved
to make an end of the sliding scale. In Durham the
dissatisfaction in the Tyneside collieries, which had
resulted in an abortive strike in the spring, broke out
again, and a county strike was only averted by the
payment, in a mysterious, anonymous fashion, of the
fines of the men who were leading the disturbance.
A second threat of trouble was silenced by agreement.
At Rough Lea, a small colliery, seventeen men were
dismissed. They were all old men, whose output was
naturally on the decline. They were leading members
of the union. The manager said they were dismissed
for exhorting their comrades to restrict their output;
the men, that he had seized an excuse to rid himself
of old and weary servants[1]. Next year the Tyneside
collieries struck again, this time over a putters' wage
dispute, and at Bowes and Partners' there was a
quarrel over a matter of principle which threatened
serious consequences. A hewer had been given permission to absent himself from work to attend a
funeral. In his absence his brother, a putter, hewed
his two shifts. By his action he transgressed a lodge
rule, which forbade any man to work longer than an
agreed maximum[2].

By the decision of the Edinburgh conference both
counties were expected to present to their owners a
list of demands, which began with the eight-hour
day and ended with a request for a weekly holiday,
and a general, temporary closing of the collieries as

[1] *Durham Chronicle*, Nov. 18th, 1887.
[2] *Ibid*. Feb. 24th and March 9th, 1888.

the first step towards a reduction of output which was to force up the price. Burt and Crawford both were of opinion that the decision should be disobeyed, and in Durham the advice of the agent was taken[1]. But the men of Northumberland, still smarting with the sense of recent failure, ordered the presentation of the whole list, with an addition, that wages should at once be increased 10 per cent. Without hesitation the owners made refusal. The bad state of the trade which had made necessary their recent demands continued unabated. By the time their reply was made public the Northumberland men had been persuaded of the folly of their action, and they made no protest at the simple refusal of their desires[2].

Four times in Durham the sliding scale brought a wage change, twice upwards, twice downwards, a despised $1\frac{1}{4}$ per cent. each time. Meantime the "County Franchise Association," its name changed into the "Durham Political Union," was busy with local politics, sanitation, and the housing question. The trouble on the Tyne continued, until the Usworth lodge fell foul of the central power of the union, the executive committee. In the face of the sliding scale agreement the unruly lodge had made a demand for a local advance, and had justified its action by a circular issued in defiance of the rules. A short strike at Hetton, hastily called, gave witness of an extension of the unrest. Its cause, concealed in the techni-

---

[1] *D.M.A. Records*, Jan. 1888.
[2] *Newcastle (Weekly) Chronicle*, Jan. 28th, 1888.

calities of the formal excuse, was wage dissatisfaction. In June the owners replied to the long list of demands, the regular presentation of which had become almost a meaningless formality, with a list as impressive. It set forth the old grievance of lodge restriction, of hasty and illegal local stoppages, of misuse of the Joint Committee. It suggested that the free house and coal should be exchanged for a general advance in wage[1].

In the spring of 1889 the Durham sliding scale agreement expired. A new hope of prosperity was in the air. In Yorkshire there was talk of a general advance. In Northumberland the men had been given back the whole of the 12½ per cent. they had lost in the strike. The hewers of Durham thought that the time had come to make an end of the wage control they so much disliked. The agents, loath to see the destruction of the system which they had devised, misunderstood the general desire. When a ballot was claimed the papers issued ignored the popular feeling. But the men were not to be entrapped into perpetuating the sliding scale by consenting to choose whether the scale was to be amended, or continued. Every colliery called a meeting of protest. The sliding scale was compared to the yearly bond. It was a shackle on the freedom of the miner. "It had done no good in the past. It would do no good in the future." Over the Tyne, where the system had at last been abandoned, the wage was 14 per cent. above the standard of 1879. In Durham the scale

[1] *D.M.A. Records*, 1888.

allowed them but a beggarly 2½ per cent.[1] Even in the presence of the agents, and in the face of their formal resolutions that the sliding scale was still the most equitable method of wage settlement, the men spoke against its renewal. The agents were compelled to issue an amended ballot paper, and on the question of abolition or amendment a vote was taken which shewed a huge majority for abolition. In place of a petition for the renewal of the agreement the agents were ordered to make a demand for a general wage increase of 20 per cent.

The owners seemed prepared to bargain. They offered to make an immediate advance of 5 per cent., and to add to it a further 5 per cent. in the autumn. The men rejected the offer and a strike seemed to be impending. In September a conference met at New-castle. The owners offered an immediate advance of 10 per cent., to include the last 2½ per cent. which the sliding scale had granted. The agents accepted the offer, and by a majority of one the men gave their sanction to the bargain. At much the same time the Northumberland men asked for a 10 per cent. increase also. Their demand too was halved. Both counties were again equal in their advance above the basis wage of 1879.

The wage dispute begat its usual crop of local strikes. At Brancepeth the "putter hewer" system had been developed to an excessive degree. There was friction already over the right to a rent allowance

[1] *Durham Chronicle*, March, April, May, 1889. *D.M.A. Records*, March, April, May, June, 1889.

where no colliery house was available. A strike was called, and all the collieries of Straker and Love joined the strikers, as their old local federation had arranged. The grievances were removed, and the obnoxious system of infringement of the hewers' work abandoned. In August, at Littleburn, there was a strike over the dismissal of an official of the local lodge. So badly were the men in the wrong that Crawford felt compelled to apologise to the Coal Trade Association for the men's unwarranted action. The lodge seemed to have fallen under the control of a violent minority, whose drunken habits had increased the ever-present tendency to groundless absence. At last Patterson, at the time Crawford's chief assistant, persuaded the lodge to tender its apology and return to work. But one trouble was ended only to be succeeded by another. In October the men at Silksworth gave the first sign of discontent which was in the end to ripen into a serious dispute[1].

After long grumbling the men had at last formulated their demands. They presented to the owners a list of suggestions and a request for a wage advance of 15 per cent. One of the suggestions, that the wages of the boys were to be standardised, and a definite age fixed at which they should commence to hew, raised an issue of such importance that it could only be decided by a county agreement[2]. The owners were willing enough to discuss the wage advance, but they were firm in their refusal to grant it. Their inflexible

[1] *Durham Chronicle*, Oct. 11th, 1889.
[2] *D.M.A. Records*, Nov. 1st, 1889.

attitude was but fresh fuel to the discontent which made 1890 so troubled a year. Serious discord threatened at Silksworth. The recent failure of a scheme for restriction of output filled the whole county with jealous recrimination. To this turmoil was added the provocation of a general wage dispute, begun at a time when prices were rising, and the men plainly dissatisfied with their share of the trade prosperity.

Already, since the depression had ended, wages had risen 25 per cent. It was natural that the public should think with the owners that every further wage demand was exorbitant, and should be confirmed in its belief by the refusal of the men to submit their claim to enquiry. It became the turn of the coal trade to blame obstinate and selfish greed for the threatened trouble, and to throw on the men the responsibility for the "disastrous consequences" of a strike[1].

That the Durham coal-field was threatened with an outbreak of war was less due to an increase of grievance and discontent than to the growth of indiscipline in the union. For some months Crawford's health had been failing. In 1887 the union sent him to the south of France, but though he returned, apparently to work, he knew that he had not long to live. In March, 1890, within a week of the meeting of the executive committee to discuss the impending crisis, he died, at the early age of fifty-eight. He was a pitman, and the son of a pitman. In his boyhood

---

[1] *D.M.A. Records*, Owners' letter. Feb. 19th, 1890.

he worked both at Hartley and Cowpen, where he met with an accident which was the main cause of his later ill-health. In the enforced idleness of convalescence he gave himself an education rare among the pitmen of his youth. At the age of twenty-four he married. He was then a temperance speaker, a preacher in Ranter chapels, an advocate of educational, social, and political reform. After the secession of 1864 he was elected secretary of the Northumberland Miners' Association. A year later he handed over his duties to Burt, and went to a co-operative store at Blythe[1]. At one time he tried his fortune as a shopkeeper, but his business failed. In 1870 he was called to Durham to act as secretary to a union which was struggling into existence in the north-east of the county.

Within two years Crawford won for this union an unquestioned recognition from the owners. In 1872 he was sitting in conference with them to settle the wage claims of the men, and the system of yearly hirings, an almost insuperable obstacle to union progress, had been for ever abandoned. Quietly, for seventeen years, he worked, in the face of strikes and trade depressions, building up a fund, educating the men, winning for himself and for them a very general, but very grudgingly given, respect. He had neither the intellect nor the education of Burt, nor perhaps the diplomatic skill of his successor, Wilson. But he had a fiery energy, an instinctive recognition of the true course of action, an intuitive grasp of affairs,

[1] *Durham Chronicle*, July 4th, 1890.

which make him a more remarkable man than any
of the other trade union heroes of the north. His
economic ideas might be vague, and at times a little
contradictory. He was obsessed by a fear of over-
production, and by a partial recognition of the evil
effects of reckless trade competition. The doctrine
that restriction of output was the cure for most
economic evils seemed perpetually to interrupt the
lessons he was learning from the followers of John
Stuart Mill. Indeed, he was of an older generation
than the individualists of the late nineteenth century.
Burt might become almost a doctrinaire Radical,
might hold, as to an eternal truth, to the teachings
of mid-Victorian economics, but Crawford was more
influenced by the ideas of Lloyd Jones, ideas which
had their origin in the socialism of Owen, their development in the aspirations of the Christian Socialists,
their popularity from some of the pamphlet literature
of the later Chartists. In 1886 he was elected member
for Mid-Durham, a working-man member in the
Liberal interest, but he found himself less suited for
the position than most of his fellows. He voted
steadily in divisions. He sat, and gained credit, on
several committees, but he never made a speech in
the House. He was never an orator, though his
writings are full of a florid rhetoric, the relic of his
early Methodism.

When he died 2000 men followed him to the grave-
side, and almost every miner in Durham came to the
unveiling of the statue which now stands in front of their
Trade Union Hall. It is a sufficient, though needless,

reply to the gibes of the journalists of his early days, to remember that at his death Crawford left his widow barely sufficient to keep her from want. A grant from the union funds, supplemented by a generous donation from the owners, alone enabled her to maintain and educate her family, and the esteem in which Crawford was held, together with the confidence existing at that time between owners and men, is shewn by the fact that the trustee of the fund was the secretary of the owners' association.

Crawford's illness had been marked by a growing unrest in Durham. His death was the signal for a strike. Patterson, his successor in office, was a lesser man, possessed of none of Crawford's readiness to shoulder responsibility. He argued where Crawford had ordered: he consulted the men where the founder of the union would more wisely have presented them with an accomplished fact. He never rivalled Crawford's popularity, which, if less steady, had been greater even than that of Burt across the Tyne. The best tribute to the memory of the first secretary of the Durham Miners' Union is the fact that during the bitter strike of 1892 men joined in saying that, Crawford alive, the trouble would never have come.

CHAPTER XV

PATTERSON'S RULE

IN the early months of 1890 the number of local strikes was so excessive that the owners threatened to break off all relations with a body which shewed so little control over its members[1]. There were many reasons and more excuses for the unrest. The size of the pits had grown. There had been a general improvement in the method of work, and a still greater subdivision of labour. A new desire for efficiency seemed to have awakened interest in the host of small expenses which, taken together, made so large a proportion of working costs. The men's counter to the managerial campaign of economy was to demand an increased uniformity of hours throughout the county, and a more accurate definition of working customs. They wished to have the demarcation between putters and hewers made plain, and the system of promotion automatic. They asked for more holidays, and for some systematic payment for the long journey from the face to the shaft. But the main quarrel began on the introduction of a new practice by which the managers hoped to increase the output. Every hewer was expected to take an empty tub into his place when he went to work in the morning, for in the past there had often been delay

[1] *D.M.A. Records*, May 15th (letter from owners, May 3rd), 1890.

through the late arrival of the putters. But the men refused to put; the older ones, indeed, said that to move even an empty tub was beyond their powers.

Last of all there was a general desire for a new agreement on the old disputed question, the hours of coal-drawing. But discussion was interrupted by a sudden strike at Monk Wearmouth[1]. At first the strike received no encouragement from the union; its root cause was the very subject which the agents were debating with the owners. But the men chose to think that Monk Wearmouth was fighting for the common cause, and they authorised the grant of strike pay. In this deep, submarine colliery the distance from the shaft to the face was so great that the fore-shift refused to wait for the coming of their relief, and ceased work at a time agreed on in a lodge meeting. Their action, said the owners, "was a distinct departure from an old-established colliery custom, that of changing at the face"[2]. They refused to proceed further with the general discussion on hours until the Monk Wearmouth men returned to work. The Joint Committee ceased to sit. For the first time since 1872 there was a complete cessation of correspondence between the union and the owners. An agitated appeal from the agents warned the men that continued obstinacy would widen still further the breach and that the unity of purpose between owners and men, which it had been Crawford's life's work to create, would be entirely destroyed.

[1] *Durham Chronicle*, Oct. 3rd, 1890.
[2] *D.M.A. Records*, July 15th, 1890.

Patterson had already issued one circular, to ask the men for support in the original dispute about the length of the working day. It was shorter than the circulars Crawford used to write[1]. It made no attempt to influence the judgment of the men. Perhaps his attitude, that of the plain statement of a disputed case, was strictly in accordance with the rules and the democratic ideals of the union. Perhaps it was an agent's duty to ascertain, and later, to obey, the desires of the men. But in an association full of ill-informed, ignorant men it would have been a higher conception of duty to have followed Crawford's example, and to have striven to persuade the men to peace. Put simply the general question which was before the county was this. If a two-shift pit drew coal ten hours, must a three-shift pit "draw" fifteen, as the men said, or twenty, as the owners desired? The men decided to support their claim by a strike[2]. By good fortune they were at last persuaded that the misunderstanding was in part due to the mixing of too many demands in one. Though they refused to settle any question of hours while the strike at Wearmouth continued, the owners said they would be willing to separate the question of coal-drawing from that of the length of the hewer's shift. Several special councils of the union were assembled, proof positive that the agents lacked the firm decision of the late secretary, and in September a qualified agreement was reached on one point. Two-shift pits were

[1] *D.M.A. Records*, 1890.
[2] J. Wilson, *Hist. of D.M.A.* p. 217.

to "draw" ten hours[1]. Other outstanding disputes were to be settled by the Joint Committee.

An "urgency" committee had for some time been investigating the claims of the Monk Wearmouth hewers. It found that the difference between the owners' system and that devised by the men was one of but two minutes a day. The county ordered the strikers back to work. Soon further enquiry proved the justice of the owners' claim in the second matter and it was agreed that three-shift pits should be allowed to draw coal for twenty hours[2]. This dispute settled the men began to look for a fresh cause of quarrel. In October, 1890, they asked for a wage increase of 20 per cent., accompanying their demand by a plain hint that if the selling price did not allow of the increase the price could be raised[3]. In Northumberland the owners had made a small concession of 1¼ per cent.[4] The Durham owners offered their men 5 per cent., and without remark it was accepted[5]. Neither on hours, nor on wages, had the malcontents been able to arouse the county enthusiasm.

But trouble they were determined to cause. In November, 1890, a general meeting of the Miners' Federation of Great Britain had been called. As usual, the main item on the programme was a motion desiring the adoption of the minimum wage, and

[1] *Durham Chronicle*, Sept. 12th, 1890, and Aug. 8th, 22nd, Sept. 5th.　　[2] *D.M.A. Records*, Oct. 30th, Nov. 21st, 1890.

[3] *Durham Chronicle*, Oct. 17th, 1890.

[4] *Newcastle (Weekly) Chronicle*, June 21st, 1890.

[5] *Durham Chronicle*, Nov. 21st, 1890.

the eight-hour day. The Northumberland Miners' Association ignored the summons, saying that where there was so great a divergence of interest and opinion there could be no agreement. The Durham men were less logical in their attitude, but they too could have no sympathy with the proposals of the Midland miners. It was obvious that the demands of the Miners' Federation, persisted in, would provoke a general strike. It was equally obvious that the officials of the north-country unions were steadily opposed to the use of the strike as an offensive weapon. Yet within their unions there were many men of a less pacific turn of mind, and not a few ambitious men who hoped by agitation to climb to power, while the new doctrines of the more militant socialists found many adherents in the north. Internal strife was bound to come. It wanted only the occasion.

The trouble began at Silksworth. Before 1884 none of the deputies of this colliery had been members of the miners' union, but about that time the majority sought and obtained admission. The men professed to believe that the few who still remained outside their association enjoyed special favour, and that on appointment new deputies were made to forswear union for ever. In November, 1890, the hewers, saying that they would work no longer under black-leg deputies, struck[1]. The black-legs joined the union. On the face of it the action of the men was a distinct breach of the tacit agreement, which had existed since the deputies' arbitration in 1887, that neither

[1] *Durham Chronicle*, Nov. 21st, 1890, and for some months.

side should compel a deputy to choose between union
and isolation. They made defence that the manager
had long ago broken the compact, though in a less
open manner. He had given the black-leg deputies
more of the extra work, and necessarily of the extra
pay, which, however, it seemed that the lodge had
refused to allow its members to accept! That the
men had no very good case is doubly proved, first
by the fact that the union refused them strike pay,
next by the persistent refusal of the enginemen, all
through the strike, to cease work. They would cease
at once, said they, if the dispute was decided in the
men's favour by the Federation Board, the committee of the unions of all the trades in the collieries.
Had the miners been certain of the justice of their
case they could easily have obtained the support of
the Federation. As it was, they dared not submit it
to the judgment even of so partial a tribunal as a
body of fellow-unionists[1]!

Lord Londonderry, the owner of the colliery, was
ready to end the quarrel, but the owners' association
elected to treat the strike as a dispute about a matter
of principle[2]. Eviction notices were served, but the
evictions were delayed until the assembly of a special
council of the men's association. But the council was
swayed more by the threat to evict than by the
courtesy of the suspension of action. It decided to
reverse the policy of the agents, and to support the
strikers. It even made threats that if the evictions

---

[1] *D.M.A. Records*, Dec. 8th, 1890.
[2] *Ibid.* Feb. 10th, 1891.

were completed, a general county strike would begin. The owners were not to be turned from their purpose by such a threat. In February the first of the men were evicted from their homes. Lord Londonderry tried to enlist public sympathy by a statement of his unfortunate dilemma. He was willing to end the strike, but he was bound by his engagement to the owners' association. He did not wish to evict the men, but the houses in which they were living were not his own, they were hired from a contractor. He was actually paying rent for the "free" houses in which the strikers were living. A simple solution of such a problem would have been the offer of a guarantee by the strikers to pay the rent during the continuance of the strike. It would have been an additional burden on the funds of the union, but it would have delayed the evictions, the justice of which in the circumstances it is hard to deny. But if the policy of the union leaders was to make the best of the existing order of society, their reply was not in strict accord with their intentions. A strike has always had a habit of exposing root differences of theory, which are smoothed over in argued agreements. The reply was that as long as no other men were at hand to occupy the houses, and the strikers had no other hope of shelter, eviction would be resisted. A contrast was drawn between the situation of the two parties to the dispute, the outcast men, and the lord who sat, "in the noble halls of Wynyard, which the labour of our forefathers helped to build, and which our labour keeps going."

There were scenes of excitement at the evictions not surpassed since the days of the first union. The Salvation Army, which had absorbed the enthusiasm of men who a generation before had filled the Ranter pulpits, tried to entice the candymen away. The women strewed the furniture with pepper, their husbands barred the doors, and in the empty houses boxes, thickly coated with tar, were placed as formal furniture to be removed. Despite the presence of both of the miners' members, Johnson and Wilson, an attack was made on the houses of the black-leg deputies. The women exhorted the men to arm themselves with their pick-shafts. Showers of stones flew in all directions. It was said that more than one pistol shot was heard. At last the mob, admittedly composed for the most part of idlers from Sunderland, became so violent that the police were compelled to charge, and in the riot which followed some thirty persons were injured.

Towards the end of March, immediately before the commencement of a second series of evictions, negotiations were resumed. The council of the union ordered the men back to work. The owners promised to make no more attempts to influence deputies in their decision to join the union. They promised further to advise the deserters to pay the arrears of subscription which the union said had become due. They recorded their protest that their promise had been made out of a desire for peace. They had, they said, been guilty of none of the malpractice from which they were now required to abstain.

In his history of the Durham Miners' Association John Wilson, who did his utmost to maintain order during the evictions, claims that the men won a victory. It was a very insignificant one. No strike has produced a bigger crop of legal actions. Policemen were charged with assault and perjury, and sued for damages. The member of parliament for Sunderland brought an action against the police superintendent, who had taken him into custody during the riot. In reply, a partisan local bench committed him to prison, to await his trial for perjury. But one by one the charges were withdrawn for want of evidence, or dismissed as devoid of all foundation. Even the committal of the irate member of parliament was quashed by a court of appeal.

A strike at Hetton, where 2000 men lay idle over the refusal of the shifts to relieve each other at the face, was patched up in a manner hardly more satisfactory. At Esh the owners closed a pit in protest against a lodge attempt at restriction. Never before, as an angry union circular remarked, had there been so many unconstitutional strikes. In one day sixteen pits had been laid idle, and only one of them had troubled to inform the agents of its action[1]. Local lodges had devised a method of defeating the rule which deprived them of strike pay for informal hasty action. They struck, and at the conclusion of the dispute they obtained from the council a grant in relief of their urgent wants. Meantime the Joint Committee was overwhelmed with complaints that

[1] *D.M.A. Records*, March 6th, 1891.

the men were leaving work before the end of the shift, or were refusing to await the arrival of their relief.

The protest of the executive brought a small improvement. There was an end for a time of the causeless disputes. But it seemed that the men everywhere were anxious for a strike and in June the men of Murton found a good excuse[1]. A deputy who had worked for thirty years at the colliery, two-thirds of the time as an under-official, was dismissed. There had been an accident for which he was plainly to blame. Either he had removed timber, or, as was more likely, he had allowed some hewer to remove it and had failed to report him for his rashness. An accident revealed his fault. The manager said that he was dismissed for inability to perform his duties. The men replied, fairly enough, that after twenty-one years it was a little late to make discovery of inefficiency. In truth it seemed that the man's crime was that of being found out in a common enough omission. The manager pleaded that the inspector of mines would not sanction the further employment of the offender, except in work of less responsibility. He offered to find him employment, but he would not re-instate him as a deputy. The men emphatically refused the offer. The executive committee of the union refused to allow the Murton men strike pay. By a large majority the council reversed their decision. In August the owners' association again threatened to break off relations with the union, unless it made an immediate end of the strike. There was more than

[1] *Durham Chronicle*, June 26th, 1891.

one broad hint that the man's neglect of duty had been caused by his fear of lodge censure, or at any rate of personal unpopularity for a display of zeal in his duty. The executive fell back on their last defence. The trustees of the union funds refused to sanction the payment of strike allowance, saying that not even a council could authorise a breach of rule[1]. Legal opinion was on their side, and at last the men were persuaded that their attitude was entirely indefensible. They went back to work, and the dismissed deputy was found other, less responsible, duties.

In Northumberland, where £50 had for several years been the average expense of the union on labour disputes, £1000 was spent in this year on a single strike. The cause of the trouble was the vexed question of house rent. It has taken many years of dispute to decide which classes of men are entitled to the rent allowance, and the free house. This strike was to settle the justice of the claim of the unmarried man on whom a family depended for support to be treated as a householder. The owners contended that if he were given rent allowance it was by charity, not of compulsion. Meantime the question of the hours of coal-drawing was troubling the northern county as much as Durham. A ten-hour day had lately been secured for all boys under sixteen years of age. The agreement was found very difficult to enforce, for it seemed impossible to work a shift of ten hours in a pit which as a whole worked ten and a half or eleven

[1] *D.M.A. Records*, Sept. 1st, 1891.

hours. The only way to shorten the day of the boys seemed to be to reduce the hours of the pit. The owners seemed little inclined so to interfere with their output. Yet to save Burt's face, and to enable him to continue the opposition to the eight-hour day, it seemed necessary to take some step towards the promised improvement of the lot of the boys. Shorter hours they would eventually get by union action, said Burt. He was to find his promise almost impossible of fulfilment.

CHAPTER XVI

A STRIKE AND A NEW LEADER

THOUGH in the early months of 1891 the Durham men obtained a wage advance of $1\frac{1}{4}$ per cent., it was the last increase they were to receive under the terms of the sliding scale. Indeed, a trade depression soon began, which threatened to rob them of all their recent gains. In April the owners asked for a reduction of $3\frac{3}{4}$ per cent.[1] They warned the men that further reduction could not long be resisted, for the price of both coke and coal was plainly about to decline. But the men refused the request. They were misled by a sudden return of prosperity to Northumberland, whose export trade had been revived by a strike in the French collieries. They forgot that they themselves were dependent on home prosperity, and at a conference in July they again refused the owners' demand. Indeed, they were so little convinced of the truth of the repeated warnings of a depression that they asked for a wage increase. As a result the owners withdrew their demands, and proceeded to prepare an exhaustive estimate of the prices at which it was likely that their future contracts would be made. It was a hint of their intentions to submit their claim to arbitration[2].

In November they made a definite demand for a

[1] *D.M.A. Records*, Owners' letter, April 25th, 1891.
[2] *Ibid.* July 7th, 1891, Owners' resolution.

wage reduction of 10 per cent.[1] It was supported by a well-reasoned account of the condition of the coal trade. At the beginning of the year, said the owners, they had made concessions amounting in all to 5 per cent. on the basis wage. They had been encouraged in their action by a hope of a further rise in the price, but their hope had been so far unfounded that in the end the movement of prices would rather have been warrant for a wage reduction than for an advance. Put simply their argument was that as the price of coal stood but $23\frac{3}{4}$ per cent. above that of 1879, the year generally taken as the norm, and as wages were some 35 per cent. above that standard, the time had come for a reduction. The men were slow in making reply. At a second meeting, in January, 1892, the owners again stated their terms. The miners could choose one of three courses. They could accept an immediate reduction of 10 per cent. They could submit the claim to arbitration. They could make a plain statement of the amount of the reduction they deemed adequate[2]. By an overwhelming majority the men declared that not one of the courses was acceptable.

In the second week of February the owners gave notice that further delay was impossible. The men's reply left them no option but to give the customary fourteen days' warning of their intention to terminate the contracts of service. They made one concession. The issue of the notice was postponed for twelve days,

[1] *D.M.A. Records*, Nov. 27th, 1891, Conference.
[2] *Ibid.* Jan. 14th, 1892, Conference. Owners' demands.

in the hope that some settlement could be devised "which would avoid the severe loss...not only to the miners themselves...but to the large...population depending on the Coal Trade"[1].

Negotiations, hastened in their progress by the threat of impending strike, brought a slight alteration in the owners' demands. They declared themselves willing to accept an immediate, though not final, reduction of $7\frac{1}{2}$ per cent., or an immediate reduction of 5 per cent., to be followed by a further reduction of 5 per cent. some two months later[2]. The men proceeded to take a ballot to make their choice between the two offers but the owners refused to suspend the issue of the notices. They acknowledged the warning of the taking of the ballot by a polite expression of hope that it would result in a decision favourable to peace[3]. On the eve of the issue of the notices the Federation Board,—the executive committee of the alliance of the unions of cokemen, mechanics, enginemen, and miners,—asked that every member of the four unions should be served with a warning. The owners would not listen to the request. They wished those men to be kept at work whose services "were considered necessary for the purpose

[1] *D.M.A. Records*, Feb. 15th, 1892, Owners' formal warning of notice.

[2] *Ibid.* Feb. 20th, 1892, Owners' final terms.

[3] *Ibid.* Feb. 25th, 1892, Acknowledgment of taking of ballot:

Feb. Ballot		Second Ballot	
Accept 10 %	605	Accept $7\frac{1}{2}$%	926
Arbitrate	2,050	Accept 5% and 5%	1,153
Negotiate	7,102	Negotiate	12,956
Strike	41,887	Strike	40,468

of maintaining the mines in a condition of safety, by drainage and ventilation." In the notice which they issued neither deputies nor enginemen were included.

By a majority slightly smaller than that of the month before the men refused the amended offer. Their attitude was simple. They would submit to no reduction. Meantime both the deputies and the enginemen who were members of the Durham Federation gave in their notices, and on March 12th, 1892, all work in the Durham collieries ceased.

It is difficult to question the correctness of the owners' attitude, and the men wisely made no reply to the explanation of the causes of the strike which their opponents at once issued. It was a careful and very reserved statement of matters of fact. In December 1890, coal prices had reached their maximum. Since then, by mistake, an advance of 5 per cent. had been made in the wage, accompanied by a slight reduction of hours. Meantime the price of coal had so far fallen that a wage reduction was unavoidable, yet

the men employed at the collieries in the county of Durham have refused all the proposals made by the employers...they have declined to authorise their own representatives to negotiate...they have refused to submit the question to arbitration....A great industry has been paralysed, and untold sufferings are being inflicted not only upon the families of the men themselves, but also upon the vast industries of the North of England.

...the foregoing statement will prove that the employers have used every endeavour in their power to avert this catastrophe...that they have shewn every willingness to treat with the men and to prove to them the justification of the demands...and finally that they have shewn great patience in the way they have preferred their claims[1].

There is no doubt that the officials of the union were not anxious to carry the dispute to a conclusion, though in a circular they admitted that "no class of men were overpaid for their work,...and that relief should come from other sources than the work-men's pockets." They advised the men to give them full power to negotiate. "No trades union," said they, "however powerful, however strong, can resist a reduction in a falling market when the fall is clearly proved"[2]. Their persuasions were of no avail. Two or three years' indiscipline had sapped the founda-tions of the agents' authority. As yet no new leader had risen, to dragoon the men in the manner of Crawford. Patterson's policy of submission to the general will made certain that the strike would con-tinue. If the hewers had lost their faith in their old remedy of restriction, they had abandoned it for another as fallacious. Their united strength was to force upon the owners a wage which was to be an essential element in the cost of production, which indeed was to govern the selling price. However little the strikers may have understood it, they were making a claim for a living wage.

[1] Owners' public letter, March 14th, 1892 (issued to the Press).
[2] *D.M.A. Records*, March 21st, 1892.

They were to find that they had made one mistake, even if they were right in their economic doctrine. They had anticipated a speedy triumph, else they would not have withdrawn the enginemen. Perhaps for the moment the men had lost sight of everything in their desire to make the strike as costly as possible for the owners. Months later there was no man who was not aware how far the foolish completeness of the strike had resulted in his own loss. As the water rose in the workings and the timbers of the roads began to decay for want of repair it became plain that every day of delay condemned hundreds of hewers to prolonged idleness until such time as the destruction could be made good.

A month passed quietly. Then, in a further letter to the newspapers, the owners stated their case again. They had been compelled to make an unusually definite demand by the temporising policy of the men. They had issued the notices in the hope that decided action would persuade the men to "recognise the necessity of the position, and come to terms." Between the month of June, 1889, and that of September, 1890, the pit-head price of coal had risen from 4s. 10·47d. a ton to 7s. 5·62d. In that time, as a result of peaceful agreement, wages had advanced 30 per cent. Since then the price of coal had fallen 1s. 2·31d. a ton. If then the owners had consented to bargain, and to increase the wage, now it had become the duty of the men to submit to a reduction. It might be

true that the men now repudiate the principle that wage should be governed by the selling price of coal, but it must be observed that they claimed and obtained advances on the ground of advances of price, and the owners apply the same reasoning to a falling market[1].

This second letter, which concluded with a regret that "circumstances point to a deepening depression of trade, rather than to any speedy improvement," was again little more than a simple statement of fact. If it gave plain warning that "on the resumption of work it will be impossible to employ all the persons who were previously engaged," the reason was simply the increasing unfitness of the mines. The charge was true that the men had carried their refusal to work to a foolish extremity of petty stupidity. They refused the owners' suggestion to allow coal to be hewed in small quantities for the sick, or for fuel for the engines which pumped up the household water supplies. Such men as dared to work —and they worked with no thought of production, merely of mine maintenance—were followed to the pits by crowds of hooting women. In several places, notably at Castle Eden, the demonstration ended in assaults. It almost seemed that it was lack of opportunity which accounted for the general absence of violence. There were few victims on whom the strikers could vent their spite. The temper of the men is shewn by the savage ferocity of the attacks on the reporters of the *Newcastle (Weekly) Chronicle*. In this strike, for the first time, the men's old champion was against them. It had tried to persuade them to peace. It had warned them that "if they succeeded in a

[1] Owners' second public letter, April 25th, 1892.

strike, with both a falling market and public opinion against them, they would do what no union had ever before succeeded in doing "[1]. It had condemned the folly of the withdrawal of the enginemen, and the lack of fairness and reason in the repeated refusal of every invitation to bargain. Perhaps its greatest crime was its boldness in comparing Crawford's independence with the timidity of his successors, who feared to oppose the men even in their better interests.

The men this time made reply, but their case was too poor to deserve respect, much less to carry conviction. "We agreed to work, and to withdraw the claim and counter claim," said the letter, "in order to keep the good feeling existing between the two associations." In some matters it was neither strictly accurate nor fair. To charge the owners with provoking rebellion by issuing notices during the taking of a ballot was foolish, for the negotiations had spread over ten months, and had been definite and continuous for three. The crux of the dispute was the statement that it was

not true that the men repudiate the principle that wages should be governed by the selling price of coal, but they do claim to have some voice as to what that price should be, and their wage should not be subject to the caprice of contractors and speculators.

We say that the public generally, and those who know the laborious toil of the miner...will not object to paying a price for coal sufficient to maintain wages at their present point[2].

[1] *Newcastle (Weekly) Chronicle*, April, 1892.
[2] Men's public letter, in reply, April 7th, 1892.

In other words the men were striking to maintain their existing wage, whatever the state of trade might be. They were resolved on upholding their recent standard of life, as the minimum which they could endure. One assertion was made which supported their claim; that if by the last agreement the wage should fall, under an older one the price of coal would have justified a wage almost at its recent level. But the arguments used by the men were in truth trifling. The strike was a definite attempt to resist a fall in the wage. It took little count of the state of trade, or the precedent of old agreement. Its solution was not to be persuasion, but force. Already it had lasted long enough to discredit the men's estimate of the endurance of the owners, and of their own fighting strength. They began to think of agreement.

On April 25th the Federation Board met the owners again, and the strike entered on its second and final stage. Public sympathy began to pass from the owners' side to that of the plainly defeated men. For the terms on which the owners were prepared to re-open the pits included a demand that the men should submit to a gross wage-reduction of 10 per cent. The original demand had been for a reduction of 10 per cent., calculated on the standard wage. The new demand, put in a form which the men could most easily understand, was for a reduction of $13\frac{1}{2}$ per cent. In addition it was proposed that a joint wage board, empowered to decide all future alterations, should take the place of the sliding scale[1].

[1] April 25th, 1892, Conference. Owners' resolutions.

The agents of the union had gone to the meeting with no power of negotiation. Indeed, their only authority for attendance was that lack of interest in the weekly ballot caused the majority for further war to sink below the necessary "two-thirds of the total membership of the union[1]." They came away enraged.

We consider that your representatives were deliberately insulted by the owners, who told them that Trade Union representatives should be influential men, and not message carriers, and that they were not prepared to give way one iota.

So ran the formal report of their failure[2]. But one of the agents, at any rate, had been convinced of the truth of the owners' gibe. He hastened to gain the influence which would be necessary, in any future negotiations.

John Wilson was at this time fifty-five years of age. The son of a tramping quarryman, he had been left at his father's death in the care of a pious and respectable uncle, who put the boy to every trade he could discover in a vain attempt to keep him out of the pits. For until that time the dead quarryman alone had disgraced the family by manual labour. But the lad, who at the age of eleven could earn in a fortnight 30s. as a pony putter, was not to be kept sweeping the floor and cleaning the windows of a small general shop. He ran away from home, and after working for several years, mostly at Sherburn Hill, he was at the age of 16½ allowed to begin to

[1] *D.M.A. Records.* Circular. Ballot, March 16th, 1892: strike, 43,056; negotiate, 11,856.
[2] *Ibid.* Circular, April 1892.

hew. It was the manager's wise provision for removing
an evil influence from among the putters, whom once
already he had persuaded to strike. Though he had
already engaged himself to be married, in 1856, at
the age of nineteen, he went to sea, first on a coaster,
then on an East Indiaman. Four years later, his
health undermined by a fever caught in the Red Sea,
he returned to the pits, married, and settled at
Haswell. He was one of the pioneers in an attempt
to found a lodge of the union, and it was perhaps
to escape unpleasant notoriety as an agitator that
in 1862 he emigrated to America. But mining in the
United States was no better paid than it was in
Durham, and the principles of union were in even
greater disfavour. In 1869 he was back in Haswell,
his old, drunken, violent habits cast aside, a Methodist
convert, and a promising local preacher. At the age
of thirty-one he undertook his own education, in a
manner strangely reminiscent of Cobbett, for he carried a small English Grammar into the pit, studied
it by the light of his lamp, and committed whole
pages to memory. A second, and this time successful,
attempt to form a lodge at Haswell lost him his employment. He was made secretary of the local co-
operative store, but he elected to leave, to rid his
neighbours of his undesirable presence. For he was
becoming well known as an agitator, association with
whom was apt to end in loss of employment. He
went to Wheatley Hill, and there tried his fortune
as a stationer. Soon he was back at his old task of
union. From organising a local lodge he passed to

assisting at parliamentary elections, and from 1875 to 1885 he was the secretary of the Durham County Franchise Association. In 1875, too, he at last consented to become a minor official of the Durham Miners' Association, and since that time he had been rapidly rising in the councils of the union[1]. A member for parliament, he went in 1887 to America, on a deputation to celebrate the signing of a treaty of arbitration. There he laid the foundations of his reputation as an orator. He was to use his gift of speech to win his way to the position which since Crawford's death no one had aspired to fill.

In a speech delivered to a mass meeting in May 1892 John Wilson told the men of the owners' offer, and of his own desperate resolution. "Rather than accept it, I will die in the gutter"; they were strong words from a respectable member of parliament, but there was every prospect that the men would do what their leader threatened. For on the funds of the union, none too high at the commencement of the strike, 64,000 men had been supported for nearly ten weeks. Not since 1879 had the Durham men, themselves always ready to give, been compelled to beg. But with a strike pay which with difficulty reached 3s. a week[2] it was necessary to issue an appeal for help[3]. It was an appeal certain of a good response. The miners were fighting for the principle that as work-

[1] J. Wilson, *Durham Chronicle*, 1909. Autobiography (weekly instalments).

[2] *D.M.A. Records*, May 28th, 1892.

[3] *Ibid*. Circular, March 31st, Appeal to United Kingdom; June 8th, Appeal to Trades Unions.

men they should have a voice in the disposal of the goods they produced. They were making their protest against the bartering away of wages by the speculations of middlemen. The Miners' Federation of Great Britain, forgetting for a time the quarrel over the eight-hour day, sent in all £33,300, though with it came a hint that but for the stupid self-sufficiency of the Durham men the strike might have been a national one. The Northumberland men, who had themselves consented to a reduction of 5 per cent., voted a levy of 1s. a man each fortnight, and hastened to get it back in a wage advance. From every lodge came resolutions, asking for wage demands which ranged from 10 to 25 per cent. The owners pleaded that the high market price was but an accompaniment of the strike, a temporary and misleading phenomenon. Burt issued a circular which restored his men to their senses.

Had we not felt bound, out of respect to the strong representations of so many collieries...we should have thought the present a most inopportune time to apply for an advance....Our best policy is to do what we can do to conserve our trade...to work so far as we can to secure the advantage...rather than to make demands for which no substantial reason can be assigned[1].

It would have been well for the Durham men if they had been dealt with so faithfully. They had spent their savings. They had drawn their dividends from the stores. They had sold their shares. Their children were dependent on charity, compelled to look to soup kitchens for their food. The extent of

[1] *Newcastle (Weekly) Chronicle*, April 1892. Burt's Circular.

the general poverty is shewn by the wild rumours
which were spread in the north that the miners were
cooking and eating their dogs. But they were not
yet disposed to treat as beaten men. On May 13th
they offered to accept a reduction of $7\frac{1}{2}$ per cent.,
and to consent to the formation of a wages board[1].
The owners refused. They would be content with
nothing less than $13\frac{1}{2}$ per cent.[2] Prices had fallen so
low that 15 per cent. would have been a more just
demand, "and having regard to the deepening depression of trade...any higher rate of wages...would
lead to serious diminution of the amount of employment." Next week the men offered to submit to the
original demand, for a net reduction of 10 per cent.[3]
Again their offer was refused. They asked for arbitration. That too was refused, on the good grounds of
the men's attitude in the early days of the strike.
To check the rapid transference of public sympathy
to the strikers, on May 26th the owners felt it ex-
pedient to issue a third general letter, in explanation
of their unrelenting attitude.

Their demand, said they,

had been raised, not as a punishment to the men for the
cost of the strike, but because of a further fall in the
selling price of coal. The reduction was not big, taking
into account the allowance of house and coal. The wage
was still $21\frac{1}{2}$ per cent. above that of 1879, yet trade
prospects were worse. At the end of three months a
court could be called to justify the continuance of the
reduction[4].

[1] *D.M.A. Records*, May 14th, 1892, offer of $7\frac{1}{2}$ per cent.
[2] *Ibid*. May 23rd, 1892.
[3] *Ibid*. May 21st, 1892, offer of 10 per cent.
[4] Owners' third public letter, May 26th, 1892.

But the refusal to negotiate, coming after twenty years of formal bargaining, was the weak point in the owners' attitude. It, too, could be defended. It was fair tactics to tell the men that after a ten weeks' strike, in which they "had determined to resist all reduction, even to the drowning of pits," their claim to arbitration had very small foundation. But it was an innovation, as great as that contemplated by the men, to say "that the owners can alone accept the responsibility of determining the rate of wages at which they can offer employment to their men." There was no doubt that the rhetoric of which the men made use in default of better reply was in part justified[1]. The owners were desirous of pushing their victory to a conclusion.

It was at this point that Bishop Westcott, who from the day of his entry into his diocese had shewn a deep interest in the affairs of his flock, took the step which ended the strike. The men in the progressive lodges of the north-east were calling for revolutionary action, and were casting out hints of a design to seize the pits, re-start the machinery, and work the coal for themselves. The bishop, in a letter which told both sides of their agreement on two points, the need for a wage reduction, and of a wage board to settle future disputes, invited owners and men alike to Auckland Castle to make a final attempt at agreement. Ten per cent. was the reduction he thought suitable as a starting-point for discussion. But it was the thought of a wages board which excited his hopes.

[1] Men's second public letter, May 28th, 1892.

Such a board would, I feel confident, call out and deepen by frank conference that feeling of trust and sympathy between master and men through which alone stable concord can be maintained in the face of apparent (though not real) conflict of material interest[1].

It is one of the rare occasions in which a churchman of modern times has meddled with success in the worldly fortunes of his flock. There was a little murmuring from the men at this uncalled for interference from a great royalty owner. The wealth of the Ecclesiastical Commissioners had long been a sore point in Durham among the Methodist pitmen. The bishop's misapprehension, that the wages board had been proposed as a settlement of this dispute, was corrected by a letter from the men, a letter which anticipated the owners' claim to be making a one-sided sacrifice by pointing out that the men too were making a concession, a wage concession of 10 per cent.[2] But the offer of mediation was willingly accepted, and the conference, at which the bishop sat as chairman, made an end of the strike. "Solely on the grounds of the...prevailing distress"[3] the owners consented to re-open the pits, at a wage reduction of 10 per cent. Their consent was given with the full expectation that in the future wage claims would be referred to a body, in some way like the bishop's suggested conciliation board.

Not all the men could be re-engaged. They paid dearly for their folly in withdrawing the enginemen.

[1] *D.M.A. Records*, Bishop Westcott's letter to owners and men, May 25th, 1892.

[2] *Ibid*. May 26th, 1892, men's reply to Bishop Westcott.

[3] *Ibid*. June 1st, 1892, owners' resolution of acceptance

Many of the pits had fallen into disrepair and for a time 20,000 men lay idle, waiting for the reclamation of the flooded seams. The old system of the lot decided which men should be re-engaged. Not more than one hewer in each family was allowed to accept his "cavil"[1]. It was some weeks before the men had recovered from their bodily weakness so far as to be able to do a full day's work. In the three months the strike had lasted they had been paid little more than 25s. a head. Their savings were spent. Many of them by accepting poor relief had lost their parliamentary vote. The funds were exhausted. As Wilson, who mourned the destruction of the union strength, wrote some years later "the gain would have been the greater by the avoidance of the struggle," and the men were convinced of the truth of his remark. They had entered the struggle, if not by their own provocation, by their own desire. They had expected a speedy compromise, even if they were not thoroughly convinced of the certainty of victory. As one by one the offers of the broken men were rejected by the owners, they called to memory the last county strike, and their hopes revived at the thought that there might again be division in the ranks of their opponents. There was one gain from the strike, it had discovered for the men a new leader. Soon ill-health gave Patterson excuse to rid himself of a task which was beyond his somewhat pedestrian abilities. Insensibly the control of the union passed into the hands of John Wilson.

[1] *D.M.A. Records*, June 3rd, 1892, owners' scheme for re-employment.

CHAPTER XVII

NATIONAL UNITY

FOR the next fifteen years Durham and North-umberland were to be ruled by two men, who compelled the obedience of their followers rather by the strength of their personality than by the plausi-bility of their economic creed. Burt, deserving of loyalty from the union which he had created, was essentially a man of practical mind. For years he had been expounding to the north the folly of thinking restriction of output a short cut to pros-perity. He was little troubled by theoretic doubts of the utility of the capitalist, though perhaps ex-perience had discovered to him the function of capital in industry. He thought it better to make the best of an existing system, and to attain such prosperity as a peace assured by goodwill could pro-duce, than to court the ruin which might follow from undue insistence on labour's rights. Wilson, who had less claim to the grateful loyalty of his followers, made up for its lack by sheer force of character. He too was convinced of the value of industrial peace. His imagination had been captured by Bishop Westcott's picture of a permanent accord between capital and labour. In the weekly gatherings in Auckland Palace, at which the bishop collected all the great men of the north, he learned to know many of the coal-owners, and in peaceful argument to thrash out the problems of society. Wages, as he was always willing to admit, were at times not as high as could be wished. It was to be deplored that competition in the markets brought violent fluctuation in prices and that the unequal balance of supply and demand condemned the miners to periodic poverty and unemployment. But life had taught him that man could make poor pretence to infallibility. He could not bring himself to believe that by sudden human effort all human misfortune could be removed. He preferred the stable earth of a prosperity which he understood to the chance of heaven promised by the prophets of the I.L.P. "If ideals were as easily attained as pointed to, and declaimed on, we should not long be outside the golden gates of millennium." It was a gibe, and a telling one, at the oratory of Tom Mann[1].

The miner might still labour under a hard lot, but Wilson could remember little but steady improvement. Morals, manners, education, comfort, all that went to human happiness, had attained a standard which would have seemed a wild dream to the prophets of his youth, and Wilson had the courage to tell the men that opportunity for improvement was greater than was the improvement itself. Was the certainty of progress to be exchanged for the promise of perfection, and that by a people so little ready to help themselves? It was with pardonable pride that he saw in himself a model of what every young miner might become. Even in the name of democracy there was little fault to be found with a

[1] *D.M.A. Records*, July, 1903.

system under which a poor boy, whose infancy had been divided between the workhouse, the road, and the navvy's hut, whose youth had been wasted in sinful folly, could rise to the fame, power, and dignity which he enjoyed,—could become an honorary doctor of Durham University, a magistrate, the Chairman of the County Council, the secretary of the strongest trade society in the kingdom. And he was not alone in his success. Across the county border was Burt, whose achievements were no less striking, who indeed had risen to the rank of Right Honourable, as a minor member of Her Majesty's government.

Armed with the hewers' fear of the Eight Hour Act these two men fought successfully against the extremists of the Miners' Federation. The theory that wages should govern prices, and that a minimum wage should assure for every man a standard of life sufficiently comfortable, had long ago captivated the imagination of the north. It was a folly of the past, this theory, which, said they, had found practical expression in the limited sliding scales long ago found unworkable. The policy of persistent aggression, of readiness to strike on any pretext, of action at the command of a bare majority, obtained in a moment of unwise excitement, had been the policy of the patriarchs of the past, in particular of Jude, on the wrecks of whose union Crawford and Burt had built. Thus the lesson began, and in a tone of patronising contempt for the deluded struggles of ill-informed youth it continued.

The miners of the north, if they chose to enter a

society blind to the lessons of the past, reckless of the prosperity of the future, could abandon all hope of peace. Without quarrel with their owners they would be swept into strike after strike, at the dictation of the unstable men of Wales. It was foolish for the pitmen to imperil their prosperity, and the existence of the unions which it had been so great a task to establish, on behalf of the men of the Midlands, who appealed for help, but would not perfect their own local organisations, and gain the victory they desired by their own exertions. It seemed unfair that every treasured possession of the north should be abandoned, the short hewers' shift, the arbitration boards, the whole machinery of wage adjustment and agreement which increased the mutual respect of master and man, because the colliers of the south, men less educated, men less skilful, of weaker moral fibre, had at last partially united, and had given their allegiance to an unsound economic theory, a theory apparently new and untried, but not so new as its advocates claimed, for it had already been rejected by the wisdom of the north.

The first task which confronted Wilson, still while Patterson remained in name but the second man in the union, was to clear away the wreckage of the strike. In December 1892 the Joint Committee, that permanent court, half of owners, half of men, before which almost every local grievance was eventually debated, was again in session, under new rules which departed little from those of the past. It began its new life with no long list of insoluble, ever-recurring,

quarrels, for all standing disputes were declared to
have been ended by the strike. But on the reconstitu-
tion of this court Wilson was reminded of an obstacle
which stood in the way of all peaceful agreement.
Partly out of gratitude for generous assistance, partly
in disappointment at their own defeat, in June the
Durham men had elected to join the Miners' Federation of Great Britain. In December Wilson issued an
appeal for direction. A recent ballot had disclosed
a two to one majority against legal action to secure
an eight-hour day. The Joint Committee was illegal
under the rules of the Miners' Federation. It was
impossible at once to fight and to agree, impossible
to serve two masters, or to halt longer between two
opinions. Was he to assume that the men of Durham
wished to withdraw from the Miners' Federation,
or was he to tell the owners that all attempts at
conciliation must be abandoned?[1]

Unfortunately, at the moment which Wilson judged
so opportune for withdrawal from an impossible alliance, fortune dealt him a severe blow. In October
the Northumberland miners had quietly submitted
to a wage-reduction of 5 per cent. In February, by
a large majority, they refused to submit further.
Argument convinced them of the weakness of their
position, and a second ballot shewed too small a
majority for a strike. The agents succeeded in reducing
the owners' demands from $7\frac{1}{2}$ to 5 per cent., and the
reduction was made[2]. The revelation of their im-

---

[1] *D.M.A. Records*, Dec. 7th, 1892.
[2] *Newcastle (Weekly) Chronicle*, Feb. 1893.

potence convinced the Northumberland men that they could no longer remain in isolation. They ordered their agents to join the Miners' Federation[1]. There had been a similar wage negotiation in Durham, as the outcome of which wages had fallen 5 per cent. So far had Wilson prevailed that the conduct of the bargain had been left to the Durham agents alone, though membership of the Miners' Federation imposed on them the duty of referring the matter to national decision. As in Northumberland, so in Durham, the increase of the depression, and of its resulting evil, unemployment and want, revived the popularity of the Miners' Federation.

In July a national conference, destined to become famous in trade union history as the "Hen and Chickens" conference, was held at Birmingham. The grand design was to impose upon the coal-fields a uniform wage, and to obtain it, if need be, by a "general stop," a strike which was meant rather to influence prices than to win the advance directly. At this conference the difference in policy between the northern unions, and the more constant members of the Federation, became plainly apparent. Discord ripened into personal quarrel. In August a second conference was called at the Palace Hotel, Westminster. Burt would not go where his presence was unwelcome, and on his persuasion Northumberland failed to send a representative. The Durham men took their seats, only to be expelled at the opening of business. For they could not pronounce the

[1] *Newcastle (Weekly) Chronicle*, July 1893.

shibboleth. They would neither promise to strike, nor to support the Eight Hour Act[1].

When the Miners' Federation proclaimed a strike Northumberland refused to support it even by imposing a levy. Durham, grateful for past favours, collected 6*d*. a fortnight from each of its members, but it refused to join in the stoppage, though the ballot of the county had surprised the agents by the size of the vote for war[2]. Not until 1907 was national unity among the miners to be regained, though more than once the quarrel seemed about to be forgotten in the mutual sympathy of strikes, or in the dissatisfaction of depression and wage decrease. In October mass meetings declared their approval of the action of the agents. A vote of confidence took the place in Durham of the proposal to discharge the whole executive. The triumph of Burt and Wilson was complete[3].

At once in Northumberland negotiations began, which promised to lead to the formation of a conciliation board similar to the one the bishop had suggested for Durham. A wage increase of 5 per cent., accompanied by one of $7\frac{1}{2}$ per cent. south of the Tyne, assured for the proposals a favourable reception[4]. The bishop continued his efforts. He hoped that his conciliation board would be more than a mere machine

[1] J. Wilson, *Hist. of the Durham Miners' Assoc.* p. 260.
[2] *Durham Chronicle*, Sept. 1st, 1893. Ballot:

Work	19,704
Strike	20,782

[3] *Durham Chronicle*, Sept. 29th, Oct. 6th, 1893.
[4] *Newcastle (Weekly) Chronicle*, Dec. 11th, 1893.

for recording wage change, that in the end it would promote a positive unity. The close accord of owners and men had a strange result, one almost laughable in the face of the union agents' respect for competitive industry. There was a last attempt by the owners to revive the old sales association, and to steady by mutual action the fluctuations in coal prices[1]. A year later it failed, as it was bound to fail where there was no stronger bond than mutual goodwill to restrain capitalist cupidity. But for a time the Durham Miners' Association was solemnly attempting to define what should be its attitude to black-leg employers, colliery proprietors who refused to share in the good work of market regulation. In July, with wages falling—the Northumberland men had lost their recent advance—the discontented minority again thrust itself to the fore. A strike had begun in Scotland, and to support it a close alliance with the Miners' Federation was suggested. In Northumberland, where Burt was less antagonistic to the minimum wage than was Wilson, a definite ballot was taken on the proposal. But the men refused to pay the price of admission, the promise of support to the Eight Hour Act. In Durham the formal assembly of the conciliation board was taken as answer sufficient to the demand. Eighteen owners sat on one side, eighteen men on the other—nine miners, three cokemen, three mechanics, and three enginemen[2].

---

[1] *Durham Chronicle*, Feb 9th, 23rd, 1894.
[2] *D.M.A. Records*, May 14th, 1895. *Durham Chronicle*, Oct. 5th, 1894.

But there was still an obstacle in the way of complete accord in Northumberland. There the negotiations for a board had broken down over the owners' refusal to suffer the appointment of an independent chairman.

Meantime smaller matters took their share of the popular interest. The foundations were laid for the Burt Hall, the headquarters of the Northumberland Miners' Association, a council chamber and a block of offices, which stands in a quiet street near the centre of Newcastle. Proposals began to be heard of the building of homes for aged miners, cottages to which in their old age they could retire, and more and more the miners turned their attention to local politics. To have some voice in the appointment of Justices of the Peace became one of the admitted objects of the County Political Associations, those bodies which had been founded in the campaign for the parliamentary vote. And the first signs of a new movement could be seen, a movement which by steady persistence was in the end to overthrow both Burt and Wilson. Here and there, mostly in the bigger colliery villages and in the districts along the banks of the Tyne, branches of the I.L.P. began to develop a strength which attracted to them the suspicious notice of the newspapers.

1895 told a sad story of unemployment, wage decrease, and depression. Except for a strike at Hutton Henry it was without incident[1]. The quiet perhaps meant that the ambitions of the local leaders

[1] *Durham Chronicle*, March 1st, 1895.

were gratified, their activities consumed, by their election to the new parish councils. In Durham, of the 615 members elected, 370, as a union circular triumphantly records, were working men. Twice the Durham Conciliation Board authorised a wage reduction, in April, of $7\frac{1}{2}$ per cent., in October, of $2\frac{1}{2}$ per cent. As a slight sop to the men it authorised the increase of the basis wage by 7 per cent., a change long overdue, for the basis had remained unaltered since 1879[1]. Its deliberations were shrouded in the most profound mystery, its decisions ushered in with careful explanation, designed to diminish the condemnation with which they were certain to be overwhelmed. But the explanations could not conceal the damning fact that conciliation was but a new name for wage reduction. Nor, as time wore on, could the suspicion be allayed that conciliation was but a device for maintaining the hated sliding scale. For, in an almost blatant arithmetic proportion, wages followed prices in their irregular, but mainly downward, movement. In June, there was a majority in Northumberland against the renewal of conciliation, but not the two-thirds majority required by the union rules for a change. South of the Tyne, where by November 1400 men were idle, and steady employment had become little more than a pleasant memory, the murmurs of the disaffected were heard again. It seemed almost as if no system of wage settlement could survive a trade depression. Arbitration and sliding scale alike had lost their appeal when they

[1] *Durham Chronicle*, Oct. 25th, 1895.

failed in turn to check a steady wage decrease. The men did not see that even strikes had failed, when begun on a falling market. To still the murmurs Wilson issued a despairing circular. If the men would not strike, would not have the board, had lost their faith in arbitration, and in sliding scales, what system would it please them to suggest? He would welcome their solution of a difficulty with which he himself could not cope[1].

His vehemence failed to quell the uproar. The new year brought neither improvement nor hope of improvement. The men, thoroughly dissatisfied, took little interest in a ballot held to discover to the agents the extent of the opposition to the board. A majority ordered its abolition, but so small was the total vote that Wilson refused to consider it decisive[2]. In May the result of a second vote made plain that the men would no longer submit to this new system of wage settlement. It had, said they, failed to give satisfaction in three material points: in the matter of the rent-allowance, of the re-engagement of "sacrificed men," men discharged for union activity, and of the wage of the "under-average" men, the sick, the weak, and the old who could not hew coal as fast as their neighbours. In reality the cause of the dissatis-

---

[1] *Durham Chronicle*, Dec. 27th, 1895. *D.M.A. Records*, Dec. 19th, 1895.

[2] *D.M.A. Records*, Jan. 15th, 1896:

	Jan.	Feb.
For Board	11,974	14,894
Against	29,064	30,586
Neutral	17,000	20,000

faction was the failure of the board to prevent wage reduction. In June Northumberland too voted for the abolition of the board they had finally set up[1], though in Durham the men were already a little regretting their precipitate action. During the taking of their second ballot the pits at Rainton, one of Lord Londonderry's oldest collieries, were closed, and the population of an entire village was at a stroke deprived of its homes and its employment. Immediate protest was made, which met with an answer as ready as it was unpleasant. To a public meeting Lord Londonderry gave a statement of costs, which shewed that for a year he had been running the pit at a heavy loss. The price of coal had fallen until it had reached a point where the saving even of the whole of the labour cost, the offer of the men to work for no pay whatever, would have been insufficient. There seemed no conceivable way of producing coal at the market price[2]. His action had been inevitable, and he deserved praise for his generosity rather than blame for his hard-hearted action. It was little praise he received, for the men were too staggered by the revelation of the coal owners' position to make comment. Next year there was a bitter quarrel over the eviction of the Rainton hewers from their houses.

In August 1896 Patterson died. Wilson might say in his praise that he had done much for the union, that he was "solid, rather than showy," but he had

[1] *Durham Chronicle*, July 10th, 1896:

For Board	3,540
Against	10,121

[2] *Durham Chronicle*, March 20th, 1896.

failed to capture the imagination of his followers. On the trivial grounds that there was danger of creating a precedent they refused to grant his widow either pension or gratuity. Wilson was elected to Crawford's place, which had seemed vacant ever since his death. The men at last could fairly join issue with their agents on the question of the Miners' Federation. A ballot was taken, which ordered the resumption of friendly relations in the hope of procuring re-admission[1]. But in Northumberland the men were still obdurate. They ordered the abandonment of the system of conciliation, but they refused to sanction agreement with the Miners' Federation[2].

The Durham men were soon to repent of their action. In January, 1897, the agents made complaint of the mistrust which compelled each one of them "to go about his work with suspicion dogging his heels at every step"[3]. In February, with some misgivings, Wilson sent the first subscription to the Miners' Federation, remarking to the men that the silence of the Federation was taken as giving consent to their continued opposition to State interference with the hours of labour[4]. As the year advanced a new distraction appeared, worthy of the men's attention,

[1] *D.M.A. Records*, Dec. 1896:
      Membership 58,228   Votes recorded 46,489
               Join Federation   29,842
               Against   16,647
                             13,195
[2] *Durham Chronicle*, Dec. 18th, 1896
[3] *D.M.A. Records*, Jan. 1897.
[4] *Ibid.* Feb. 25th, 1897.

the Workmen's Compensation Act, but unrest and dissatisfaction continued to grow. With every increase in rents, and ultimately with every improvement in housing, the question of the rent allowance became more and more important. It could not be allowed to remain at the traditional 2s. a week, when the man himself was paying three or four times as much for his house. In August the agents found themselves compelled to make protest at the unreasonable frequency of local strikes[1]. There was every sign of factious opposition to Wilson when suddenly the Miners' Federation thought fit to revive the old quarrel which had begun at the "Hen and Chickens."

With the remark that the men were anxious for national unity, though in the north the agents were not, the secretary of the Federation returned the quarterly contribution, saying that it would be accepted only if it were returned with a promise of support for the Eight Hour Act, and of submission to the majority vote of the Federation[2]. It was too good a chance to be missed. Wilson replied to the challenge, for challenge it plainly was, by a demand for the return of the entrance fee, which, said he, the Federation had no right to retain if Durham had never properly been accepted into its ranks. His demand was refused, and the battle was for a second time fairly joined. If the Federation counted on a revolt from Wilson's rule it counted in vain. The threat of the Eight Hour Act secured for him the

[1] *D.M.A. Records*, Aug. 13th, 1897.   [2] *Ibid.* Aug. 1897.

firm adherence of the majority of the hewers in the county.

Fortune this time fought for Wilson. The trade boom which accompanied the Boer War was about to begin, and with it a steady wage increase which in the end carried the earnings of the men to a point unrivalled even by the fabulous prosperity of 1872. But in the early months of the year, while the feeling of prosperity was not yet reflected in the wage, the opposition to Wilson and his cautious policy was as loud as ever. A new inner association, the Durham Miners' Progressive Federation, was formed to bustle the union out of its conservative formalism. It organised local meetings, it attacked the leaders, it cried out for an increase, both in the actual wage and in the basis upon which it was calculated. Wilson was too busy to listen to such noisy protest. He was making the initial experiments with the Workmen's Compensation Act. As soon as it was passed he and the owners worked out a scheme, whereby a private tribunal was authorised to assess the award to be made in each case of accident. For a time this tribunal, the Durham Compensation Committee, was to command his whole attention, and to deserve his almost exaggerated pride. From the first it was an unqualified success. There was nothing like it in any other district. Bereaved relative and injured miner alike could plead their case before a private court; there was no appeal to the law to enforce a payment as a rule sufficiently well earned. For years to come Wilson was to find it one of his most pleasing tasks to recite the financial benefits which each month the Committee dispensed, to make careful distinction between appeals which had failed, and appeals, similar, but not exactly alike, which had been advanced with success.

Except for a strike at Sherburn there was little open trouble in the later months of the year. Wages were beginning to advance, and by Christmas 1898 an increase of $7\frac{1}{2}$ per cent. had been secured. But at a Primitive Methodist Conference, held in October, the rise of a new interest was in more than one speech blamed for the religious decline which had evidently begun[1]. There was a noticeable increase in Socialism. That year, at the annual gala, at which the speakers were chosen by popular vote, Tom Mann appeared upon the platform, the first of a series of intruding demagogues who were year after year to make savage attack on the union policy[2]. It was curiosity in these early days which drew the largest crowd to hear the violent oratory of this socialist pioneer. Soon it was to be the less critical interest of conviction. Meantime the year had passed quietly enough in Northumberland, where the advance in wage had also begun. One relic of the past disappeared, the Miners' National Union. As the Miners' Federation grew, the National Union became no more than a close alliance between its two surviving members, Northumberland and Durham. This year Durham withdrew, and the "National" was no more.

[1] *Durham Chronicle*, Oct. 14th, 1898.
[2] *Ibid.* July 17th, 1898.

1899 was Wilson's year of triumph. After 32 weeks
the strike at Sherburn was settled. It had cost the
union £4694 to settle this petty dispute, which arose
out of the dismissal of two men personally obnoxious
to the manager[1]. But the strikers, though they were
ready enough to strike when wages were low, did not
wish to stand idly by, living on the poor support of
their strike pay, while in the rest of the coal-field a
period of unexampled prosperity had so plainly
begun. In February Wilson was delighted to note
that the miners were anxious to re-establish the conciliation board. In September he was able to take
a holiday in America, secure in his belief that the
ballot then being taken would end in his favour. It
did so; and the conciliation board became again the
official means of wage settlement. In December
Northumberland thought fit to follow the example of
its neighbour. The prosperity was to lead to a notable
experiment in philanthropy. For some years the
desire to make provision for miners who had been
compelled by old age to retire from active work, had
been steadily increasing, both among the owners and
the men.

The inception of the idea and its successful accomplish-
ment were both due to Joseph Hopper, of Felling. For
years he battled against prejudice and ridicule, but he
was a man of both intellect and force of character.
Hopper and his homes were thought a good joke, but
he kept at it, formed an Association, and in time secured
the support of the Union and its agents[2].

[1] *D.M.A. Records*, 1899.
[2] Letter from Mr R. Gray, Chief Clerk to the D.M.A.

A chance came to purchase an entire village, at a recently abandoned colliery. At the small cost of £25 a house Wilson promised he could provide a whole settlement for these worn-out workers[1]. His appeal for help was well received. Owners, men, and general public alike made certain by their subscriptions that so good an opportunity should not be lost, and in October the Bishop of Durham declared the first of the homes open. Soon the chronicle of his yearly triumphs, as more and more homes were erected in every corner of the county, was to delight Wilson more than the story of union victories or the benefits of the compensation committee. To the north-country Miners' Unions is due the first successful attempt to provide on a large scale for the pensioners of industry. Before Wilson died there were several hundreds of these cottage homes in Durham, each with its aged couple, happy that in their declining years they had not lost the privilege of the "free house and coal" on which the miners' system of domestic economy has always been based.

But again Tom Mann had appeared at the gala, to expound the doctrine that Conciliation Boards were but palliatives for evils produced by a Capitalist system which was itself marked out for destruction, and to point out the folly of the masquerade of working men as Liberal Members of Parliament.

In 1900 the high-water mark of prosperity was reached. In November wages were 6 per cent. above the highest summit of previous prosperity, that of

[1] *D.M.A. Records*, March 1899.

the boom of 1872, and two of the recurring quarrels of the pits had been settled by agreement[1]. In April it had been decided that when a hewer was made, temporarily, to "put," he should be paid the average daily wage of a hewer. And in August a list was compiled which defined the classes of men entitled to the free house, or its equivalent the rent allowance. In Northumberland, by a large majority, the men decided to give a further trial of the conciliation board, confident that on the last occasion it had not been given a fair chance, during the trade depression which existed, to demonstrate its advantages. But warnings were not wanting that such prosperity could not last, and that the height to which wages had been raised would only intensify the resentment sure to be occasioned by their fall. Tom Mann again appeared at the gala. In South Shields, at a conference which became an annual function, the Durham Miners' Progressive Federation[2], soon to become the Durham Miners' Reform Association, was as urgent in its demands as in days of misfortune. It wished for still greater wage increase, and for a revision of the standard by which the wage was assessed. And it demanded a more democratic constitution for the union. It was not too well pleased at Wilson's steady insistence on the benefits of industrial goodwill, and the folly of the doctrine of the minimum wage. It thought that there was a sufficient body of opinion in the county favourable to the doctrine of the

---

[1] *D.M.A. Records*, Nov. 1900.
Durham Chronicle, March 30th, 1900.

minimum wage, to make open and official expression of other opinions by the agents, unwise, if not distinctly improper. Month by month, in the lodge meetings, the secretary's letter would be read, and month by month it was found to contain more definite expression of the old individualistic creed, "there never had been, and there never will be, a system...which can fix wages at a point and say ...there they shall remain[1]." It was a solemn reproof to those lodges of the north-east which at each quarter day made appeal to be allowed to join the Miners' Federation, a federation whose president was beginning to boast that he would win by force what persuasion could not obtain. Pickard, who was in the Miners' Federation an autocrat only less despotic than Wilson in his own county, began to warn the Durham men that he would be compelled to provoke a schism in a union which stood so stubbornly in the way of progress. 20,000 men, said he, would at his word refuse any longer to obey Wilson's commands.

Next year, in February, the first wage reduction took place. It was but $1\frac{1}{4}$ per cent., little enough in itself, but it was plainly the signal for more. By the end of April, both in Northumberland and Durham, wages had fallen over $12\frac{1}{2}$ per cent., and they fell almost as much more in the course of the year. Wilson thought fit to forestall the inevitable request, that a return should be made to the Miners' Federation. In February he made reply to the advocates of the Eight Hour Act that they could have

[1] *D.M.A. Records*, Nov. 1900.

had their shortened day in 1893 had they not refused the northern unions' suggestions for an act which allowed local option[1]. As to Smillie's prophecy, that some day the miner would enjoy a minimum wage of 10s. a day, Wilson could only gasp in amaze. "Ideals are good things, but they should have at least an element of probability about them"[2]. Mann was not allowed such an uninterrupted liberty of speech as in the past. After a condemnation of the mine-owners as "the biggest thieves in creation," and an exhortation to the men to work for the day when the mines should be the property of the nation, he was stopped by the chairman, House, who told him that he had broken faith with Mr Wilson, by the extravagance of his language. But the sympathy of the crowd was with Mann. "It was no secret," said he, "that I have never been to the gala by the wish of the executive...and that I should not be here if the officials could prevent it"[3].

It was some consolation to the old leader, who saw his popularity slipping away, to be able to watch the Northumberland men, as they too began to erect homes for their aged members. It perhaps was some relief to quarrel with his ancient respected enemy, Pickard, the Yorkshireman who ruled the Miners' Federation. One friend had gone, Bishop Westcott, the "Pitman's Bishop," the scholar at whose death the union could remark with all official gravity "there

[1] *D.M.A. Records*, Feb. 1901.
[2] *Ibid*. May 1901.
[3] *Durham Chronicle*, July 20th, 1901.

is not a single miner in the whole of the county who
will not realise that he has lost a friend"[1].

In 1902 the wage decrease was still continuing and,
as usual, it was bringing its usual crop of troubles.
Among them was the request that the miners' leaders
should leave the Radical party, and join with the
independent labour men, who, as Wilson told Keir
Hardie, were less independent than was any one of
the old Radicals. He himself was

not one who preached the doctrine of class interests. He
would not vote for a working man who represented the
working class interests only, and he did not think that
a man should go to parliament for that, and put himself
on a level with the landowner and the aristocrat[2].

Next year, in the spring, a strike of the American
miners brought a sudden, and completely unexpected,
wage advance. The miners were a little alarmed at
the recent improvements in the efficiency of the coal
cutting machines, and watchful of any infringement
by a new class of workmen on the traditional privi-
leges of the hewers. In June they were formally
giving approval to the doctrine of the living wage,
and the defeat of Wilson was plainly only a matter
of a few months. It was deferred for a while by a new
ballot on the Eight Hour Act, when by a substantial
majority the hewers of the north shewed that they
still thought union effort a more suitable way to
industrial change than the interference of the State.
Local disputes, provoked by the fall in the wage,
a recrudescence of the old trouble of restriction of

---

[1] *D.M.A. Records,* July 1901.
[2] *Ibid.* Oct. 1902.

output, and a general absence of confidence, caused
the Joint Committee to suspend its sittings during
the early weeks of 1904[1]. The Miners' Reform Association was steadily exhorting the union to put its pride
away, and join with the Federation in the attempt to
obtain a minimum wage. In April, as Wilson said
by I.L.P. influence, the first of the votes for the
abolition of the conciliation board was passed.
Wilson's outcry against Chinese labour, and the oppression of the Coal Tax, had failed to divert the new
politicians from matters which they considered to be
of greater urgency, and he became convinced that if
the Socialists were as yet in a minority the day of
their triumph was at hand.

1905 and 1906 passed, with the same tale of resolutions against conciliation, and against political alliance with the old parties. Northumberland quietly
joined the Miners' Federation. Wages were again on
the increase, but the pace of the improvement did
not satisfy the eager minds of the reformers. The days
had gone when an addition of $1\frac{1}{4}$ per cent. to the
basis wage could arouse feelings of satisfaction. The
list of speakers at the gala more and more plainly
witnessed that Wilson's hold on the county was no
longer unquestioned. He had changed Tom Mann for
Keir Hardie. In November, 1907, a little more than
a year after Northumberland had made its decision,
the Durham Miners' Association formally applied for
admission to the Miners' Federation of Great Britain.
It made unconditional surrender. Eight Hour Acts,

[1] *D.M.A. Records*, Feb., June, 1904.

Minimum Wage demands, and strikes might come in turn. The local independence of the north was at an end. Henceforth neither in Burt Hall, nor in Durham City were the fortunes of the northern pitmen to be decided. The centre of interest shifts to Russell Square, to the offices of the Miners' Federation of Great Britain.

SOURCES

(1) THE RECORDS OF THE DURHAM MINERS' ASSOCIATION.

A collection of financial statements, beginning in 1875, minutes of committees, minutes of councils, books of courts of arbitration, and handbills and leaflets. In particular there is a valuable series of "Monthly Circulars," mostly written by Crawford and Wilson, summarising recent progress, past history, and future policy, whose object seems to have been mainly educational. These records are kept in the Miners' Hall, Red Hill, Durham, but many of them have been issued to the local press.

(2) LOCAL NEWSPAPERS.

(a) *The Durham Chronicle*. A weekly newspaper, whose files begin in 1823. A Liberal journal, with a Whig interest, it gradually turned into a definitely Radical party newspaper. Until the '60's it had the usual middle class bias against the miners, but by degrees it began to take their side, and in the days of Crawford, and of Wilson in particular, it was almost the official journal of the Miners' Association, among whose members it found its main circulation, and of whose officials it was the political supporter, as local Liberal members of Parliament.

(b) *The Newcastle* (*Weekly*) *Chronicle*. A paper less directly interested in mining, used to supplement the *Durham Chronicle*. In the 1870's and '80's, in the hands of Joseph Cowen, it was a most remarkable paper, with a very individual political and social outlook. In those years it made a definite attempt to assist the spread of education among the local industrial peoples, printing articles in regular series on every subject, from arithmetic to elementary chemistry. In 1882–3 there was a notable fortnightly contribution by Lloyd Jones, in ex-

position of his somewhat peculiar economic ideas, which
provoked violent controversial replies from men of all
classes. Joseph Cowen made great efforts to maintain
an interest in local tradition and history, printing
reminiscent interviews with every local patriarch who
could be discovered, in particular with the survivors of
the Chartist movement, and the trade union activity of
the earlier years.

(c) *The Durham City and County News*. A weekly
newspaper, calling itself the "official organ of 35,000
miners," which lived for two years, 1870 to 1872, and
in which there were a great many articles by Crawford.
It died, probably as a result of the change in the attitude
of the *Durham Chronicle*.

(d) Incomplete files, in the late eighteenth century,
of the *Newcastle Courant*, the *Newcastle Journal*, the
Newcastle Advertiser, the *Newcastle Intelligence*, and the
Tyne Mercury.

(3) PARLIAMENTARY PAPERS, ETC.

Hansard.

Children's Employment Commission, 1842.

Report of the Select Committee of the House of
Lords on the Prevention of Accidents in Mines,
1849.

Report of Commissioners to enquire into the state of
Popular Education, 1861.

Final Report of the Commission on Labour Laws,
1875.

Report (Preliminary) of the Royal Commissioners
appointed to enquire into accidents in Mines, 1886.

Report of Royal Commission on Mining Royalties,
1890.

Report of Royal Commission on Labour, 1892–94.

Report of Departmental Committee to enquire into
the probable economic effects of a limit of eight
hours on the working day of the coal miner, 1907.

Report of the Royal Commission on Mines, 1907–8.

Reports of the Commissioners appointed under the

provisions of the Act 5 and 6 Victoria, to enquire into the operation of that act, and the state of the population in the mining districts. (Tremenheere), 1845–58.

Reports of H.M. Inspectors of Mines, annual since 1851.

Various Statutes, Bills proposed, etc.

Various statistical reports on Unions, Strikes, Hours of Labour, etc.

(4) Books.

A most Pleasant description of Benwell Village. Q. Z. 1726.

The Oppressed Man's Outcry. J. Hedworth. 1651.

An Exhortation to Christian Love. Sermon. 1720.

Essay on Burns. Edward Kentish. 1817.

The Compleat Collier, or the Whole Art of Sinking, Getting, and Working Coal Mine, as is now in Use in the Northern Parts, especially about Sunderland. J. C. 1708.

Plan and Report of the Greymare Colliery. 1761. Newcastle Antiquarian Society Library.

Voyages Metallurgiques, ou Recherches et Observations sur les Mines. Gabriel Jars. 1781.

View of the County of Durham. J. Bailey. 1810.

The Funeral Sermon of the Felling Colliery Sufferers. Rev. John Hodgson. 1815.

Pamphlet on Proposed Accident Insurance. Thomas Whittell. 1815.

The Newcastle Songster. A choice collection of Songs. 1812–21.

Rules of Newcastle upon Tyne Miners' Society. 1812.

A Treatise on the Coal Mines of Durham and Northumberland. J. H. H. Holmes. 1816.

Tour of Scotland and the Four Northern Counties. William Cobbett. 1833.

Fossil Fuel. John Holland. 1835.

An Historical View of the Coal Trade. Matthias Dunn. 1844.

A Treatise on the Winning and Working of Collieries. Matthias Dunn. 1848.

Gatherings from the Pit Heaps, or the Allens of Shiny Row. Coleman Collier (James Everett). 1861.

A Few Brief Observations, illustrations and Anecdotes respecting Pitmen in a Northern Colliery Village. (Anon.) 1862.

The Progress of the Working Classes. Lloyd Jones (and Ludlow). 1867.

The Coal Mines. James Mather. 1868.

A Choice Collection of Tyneside Songs. Joseph Wilson. 1872.

The Pitman's Pay. Thomas Wilson. 1872.

The Miners of Northumberland and Durham. R. Fynes. 1873.

Life and Correspondence of T. S. Duncombe. T. Duncombe. 1868.

The Conflicts of Capital and Labour. George Howell. 1878.

Accidents in Mines, their causes and prevention. Alan Bagot. 1878.

Coals and Colliers. S. J. Fitzgerald. 1881.

Treatise on Ventilating and Working Collieries. J. A. Ramsay. 1882.

Sliding Scales in the Coal Industry. J. C. Munro. 1885.

The Northumbrian Pitman. R. F. Wheeler. 1885.

Explosions in Coal Mines. W. M. Atkinson. 1886.

Glossary of Terms used in the Coal Trade of Northumberland and Durham. G. C. Greenwell. 1888.

History of the Chartist Movement. R. G. Gammage. 1894.

A Sketch of the History of the Coal Trade of Northumberland and Durham. Mark Archer. 1897.

Coal Pits and Pitmen. R. N. Boyd. 1895.

The Annals of Coal Mining and the Coal Trade. R. Galloway. 1904.

Capital and Labour in Coal Mining during the Past 200 years. J. B. Simpson. 1900.

Coal Cutting by Machinery. S. F. Walker. 1902.

The Company of the Hostmen of Newcastle. Surtees Society. 1901.

Dusty Diamonds. True Tales from Pit Life. David Addy. 1900.

Papers Relating to the History of the Coal Trade and the Invention of the Steam Engine. R. L. Galloway. 1906.

History of the Durham Miners' Association. J. Wilson. 1907.

Wesley's Journal. 1909.

The Cranstons. 1909.

Davie Graham. Pitman. 1904.

Elsie Magregor. 1904.   By Ramsay Guthrie.

Brotherhood Stories. 1916.   (Novels with very

The Canny Folks o' Coal Vale. strong local colour.)
    1910.

Black Dyke. 1904.

Colliery Accounts. H. G. Judd and J. Mann. 1909.

Profits and Wages in the British Coal Trade. T. Richardson and J. A. Walbank. 1911.

Colliery Working and Management. H. F. Bulman and R. A. S. Redmayne. 1906.

The Collier's Wedding. Edward Chicken. 1764.

INDEX

For EU product safety concerns, contact us at Calle de José Abascal, 56–1°,
28003 Madrid, Spain or eugpsr@cambridge.org.

www.ingramcontent.com/pod-product-compliance
Ingram Content Group UK Ltd.
Pitfield, Milton Keynes, MK11 3LW, UK
UKHW042209180425
457623UK00011B/106